-2

THE LAZIER MURDER

Prince Edward County, 1884

THE LAZIER MURDER

Prince Edward County, 1884

ROBERT J. SHARPE

Published for The Osgoode Society for Canadian Legal History by
University of Toronto Press
Toronto Buffalo London

ISBN 978-1-4426-4421-2

Library and Archives Canada Cataloguing in Publication

Sharpe, Robert J.
The Lazier murder : Prince Edward County, 1884 / Robert J. Sharpe.

(Osgoode Society for Canadian legal history)
Includes bibliographical references and index.
ISBN 978-1-4426-4421-2

1. Murder – Ontario – Prince Edward – History – 19th century.
2. Trials (Murder) – Ontario – Prince Edward – History – 19th century.
3. Criminal justice, Administration of – Ontario – Prince Edward – History –
19th century.   4. Thomset, Joseph – Trials, litigation, etc.   5. Lowder,
George – Trials, litigation, etc.   6. Lowder, David – Trials, litigation, etc.
7. Lazier, Peter.   I. Title.   II. Series: Osgoode Society for Canadian Legal
History series.

HV6535.C33P76 2011   364.152'30971358709034   C2011-904006-9

University of Toronto Press acknowledges the financial assistance to its
publishing program of the Canada Council for the Arts and the
Ontario Arts Council.

 Canada Council   Conseil des Arts   ONTARIO ARTS COUNCIL
for the Arts   du Canada   CONSEIL DES ARTS DE L'ONTARIO

University of Toronto Press acknowledges the financial support of the
Government of Canada through the Canada Book Fund for its
publishing activities.

Contents

Photos follow page 82

Foreword

THE OSGOODE SOCIETY
FOR CANADIAN LEGAL HISTORY

Robert J. Sharpe is one of the Osgoode Society's most prolific authors, and his latest offering is a compelling account of a late-nineteenth-century murder case in Picton, Ontario. This very thoroughly researched and engagingly written case study details the murder of a local resident and the subsequent court and governmental proceedings. What emerges is a fascinating insight into the operation of the policing, prosecution, and trial processes of late-nineteenth-century Ontario, one that shows how much public opinion and courtroom atmosphere could at times affect the outcome of a trial. *The Lazier Murder* also looks at the executive commutation process by which it was decided if those sentenced to be executed would be hanged. Sharpe's account suggests that this may well have been a case of what we would now call a 'wrongful conviction.'

The purpose of the Osgoode Society for Canadian Legal History is to encourage research and writing in the history of Canadian law. The Society, which was incorporated in 1979 and is registered as a charity, was founded at the initiative of the Honourable R. Roy McMurtry, formerly attorney general for Ontario and chief justice of the province, and officials of the Law Society of Upper Canada. The Society seeks to stimulate the study of legal history in Canada by supporting researchers, collecting oral histories, and publishing volumes that contribute to legal-historical scholarship in Canada. It has published eighty-four books on the courts, the judiciary, and the legal profession, as well as on the history of crime and punishment, women and law, law and economy, the legal treatment of ethnic minorities, and famous cases and significant trials in all areas of the law.

Current directors of the Osgoode Society for Canadian Legal History are Robert Armstrong, Christopher Bentley, Kenneth Binks, David Chernos, Kirby Chown, J. Douglas Ewart, Violet French, Martin Friedland, Philip Girard, John Honsberger, Horace Krever, C. Ian Kyer, Virginia MacLean, Patricia McMahon, R. Roy McMurtry, Laurie Pawlitza, Paul Perell, Jim Phillips, Paul Reinhardt, Joel Richler, William Ross, Paul Schabas, Robert Sharpe, Mary Stokes, and Michael Tulloch.

The annual report and information about membership may be obtained by writing to the Osgoode Society for Canadian Legal History, Osgoode Hall, 130 Queen Street West, Toronto, Ontario, M5H 2N6. Telephone: 416-947-3321. E-mail: mmacfarl@lsuc.on.ca. Website: www.osgoodesociety.ca.

R. Roy McMurtry
President

Jim Phillips
Editor-in-Chief

Acknowledgments

I wish to thank a number of people who have provided me with invaluable assistance in the writing and production of this book.

I am especially grateful to Jim Phillips, who encouraged me to turn what began as a modest project on local history into a case study on nineteenth-century criminal justice and guided me through the process with constant support and many helpful suggestions.

Several people reviewed the manuscript in draft and generously offered insightful comments and editorial suggestions that made this a better book: Earl Cherniak, David Doherty, Martin Friedland, Patricia McMahon, Kent Roach, Geraldine Sharpe, Stephen Waddams, and two anonymous referees. David Warwick helped me with information on Edwards Merrill and Sir John A. Macdonald, and Peter Lockyer provided me with several photographs and information about George Lowder's gravestone.

I also thank Andrea Bolieiro and Rosemary Legris who helped me with the proofreading and Marilyn MacFarlane who provided her usual cheerful encouragement and support throughout.

Abbreviations

AO	Archives of Ontario
British Whig	Kingston *British Whig*
CCF	Capital Case File, Lowder, George, and Thomset, Joseph, Library and Archives Canada, RG 13, vol. 1420, files 183A and 184A (1884)
Daily Ontario	Belleville *Daily Ontario*
Gazette	Picton *Gazette*
Globe	Toronto *Globe*
Intelligencer	Belleville *Daily Intelligencer*
LAC	Library and Archives Canada
PECA	Prince Edward County Archives

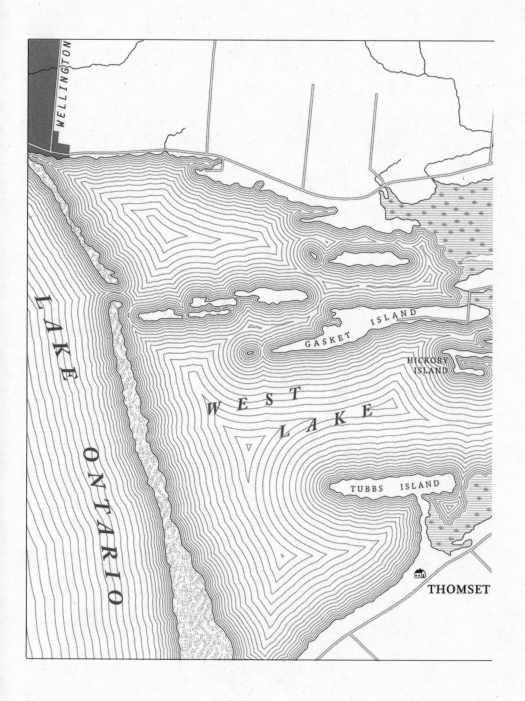

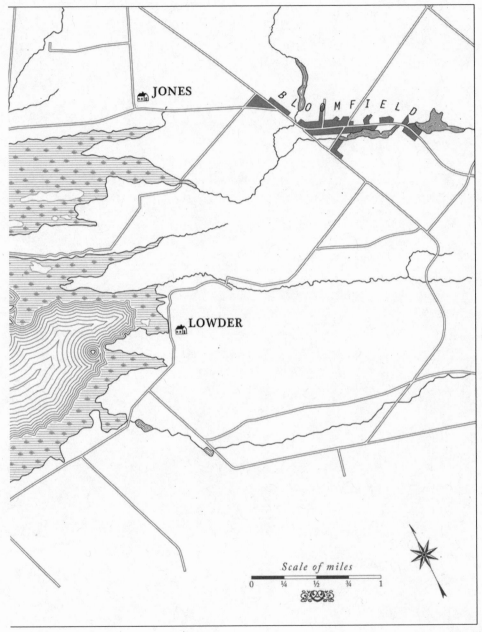

JONES

B L O O M F I E L D

LOWDER

Scale of miles

0   ¼   ½   ¾   1

As the Crow Flies cARTography

THE LAZIER MURDER

Prince Edward County, 1884

1

Introduction

Peter Lazier was murdered at Gilbert and Margaret Jones' farmhouse near the village of Bloomfield, Ontario, six miles west of Picton, at about 10 p.m. on 21 December 1883. A group of concerned citizens eagerly responded to an immediate hue and cry from the coroner. The neighbours of Gilbert and Margaret Jones, assisted by local constables, went out into the night to try to track footprints in the snow left by the culprits. With considerable coming and going, and despite losing the trail at various points in between, the trackers were convinced that the trail that led away from the Jones' farmhouse could be traced to the homes of Joseph Thomset and the Lowder family near West Lake, some five miles from the scene of the crime. Early the next morning, Thomset and David Lowder were arrested and taken to the Bloomfield Town Hall. By noon, David's brother George was apprehended. All three were charged with murder.[1]

The legal process moved with remarkable dispatch. A coroner's inquest was convened on 22 December and committal proceedings began six days later on 28 December 1883. Less than five months after the murder, in early May 1884, the three accused were tried before a judge and jury at the Prince Edward County Courthouse in Picton.

The prosecution's theory was that the murderers had intended to rob Gilbert Jones of $555 he had been paid at the Bloomfield station for a load of hops earlier on the day of the murder. That was a substantial sum of money, in modern terms, certainly many thousands of dollars.

While difficult to convert precisely into present value,[2] it was about 20 per cent more than the average annual tradesman's wage.[3]

Lazier, an overnight visitor at the Jones farm, had simply been in the wrong place at the wrong time. The central issue in the case was identity: were Joseph Thomset and the Lowder brothers the men who came to rob Gilbert Jones and who shot Peter Lazier? Margaret Jones saw Lazier's two assailants on the night of the crime, but could not identify any of the three accused as perpetrators of the crime, nor could Gilbert Jones, who had only seen the man who fired the fatal shot. The evidence against the accused consisted of little other than the footprints in the snow near the Jones farm, near their own homes, and at various points in between.

This book tells the story of the apprehension of Thomset and the Lowders and of the legal process that followed. It is a case study,[4] based upon archival and contemporary newspaper accounts, that attempts to reconstruct the case and to place the legal issues in their proper historical context.

Every lawyer trained in the common law tradition is familiar with the case-study method. Past cases stand as precedents and can be best understood by careful dissection of the underlying facts and circumstances and debated in the classroom and in moot-court exercises. Scholarly studies that probe beyond the bare facts revealed in official law reports to explore cases in their broader social and political context and see the cases 'as events in history and incidents in the evolution of the law'[5] have become a significant genre of legal writing.

Case studies often focus on well-known leading cases,[6] but increasingly, legal historians have adopted a method developed by social historians and turned to the study of ordinary cases that have faded from modern memory.[7] 'Ordinary' cases have the advantage of focusing on the circumstances of 'ordinary' people and events, providing insight into the relationship between ordinary people and larger events and issues.[8] This book is about such a case. Some of the characters in the story were prominent and well-known contemporary figures. The trial judge, Christopher Patterson, was a highly respected jurist who later served on the Supreme Court of Canada. Defence counsel D'Alton McCarthy was a politician and highly regarded lawyer with a reputation as one of Canada's leading advocates. Prime Minister Sir John A. Macdonald makes a brief but crucial appearance, as does Macdonald's political confidant and justice minister, Alexander Campbell. But the central characters are very ordinary people: Peter Lazier, a farm-implement salesman, Gilbert and Margaret Jones, farmers, Joseph Thomset, a fisher, George Lowder, a mason, and David Lowder, a farm-worker. In an instant, one of those people was dead and the others were embroiled in the legal process, a process that was profoundly influenced by the mood of an outraged and threatened community.

The story of the Lazier murder and the trial of Joseph Thomset and George Lowder provides a window for the exploration of how the legal process unfolds and how it affects, and in turn is shaped by, the ordinary people involved. Several significant themes emerge: community justice and the impact of popular mood and opinion, the changing pattern of criminal justice in late-nineteenth-century Canada, and the enduring problem of wrongful convictions and miscarriages of justice.

In the 1880s, the English model of community justice based upon local constables, coroners, and justices of the peace, essentially untrained volunteers who reflected the values of the community, still prevailed in Prince Edward County. But that model was fading in Ontario. There was a clear shift towards full-time, professional police, a development that is dramatically revealed in the Lazier case. Prince Edward County's constables, overwhelmed by the responsibility of investigating a crime of this magnitude, did not resist the intervention of Belleville's chief of police Hugh McKinnon. As we shall see, McKinnon was a man bent on establishing a reputation as a fearless and effective crime-buster, and was willing to use dubious tactics to achieve his goal.

The Lazier case also reveals another aspect of community justice, the powerful influence that popular opinion can have in a case involving a major crime that threatens a community to its core. In 1884, Prince Edward County was a peaceful, prosperous, and relatively isolated community, proud of its United Empire Loyalist roots and with a strong sense of its own character and identity. The local economy was built on the production of barley and hops. By attempting to rob Gilbert Jones of the proceeds of his hops crop and killing an innocent bystander who was a Loyalist descendant, the men who murdered Peter Lazier shook the residents of Prince Edward County. The reaction was swift and severe. The community was out for blood and a hostile mood prevailed throughout the trial. The courtroom audience cheered the prosecution and jeered the defence, and in the evenings, hotel barroom patrons impatiently anticipated the hangings they so wanted to occur. The trial judge and the lawyers urged the jury of twelve men who determined the fate of the accused men to decide the case on the basis of the evidence and not be swayed by the community's hostility, but the jury took little time to convict. Prominent members of the community were appalled by what they perceived as a miscarriage of justice that had resulted from the pressure of public opinion and pleaded with the prime minister and the minister of justice for mercy.

The case also involves two of the burning issues in nineteenth-century criminal law. The first was the rule, highly contested at the time, that an accused person could not testify in his or her own defence. Joseph Thomset and George Lowder protested their innocence, but the law of the day did not permit them to tell their side of the story to the jury that would determine their fate. Supporters of the rule argued that it was required by the presumption of innocence and by the basic right of an accused person to remain silent in the face of an accusation. It was not until nine years after the Thomset-Lowder case that the law was changed to allow the accused to testify.

The second burning legal issue was the question of appeals and post-conviction review. The law did not afford Thomset and George Lowder a right of appeal from their conviction. The prevailing view at the time was that allowing for appeals would result in unnecessary cost and delay that would undermine the deterrent effect of punishment. Those convicted of crime could petition the governor-in-council and the minister of justice, assisted by officials in the Department of Justice, would conduct a review of the case. As we shall see, the trial judge played a central role in this process, and in many cases the cabinet did commute the sentence. But the process of executive review rarely responded positively to pleas of trial unfairness or wrongful conviction.

Finally, the Lazier murder case opens a historical window on one of the most troubling and enduring issues in criminal justice, the possibility of wrongful conviction. Were Thomset and Lowder wrongfully convicted? Regrettably, that question remains unanswered. The case does, however, provide a historic setting for the consideration of many of the features still commonly found in cases of wrongful conviction – outraged public opinion, a rush to judgment, a tunnel-visioned police investigation, 'expert' forensic evidence of dubious value, inadequate Crown disclosure and defence preparation, and flaws or shortcomings in criminal law and procedure.[9]

2

The Crime

Gilbert and Margaret Jones lived on a farm on what was then called Danforth Road, about one mile west of Bloomfield, Ontario, the third largest community in Prince Edward County, and about six miles west of Picton, the county seat and largest town. Their house, built in about 1855, is said to be 'noteworthy for its expression of County building tradition' – with a kitchen wing on the side of the building and the diagonally mounted window in the gable of the upper storey[1] – but is best known as the scene of the crime that occurred on 21 December 1883, when Peter Lazier met his death at the hands of two intruders.

Gilbert and Margaret Jones were members of the Quaker community. Gilbert came from nearby Brighton to Prince Edward County after his wife died to marry Margaret Hubbs, who had also lost her first spouse.[2] They were actively engaged in Quaker affairs,[3] opposed to the death penalty, and profoundly shocked by what had happened to Peter Lazier at their home. They found it difficult to testify in a proceeding that could lead to the infliction of capital punishment, which they regarded as a cruel and immoral penalty, yet they knew they had a legal duty to do so. Margaret Jones's grandson later wrote that the trial was a 'harrowing experience' for them that probably shortened their lives.[4]

Gilbert and Margaret Jones described the murder of Peter Lazier to their friends, neighbours, and the local constables who visited their home the night of 21 December and the next morning. They testified three times – at the coroner's inquest conducted at their own home and in the Bloomfield Town Hall within hours of the horrific event, at the committal proceedings conducted a few days later at the Picton court-house, and then at the trial of George and David Lowder and Joseph Thomset before a judge and jury in May 1884.

Here is their first-hand account of the Lazier murder, distilled from the transcript of their testimony at the trial, with editing for syntax and context and with some passages taken from the questions that were posed.[5]

GILBERT JONES: My name is Gilbert Jones. I am a Quaker and a farmer and I reside about a mile west of Bloomfield about 6 miles from Picton on a farm in the township of Hallowell, County of Prince Edward. The house is on the north side, as I could judge, ten or fifteen rods [a rod is 5½ yards] from the main Bloomfield road. To approach the house with a team, we have a gate at the road that comes up alongside a fence opposite to the front of the house. To enter the house, there is a gate to the dooryard.

On the morning of the 21st of December last, I got my mare shod down at the blacksmith shop. I got home between 10 and 11 o'clock and the men who work for me on the farm were loading up the hops to take down to the station. They had it pretty well loaded when I got home.

I went down to Bloomfield between 11 and 12 o'clock with this load of hops and I stayed there until about four o'clock when we got through weighing. I only took one load down but there were quite a number drawing hops and we had to wait till they would weigh a load and pay them off and then weigh again. Mine was the last load weighed. There were quite a number of people at the station just at noon, including several strangers eating dinner, and several men around the station when I got my money.

I was paid $555 for the hops in a store-room that opens off the platform. I could not say who was in the room other than the man paying me and John Miller – whether there were any more men in there or not I could not say. I do not recollect whether there were strangers there at that time and I do not mind of a stranger being at the scales when we were weighing the hops. I was very busy and I was in a hurry. My horses were shivering with the cold and I did not pay much attention to who was around. It was pretty near four o'clock when I was paid. I was paid cash, large bills, including one hundred dollar bill. I went direct home after I got my pay and got home about half an hour or so before sundown. As I took care of my team it began to get dusk.

In the forenoon earlier that day it was very handsome, and the sun shone very nicely but when the clouds got up in the afternoon it was colder. In the afternoon between two and three there came a great cold out of the west and it blowed and snowed. It seemed to come up in blasts. It would snow quite briskly for a while, and then slack up again. I think it was freezing at night. The next day it was quite a bit colder and on the next day following on Sunday it was a very cold day. There had not been a great deal of snow up to this point. The turnpikes were bare generally, and the ditches had snow in [them].

Peter Lazier, who is married to a niece of mine, came about dusk. I got up from the table and went out to help him put out his horse. It was snowing and blowing. I went up a scaffold to the loft to throw down some hay for the horse but missed my calculation in coming down and slid and fell about 10 or 12 feet. I hurt my back and could not get up for a while. Peter helped me to the house. I sat in an armchair and him and me conversed for a while and my wife got supper. At about eight o'clock Peter went out to attend to the horse and I went to bed. John Wallace, the man that works the place, came in directly after Peter returned and sat in the sitting room conversing with my wife and my wife's niece. I was awake and the door was opened from my room into the sitting room. Peter was sitting just behind the coal stove and could not have been seen from the windows on the north side of the house.

Wallace remained until pretty near 10 o'clock. Peter retired almost immediately after Wallace left. My wife came into the room to retire at the same time. She had not been in but a very few minutes before we heard a rap at the door, not much difference of ten o'clock. She took the lamp and started towards the back door. Then they rapped quite loud at the front kitchen door. When she opened the kitchen door she gave such a frightful scream out of her that it struck me at once that someone had come to rob us.

MARGARET JONES: At about eight o'clock Lazier went out to water his horse and I helped my husband to bed immediately. Wallace came over and sat for a while and talked with Lazier and me. Lazier could not be seen from either of the windows at the back of the house where he was sitting, but Wallace was sitting nearly opposite to the window and likely could be seen. Wallace left about 10 o'clock. I could not say whether the clock had struck or not and our clock was ten minutes faster than standard time. Wallace went out of the back door going out of the kitchen to get over to his own home to the east. I gave Lazier a light immediately on Wallace leaving and he went right into his own room. I took the lamp and went into the bedroom where my husband was.

After I went into my room I commenced unfastening my dress and heard a rap. I buttoned again, took my light, and came out to the kitchen thinking that Wallace had come for something. I started to go to the door but a second rap told me it was at the front door. I thought the first rap was at the back kitchen door but I am satisfied now that both raps were at the one place. I set my lamp down on the table and opened the front door and saw two men, one with what appeared to me a linen mask on his head standing perhaps 6 inches above his head. He was on the west side. They were both facing me. They both stepped in. The one with the mask had a pistol in his left hand and the other had a shotgun in his right hand. The weapons were on the outside. The man with a shotgun had a hat or a cap but from the way it covered his face I should think it was a hat. He had a hat down over his head and his eyes and his body stooped. To appearance it made more difference in his height than there really was but at first sight you would think there was quite a difference in their height. The mask looked like a linen bag with oblong holes for eyeholes. It came right down to his shoulders so that you could not see anything at all of his neck nor head nor face.

Neither man spoke. I looked at them and gave a scream. I knew what they wanted. I took up the lamp and rushed for the other room. As I went through the door, the chimney fell off but I still kept the lamp in my hand. Knowing my husband to be helpless, as I thought, from having to help him to bed, I stopped at Lazier's door for protection. He had evidently been in bed from the bed being mussed. I shoved the door open and he stood there right in front of me. I said nothing nor he to me. We merely looked at one another. I passed on to my own bedroom and just as I was going to go in I looked over my shoulder and could see Lazier coming out of his room. The man with the shotgun was standing erect and fetching the gun down over the sideboard as though to strike Lazier's head. I could see the shotgun coming down very near his head but I did not see him hit. The man with a shotgun was not as tall as Lazier. The man with the mask and the pistol stood at his side.

I went right into the bedroom. As I shoved the door, I turned the key, set the lamp on the stand just beside the door and fetched my hand to my heart. I saw that my husband was out of bed and in the act of getting down his shotgun.

GILBERT JONES: When I heard my wife scream at the men who rapped on our door, I sprang right out of bed and my first thought was to get something to defend myself. I thought of the shotgun although I knew I had no load in it. I could not see to get the shotgun loose and I jerked at it to get it off. My wife came in and quickly slammed the door and locked it. I had not more than got the shotgun down before she unlocked it and let me out. My wife brought the lamp into the bedroom but I had the light from the coal stove. The moment I came out into the room I saw Peter Lazier and this man with a mask. Peter had him by the hands holding him back. The man was trying to go on. Then he broke loose and they were separated by some six or eight feet I should judge.

Peter stood by the sideboard and I went towards him. I never heard a word said, only when my wife came out of the bedroom after me and said 'Shoot him, shoot him.'

The moment I came, the man with a mask went back into the kitchen. It appeared to me as if he frightened when I came out of the bedroom with a shotgun that I was holding up just as though I was going to shoot. He ran back and fired the pistol – I expect it was a pistol but I could not distinctly see. I suppose Peter and I were about side-by-side, not more than a foot or two apart, when the shot was fired. I saw the flash and heard the report. I rushed right by Peter after this man with a mask. I got to the kitchen door and he was looking over his shoulder towards the room. He kind of hesitated. But as I got closer to him he ran out of the room and then left the house. I followed him to the door. He took out the gate into the driveway we use to drive out into the road. I could see him running until he got, I should think, about halfway to the road. The trees hid my view so that I could not see him any farther. He made such an awkward movement running, a kind of a rolling gait. He was trying to run fast but he could not make a fast run of it.

I heard but one shot but I now know that two shots were fired because there was a shot fired in the bedroom door that went in half an inch and then came out and struck the wall and then fell to the floor. It must have been fired after my wife shut the door. I turned around, came in and hollered to my wife 'Go for Wallace.'

Peter Lazier had fallen into the bedroom and lay right on his back on the floor. He had his nightshirt on and I could see the bullet hole in his breast and a little blood. I said 'Oh Peter, Peter, is thee shot?' He kind of threw up his head and said 'It's me' and then threw his head back. I think he lived but a little while after that. My wife went to the Wallace's and they came right over. Young Wallace got hold of Peter's pulse and said 'He ain't dead yet.' I said 'Go for the doctor as quick as you can.' I do not think Peter lived 10 minutes. I just saw him move his head once or twice. In a short time Dr. Noxon came in and said he was dead.

The neighbourhood was alarmed. I was not able to get out myself but there was quite a number came in very shortly.

I never saw the prisoner Thomset until we came down here to court for the investigation. I had not a very good opportunity of seeing the intruder that night such an exciting time as that was. He went back into the kitchen so quick and had this mask up over his head and that rose I should think perhaps five or six inches above his head but I would say he was nearly my height, he might be a little taller. The mask had the appearance of a bag, the bottom of a bag pulled over his head and it came down to his shoulders when he was running. I could see the ends of it kind of flapping on the shoulders, it covered his whole face and down on his chest.

MARGARET JONES: My husband being lame there was no one but myself to go for anything and the two lamp chimneys were crashed. I took the broom and drew the glass to one side and then put on my bonnet and ran over to Wallace's. Robert Wallace, one of the sons, came with me. The father, John Wallace and his other son, Samuel, came immediately after. I immediately started Samuel for Dr. Noxon. Before Dr. Noxon came, my husband requested me to go out to get his crutches in his storeroom. He had inflammatory rheumatism last winter and could not walk and he thought after this accident that if he had the crutches that had been made, he could maybe go about. Wallace went out for them but did not return.

After Dr. Noxon came, he and I went out to the storehouse but Wallace had taken the key and gone home. Just as we turned around to go in Dr. Noxon said 'What is the meaning of all these tracks?' There were tracks under the windows that seemed to follow from the outbuilding. The tracks led to a point close enough for anyone to see in through the window and our curtains were only half drawn. It looked as though there might be two persons going and retreating. The next morning Abram Saylor said they were going to cover the tracks and I went out with him and saw him cover one.

There was no one else about the premises that afternoon that would make those tracks. Wallace would go out the kitchen door and go east – he had no occasion to go there. I was home all the afternoon and I did not see any person from the time my husband went away until he came back. There was not a track to be seen in our yard. It had been squally during the day and the ground was all white with snow, fresh snow. I could not say how much snow had fallen, not very much depth, though behind the house the tracks sunk down maybe an inch and a half in this new fallen snow. It was not snowing when I went over to Wallace's after this occurrence that was a few minutes after 10 o'clock; it was clear enough even to see a man across the road from our house.

Peter Lazier was in good health. His hair was very white, whiter than common for persons of his age. He was a tall man rather above average height and slim.

It is my impression that the man I saw with the shotgun was about the size of George Lowder. The one with the shotgun had dark clothes on. He might have had a false beard on. I did not see the skin and I could not say whether it was a false beard or hair. The other one's clothes were a sort of mixed gray – I could not say whether it was striped or checked. I took it to be a sort of tweed, common clothes, coarse clothes. The other man was dressed in dark clothes, I should suppose the same material, only dark. Neither man had on an overcoat – they just wore their underclothes. Their hands were bare.

Identifying Features?

The Jones' account of the crime and their description of the intruders revealed several features that might be used to identify the culprits. There was considerably more detail about the masked man with the pistol who fired the fatal shot. Gilbert and Margaret Jones both thought that the shooter was tall. Gilbert Jones thought he was about his height – 5 feet, 9 inches – and that would make the shooter 3 inches taller than Thomset and 4 inches taller than George Lowder. That man had difficulty running away and had an awkward way of running described by Gilbert Jones as 'a kind of rolling gait.' He was holding the pistol in his left hand, an indication that he was likely left-handed. Margaret Jones gave fewer identifying features of the other man who carried the shotgun and who fled before Gilbert Jones came out of his bedroom. She thought he either had a beard or was wearing a false beard.

The Jones' description of the clothing the intruders were wearing was not detailed, but was still potentially useful. The masked man with the pistol had striped or checked grey clothing made of tweed or some other coarse cloth and the man with the shotgun wore darker clothing. The fact that neither man wore an overcoat or gloves or mittens might suggest that they had not come from far away and that they did not have far to go once the crime was committed. Was it significant that neither man spoke? Could they have been afraid to reveal their voices because they were known to Gilbert and Margaret Jones?

What is surprising is that none of the features that could have identified the intruders or excluded Thomset and the Lowder brothers appear to have been investigated. The investigation of Peter Lazier's murder consisted almost entirely of the efforts of the concerned neighbours who went out into the night soon after the fatal shot had been fired to track footprints in the snow.

Hue and Cry

John Wallace, the man who worked on the Jones farm, was the first to arrive after Peter Lazier was shot. Wallace rushed with horse and cutter to Bloomfield to get Dr Allen Noxon, a physician who practised in the village of his birth. By the time Dr Noxon arrived at the Jones farm-house, it was too late for medical assistance. 'When I got there Lazier was dead and I found Mr. and Mrs. Jones alone in the house and of course very nervous and frightened.'[6]

Dr Noxon also happened to be the local coroner and was the first to notice footprints in the snow behind the Jones house. Although he was unaware of their significance at the time, the footprints quickly became the key investigative tool to track down the killers. Mrs Jones asked him to go out to the shed to get a pair of crutches for her husband. Noxon noticed tracks in the snow near the windows and the shed. He saw no tracks in the lane but did notice some tracks in front of the house around a clump of cedar trees, perhaps 20 to 30 feet from the house. He took a lantern to rouse neighbours James and Stephen Bowerman from their beds and inform them of the tragedy and to get help to track down those responsible for Lazier's death.

James Bowerman carried the message to Abram Saylor and his son Charles, who lived a half mile east of the Jones farm. Abram Saylor rushed over to his neighbour Jones as soon as he was called: 'When I got there I found Peter Lazier lying on the floor, his feet in the door of a bedroom on his back with his head back in the bedroom. He was dead.' Dr Noxon proceeded to the home of Constable Edmund Bedell in Bloomfield to inform him of the crime.

Within minutes, more neighbours gathered at the Jones house. Shocked to see Lazier's dead body lying on the floor, they immediately launched their pursuit of the culprits. When Saylor's son Charles arrived with Stephen Bowerman, Mrs Jones took them outside with a lantern to see the tracks she and Dr Noxon had observed earlier. They found what appeared to be the tracks of two persons at the back of the house near the windows and near the shed. Abram Saylor also saw what appeared to be the print of a bare hand in the snow on the sill of one of the windows. He could find no tracks to indicate how the intruders got to the Jones farmhouse. The snow was 2 to 8 inches deep. The Saylors and Bowerman saw the tracks Dr Noxon had observed behind the house to the north. One was a round-toed boot and the other a square-toed boot with a patch-bottom. The tracks were positioned close together near the windows. Abram Saylor later covered the tracks at the rear of the house near the windows with boxes and lids he found in the shop.

Saylor traced two tracks leading away from the house. One led from the kitchen door on the south side and through the front yard. The other went out the gate and down the driveway to the road. Saylor, his son Charles, and Stephen Bowerman were the first of many who would attempt to follow the tracks in the snow that night and the following morning. Believing that hot pursuit of the killers was imperative, they did not think it necessary to wait for the local constabulary to arrive. The rush to follow the trail by many well-meaning but amateur detectives led to considerable traffic back and forth along the trail from the Jones farm leaving many footprints in the snow and resulting in confusion later over who saw what, when, and where.

The detailed accounts of the various neighbours who attempted to track down the culprits were difficult to follow. The location of the Jones farm, the homes of Thomset and the Lowders, and various points in between is shown on the map found after the Foreword, above. The trackers believed that they could follow the tracks across the Danforth Road, then for a short distance along the railway line that led towards Wellington from Bloomfield. After a distance of less than a mile, the trackers proceeded south, across frozen marshlands, a peninsula of land, and the frozen lake to the homes of Thomset and the Lowders on the shores of West Lake – a Lake Ontario bay called a lake because it is protected and more or less cut off from the open lake by a long peninsula formed by the Sandbanks dunes.

Constable Edmund Bedell and the Arrest of Joseph Thomset

The first constable to arrive at the scene of the crime was Edmund Bedell, a typical rural constable – a well-meaning volunteer with virtually no training in police work.[7] Bedell observed Lazier's dead body and learned of the tracks in the snow. He immediately went out with a lantern and saw the tracks near the house. He saw no tracks between the house and the road, but followed three tracks along the road, over the fence, and into the orchard where he found Charles Saylor and Stephen Bowerman who, presumably, had left two of the tracks that Bedell was following. Bedell found the single track difficult to follow, but it seemed to go along the rail line, where he saw another track that came in from the field to the north. The two tracks then joined and, together with Saylor and Bowerman, Bedell followed them. The tracks went along the railroad and then south through the marsh. With only a lantern to light the way in the dark, the three pursuers lost the trail. At that point, Saylor and Bowerman abandoned the search and returned to the Jones farm. Bedell continued on to the McDonald farm, where he roused Aaron McDonald from his bed.

Aaron McDonald knew every corner of this part of the County and Bedell enlisted his help. It was at this point, very shortly after the crime occurred, that the investigation started to focus on Joseph Thomset, a thirty-four-year-old fisherman who lived near West Lake with his wife and their young daughter. Thomset was the son and oldest child of John Thomset, an English immigrant, and his Canadian wife Pamilla.[8] Thomset and his two sisters, Sarah and Margaret, had been raised in the area and, like McDonald, he knew the terrain very well.

Aaron McDonald would later admit at the trial that he had a history of serious conflict with Joseph Thomset that had led to fights and criminal charges. Bedell also knew Thomset. Thomset did not enjoy a good reputation – he was the sort of man a good constable would keep his eye on. Although McDonald would later deny that his enmity towards Thomset played any part in the tracking that night, he admitted that as he and Bedell wandered about in search of the trail, they discussed Thomset as a likely suspect and their instincts led them in Thomset's direction.

Bedell and McDonald followed the road leading to Gaskett Island, about half a mile from the McDonald farm, and found tracks again at a place called Springbrook, where the marsh projects out into the lake. The tracks led to clear ice on the lake and could not be followed. They proceeded to Tubbs Island, but found nothing until they got to the south side, where they saw the tracks of one man leading south along the sand bar connecting the island to the mainland. The track was lost in places, but seemed to lead to the main road and then to Thomset's house.

Bedell wasted no time in arresting Thomset for the murder of Peter Lazier very early on the morning after the murder. When he knocked, Thomset came to the door and said, 'Hey is this you? Take a seat.' Bedell replied: 'No Joe I have come to arrest you.' When Thomset asked what for, Bedell told him that there had been a couple of men out at a house near Bloomfield who had frightened some people with firearms. Thomset complained that he always seemed to be a suspect. Before he got dressed Bedell told him, 'Joe, there is a man dead over there at the house.' Thomset turned pale and demanded to know the grounds for the arrest. Bedell told him that he had found tracks leading from the Jones' farmhouse to his. He asked Thomset where he had been the previous evening and told him the time the murder had been committed. Thomset denied any involvement. Bedell told him that there would be no problem if he could give a satisfactory account of where he had been last night. Thomset told Bedell that he had been at the Lowders' and mentioned that he had passed by the Hicks' residence on his way home. Bedell arrested Thomset and took him to the Lowder residence.

Chief Constable Horatio Babbitt and the Arrest of David Lowder

Horatio N. Babbitt, chief constable for Prince Edward County, got to the Jones house at about 3:30 a.m. the night of the murder. As chief constable, it was Babbitt's responsibility to take charge of the investigation, although both Babbitt and Bedell lacked experience and training in the investigation of such a serious crime.

There was considerable coming and going to and from the Jones farm on the part of the trackers, so Babbitt knew something of what they had found and the direction they had gone. Abram Saylor gave Babbitt the stick he had used to measure some of the tracks. Yet it is by no means clear how or why Babbitt proceeded directly to the home of Joseph Thomset. Bedell and McDonald, the first to claim that the tracks led in that direction, had not returned. The local constabulary, it would seem, had quickly fastened on Joseph Thomset as the likely culprit. As Babbitt would later explain:

The first thing I did was to drive the cutter to Thomset's to meet some people who had tracked to this track down the lake. I did not know I would meet them there.

I went into Thomset's house and found Thomset in charge of the constable Bedell. Mrs. Thomset and the little girl were there. I asked Bedell if he had him under arrest. He said he had. I told him to get his clothes on, for I was in a great hurry and he would have to go with us. I saw a shotgun there and I brought it with me. I brought him out, put him in the cutter, and told Constable Bedell to get in with him.

Babbitt saw some tracks coming to and from Thomset's place, but made no effort to trace them. He proceeded back along the road to the home of John Lowder, a sixty-year-old fisherman and farmer who had immigrated as a child to Canada from England. Lowder and his Canadian-born wife Margaret[9] had eight children, two daughters and six boys. The four youngest sons, George (23), David (21), Christopher (19), and Allan (17) still lived at home.[10]

Babbitt heard David Lowder say something to Thomset about them having been together the night before. Bedell heard Thomset say, 'You remember, Dave, my being at your place about ten o'clock last night.' David answered him that he did. Babbitt asked David to lift his boot so that he could measure it with a stick Abram Saylor had used to measure the tracks. 'I measured one of the boots on his feet and they did not correspond with my measure.' Despite the discrepancy of the boot size and the lack of any other evidence to link David Lowder to the crime, Babbitt arrested him on the spot:

I came up into the house to get his overcoat and while in the house he wanted me to examine a pair of boots he had there. They were brought out – an old pair of boots with a hole in the side. They did not correspond with the measure. I went back to the cutter and started for Bloomfield.

Patch-bottom Boots and the Arrest of George Lowder

Babbitt explored the tracks near the Jones' farmhouse and some time the next morning returned to the Lowder house, where he found a pair of boots that he thought could have made the tracks. He measured the boots with the stick and examined the patch-bottom. He put the boots back where he found them. Babbitt then returned to Bloomfield, where he asked Adam H. Saylor, a prominent Bloomfield businessman and justice of the peace, to exercise his legal powers to seize the boots. Babbitt did not know who the boots belonged to, although he naturally assumed that they belonged to one of the Lowders.

Thomset and David Lowder were taken by sleigh to the town hall in Bloomfield, the closest public building. As Babbitt had requested, Adam Saylor went with John Fralick to the Lowder residence, where he seized the pair of patch-bottom boots that Babbitt had found earlier that morning. Saylor put the boots under the seat of Fralick's cutter and drove back to Bloomfield. Fralick lived opposite the town hall, where the prisoners were being held. He left the cutter in his yard while he went to the stable to tend to his horse. When he had finished with the horse, John Fralick removed the boots from the cutter and gave them to his wife.

Outside the town hall, Saylor and Fralick encountered George Lowder. George had been to Picton earlier that morning to retain a lawyer for his brother David and Joseph Thomset. Fralick heard George say, 'Who has got my boots?' The other young men milling about told George that Saylor and Fralick had his boots. Saylor told George, 'Your boots are in the cutter across the yard into Fralick's cutter,' to which

George replied, 'If I should see them, I would know them.' Saylor told him that he could go and have a look at the boots he had seized. Neither Saylor nor Fralick saw George approach the cutter to inspect the boots, but Fralick's wife would later testify that she saw a young man whom she could not identify walk up to the cutter, peer in, and then walk away.

Fralick later encountered George Lowder opposite the post office, and related this conversation: 'He asked me what I was doing with his boots. I said "George, I did not get your boots, Mr. Saylor got them." Said I "Are they your boots?" "Yes" said he. "They are, and I would like to have them to do the chores, but" said he, "You can have them and welcome."'

George Lowder was arrested later that day at Bloomfield, and became the third man charged with the murder of Peter Lazier.

3

Hugh McKinnon, Detective

The morning after the murder, George Pope, Peter Lazier's brother-in-law, was eating his breakfast at his home in Belleville, a town of 12,000 inhabitants on the north shore of the Bay of Quinte, less than twenty miles from the scene of the crime. Pope received a telegram from Gilbert Jones conveying the shocking news of Lazier's death. Pope had the dreadful task of informing Lazier's widow that her husband had been murdered. Horrified and devastated by the crime, Pope engaged Hugh McKinnon, Belleville's chief of police and a detective with nineteen years' experience, to investigate the murder. There is nothing to indicate that Pope or anyone else paid McKinnon for his efforts, but as the trial approached, Philip Low, Prince Edward County's crown attorney, got permission from the deputy attorney general 'to employ' McKinnon to prepare the case for trial.[1]

'Sleuth and strongman'

Hugh McKinnon,[2] Belleville's forty-year-old chief of police, was a formidable figure standing 6 feet, 3 inches tall and weighing 225 pounds. He had demonstrated his strength and athletic prowess as a regular champion in the Scottish sport of heavyweight tossing in the 1870s. McKinnon had briefly articled with his older brother's law firm in his home town of Hamilton, but after three years, deciding that he 'was a born detective' and 'hunger[ing] for a chance to distinguish himself in police and detective work,' he abandoned his fledgling legal career to become a private detective. [3] After a rather uncertain and undistinguished start, he gained notoriety when he was engaged by a group of concerned citizens in Lucan, a town in south-western Ontario, to investigate the infamous Donnelly gang. He went 'underground' and attempted to infiltrate the Donnellys. Whether he succeeded in duping the gang members is a matter of debate, but five members of the Donnelly family and several associates were brought to trial and convicted of various offences.[4] McKinnon found himself charged with assault as a result of a gang-related fight, but he was acquitted at trial.

McKinnon was appointed as Belleville's chief of police in 1877 to deal with a crisis. The police chief, the town council, and the local magistrate were at loggerheads. McKinnon's predecessor had tried to hold on to his office after being fired by the town council amid a crisis of confidence arising from his refusal to arrest striking Grand Trunk Railway workers. The mayor proclaimed an emergency and brought in the troops. The police force was demoralized and leaderless. McKinnon quickly rallied his force of two sergeants and five men by providing them with clear orders and updating their uniforms and equipment. The local newspapers lauded his efforts and McKinnon's name soon struck 'terror into the hearts of evil-doers.'[5]

McKinnon was a man of courage and conviction, a tough policeman who did not hesitate to assert his authority or his imposing physical presence even to the point of intimidation. 'He was a walking blend of sleuth and strongman – a Pinkerton and a Wyatt Earp.'[6] In 1886, after almost ten years in Belleville, McKinnon returned to Hamilton as chief of a much larger police force, where he earned a solid reputation as a good administrator and popular figure, only to come unstuck in 1895 when he was absent for five days and found to be in a Toronto hotel with two women. He returned to private detective work and ended his days in Dawson City, Yukon, where, despite his penchant for drink, his job was to take charge of controlling illegal alcohol.

Community Justice

As in most rural Ontario communities in the 1880s, Prince Edward County had no organized police force. Chief Constable Babbitt and Constable Bedell were not full-time peace officers. They were essentially community volunteers who lacked training and experience in the investigation of such a serious crime, and despite the County's wariness of outside influence, they did not resist McKinnon's intervention in the case.

Babbitt and Bedell had been appointed as constables by the General Sessions of the Peace, or Quarter Sessions, the local county court judge presiding, on the recommendation of the local justices of the peace. Justices of the peace were men of solid standing who were expected to reflect and uphold the values of the community. They were required by statute to be 'of the most sufficient persons resident in the county' and property qualifications were used to ensure that those appointed were up to the task.[7] Although untrained in the law, they were on the front line of law enforcement and exercised administrative, policing, and adjudicative functions. Justices of the peace were responsible for building and maintaining courthouses and local jails, highway planning and maintenance, regulating liquor licences and taverns, and inspecting weights and measures. In the administration of justice, they were responsible for investigating crimes and appointing constables, and they had the power to decide issues arising in the early stage of the criminal process – bail and committal for trial for serious offences – as well as the final adjudication of minor offences. The investigative functions could be exercised by a single justice of the peace, while the judicial functions were carried out by two or more justices.

Unsalaried local justices, modestly and, for the most part, inadequately compensated on a fee-for-service basis, remained the cornerstone of the administration of justice in the late nineteenth century. Responsibility for the investigation of crime rested with the amateur, quasi-volunteer efforts of the justices of the peace, constables, and, in homicide cases, the coroner.[8] Constables like Bedell were not paid a salary, and they only received modest fees, fixed by a provincial tariff that often failed to match their out-of-pocket expenses. Chief constables like Babbitt were sometimes, but not always, paid a modest salary from the county.

From the mid-1850s, the establishment of a more professional and uniform province-wide police service along the lines of the Belleville force headed by McKinnon was under active consideration by the provincial government. At first, many municipal authorities who distrusted centralization and wished to maintain local control over the administration of justice resisted change.[9] However, by the 1880s, there was a growing feeling that professional police forces were required and that the provincial government should assume more responsibility for the administration of criminal justice. Many cities and towns, such as

Belleville, had established paid police forces, and from 1859, in some of the larger communities, including Picton, the provincial government appointed stipendiary police magistrates to deal with a wide range of criminal cases.[10] Although their jurisdiction was significant, police magistrates were only paid $400 per year – less than the average annual wage of a tradesman and less than one-tenth of the salary paid to a Superior Court judge – and even that was thought to be inadequate.[11]

McKinnon's intervention in the Lazier murder case reflected the change that was occurring in the administration of justice in late-nineteenth-century rural Ontario. The community-based approach inherited from England that relied on respectable local citizens to serve as justices of the peace, coroners, and constables was yielding to specialization and professionalization. Constables Babbitt and Bedell were, no doubt, honest and upstanding citizens who faithfully served their community by reliably enforcing the law under the supervision of the justices of the peace. The offices they held were meant to reflect the values of the community and to bring to bear the community's sense of decency and fair play in the administration of justice. But they were clearly amateurs, drawn from the ranks of artisans, tradesmen, and small businessmen who served part-time and worked on an inadequate fee-for-service basis, and who had no training in law enforcement or criminal investigation.[12]

If Babbitt and Bedell reflected a fading model of policing and law enforcement, McKinnon represented the future of policing in Ontario. He worked as a trained professional who had no deep roots in the community. He embraced quasi-military organization and discipline, and was reputed to be possessed of a cool, dispassionate understanding of criminal behaviour with the skills and knowledge required to track down the evil-doers. As we shall see, McKinnon's professional approach was also quite ruthless.

Pleas for Professionalism

A year before the Lazier murder, J.G. Scott, Ontario's deputy attorney general, sent a circular letter to the province's judges, crown attorneys, sheriffs, and chief constables to 'ascertain the opinion throughout the Province who are best able to judge, as to the efficiency or otherwise of the present system of detecting crime and bringing the offenders to justice.' Was the constabulary force now in place adequate or should it 'be supplemented by the appointment of detectives or constables paid by salary instead of fees?' Was there any reason to believe that 'criminals now escape detection or conviction, who under such an arrangement would probably be brought to justice?'[13]

The overwhelming view was that the current system was inadequate. Most local law enforcement officials stated that constables should be more carefully selected and better paid, and that more satisfactory arrangements were required for reimbursement of the expenses they incurred in the detection of crime. Many complained that constables lacked training, aptitude, and motivation. Constables appointed under the influence of local politicians lacked independence and tended to be 'subservient to the wishes of councillors and their friends.'[14]

Most frequently mentioned was the absence of a proper scheme of remuneration for both constables and justices of the peace. A salaried police magistrate from Owen Sound thought that the rural justices of the peace lacked impartiality and were subject to being 'swayed by private friendship or by private enmity' as well as avoiding cases that did not offer significant fees.[15] Others reported that the county justices were 'not very well up in the knowledge of their duties.'[16] Typical were the views of Kent County Sheriff John Mercer: 'The present system of indiscriminate appointments of both the rural magistracy and constabulary, puts a certain amount of power in the hands of a great number of men, ignorant alike of letters and law, which is in many instances used for the furtherance of their own desires and designs instead of the legal benefit of the residents.'[17] The English model, based upon the noblesse oblige of the landed gentry, was difficult to replicate in nineteenth-century rural Ontario. Renfrew's crown attorney recommended the appointment of properly trained and paid magistrates: 'In this comparatively new country the position of a Justice of the Peace is not regarded in the same way as in Britain [and] it is almost impossible to get farmers or others in most of the outlying townships to perform the duties of a J.P.'[18]

The fee-for-service payment scheme for constables was regarded as problematic and the principal weakness in the existing scheme of law enforcement. Prince Edward County Sheriff James Gillespie thought that it was unfair, both to the magistrate and to the litigants, that the magistrate should depend upon the fines he levied for his own remuneration. Magistrates should not, he argued, be 'subject to the accusation of having inflicted a fine in order to secure his own costs, or being told, or having it generally believed the case would never have been brought if he had not acted as detective as well as police magistrate.'[19]

The county court judge from Napanee described the present system as 'utterly useless'[20] and the county court judge from Cobourg reported that constables were 'utterly wanting' in their knowledge of the methods of crime detection, adding: 'It cannot be expected that men engaged most of their time in other avocations, can be properly skilled in the detective art.' He advocated the employment of properly paid individuals who were required to devote their full-time attention to law enforcement.[21] Many correspondents pointed out that constables were reluctant to pursue suspected criminals in contentious cases as they would only get paid if they were successful in apprehending a suspect and securing a conviction. Constables had no advance for expenses and even the modest fees and expenses allowed by the tariff were often reduced by local audit authorities.

Some constables promoted 'frivolous and vexatious prosecutions for the sake of making fees'[22] or devoted their time and attention to trivial cases requiring little work and certain remuneration while ignoring the more difficult cases. London's police chief, who claimed twenty years' experience as a constable in England and in Canada, reported that the fee-paid constable often 'simply executes the process of the court after the real detective work has been done, or attempted to be done, by the complainant or some other interested person.'[23]

Some suggested that the crown attorney, rather than the justices of the peace, should be given the power to authorize investigations or conduct further inquiries in difficult cases. Many felt that a select number of trained detectives should be hired in the more heavily populated areas, and in areas where there was no need for a permanent detective, one should be made available when required for the investigation of serious crimes.

Chief Hugh McKinnon responded to the circular letter with a strong recommendation for a professional police force. McKinnon reported that many criminals escaped detection in rural areas policed by volunteer constables. He explained the situation as follows:

The constable (who is usually a poor man financially), without a dollar in his pocket for disbursements, can only take a look about the immediate neighbourhood and if he fails to discover the culprit, then that ends the case, he has not the means to pursue any further and the fees are totally inadequate to reimburse him for either his time or necessary expenses. When the work is done, he has to wait from two to five months for his miserable fees made more so by the Audit of Criminal Justice Accounts.[24]

But in 1882 in Prince Edward County, the tradition of community policing and a wariness of outside influence reigned supreme. The local judge, sheriff, and constabulary staunchly resisted the tide of opinion in favour of reform and resisted any move to greater centralization or professionalization. The County's legal establishment resoundingly answered that things were perfectly fine as they were. County Court Judge Robert Jellett pronounced the constabulary force to be 'ample' and further assistance to be 'unnecessary.'[25] Sheriff James Gillespie allowed that criminals did escape justice, 'but not from any defect in the constabulary.'[26] Chief Constable H.N. Babbitt reported that 'the present constabulary force for the County of Prince Edward is sufficient for bringing criminals to justice.'[27]

It became clear, however, that these attitudes were premised on the belief that Prince Edward County was a peaceful place and essentially crime-free. The murder of Peter Lazier in 1883, the third homicide since the early 1860s,[28] pointed to the need for a new approach. When the need arose, the local authorities readily admitted their need for professional help, and when it was proffered in the form of the famous detective Chief Hugh McKinnon, they did not refuse it.[29]

McKinnon Takes Charge

On Saturday, the day after the murder, McKinnon travelled to the Jones residence from Belleville with Pope, Mrs Lazier and Lazier's son from an earlier marriage. They arrived at about 1:30 p.m. Peter Lazier's body was still lying in the house. The coroner's investigation was already under way and there were many people milling about. McKinnon was told that Lazier's assailants had left tracks in the snow at the rear of the house, where they had lurked to await the opportune moment to attack, and at the front of the house as they fled. Those tracks had led to the arrest of Joseph Thomset and David Lowder. McKinnon immediately started to gather the evidence he thought necessary to convict them. After finding out what he could at the Jones farm, McKinnon drove to the Bloomfield town hall, where Thomset and David Lowder were being held. 'I requested them to remove their boots which they did.'

George Lowder Arrested

McKinnon met Constable Edmund Bedell at Bloomfield and then returned to the Jones farm by horse-drawn cutter to commence his investigation. He took the boots he had removed from the two prisoners and proceeded from the farm to a point in the marsh where he had been told tracks could be found. The scene was covered with as many as twelve to fifteen different sets of footprints left by those who had attempted to follow the trail. One tracker, Frank McDonald, had worn a pair of patch-bottom boots. However, McKinnon was confident that he could distinguish the tracks left by the culprits from the others. He measured fifteen or twenty tracks extending over a distance of about an eighth of a mile. The trail was broken and there were places through the marsh where no tracks could be seen. Some of the tracks were frozen in the ice and he had to blow snow out to examine them. It quickly became clear that the case against David Lowder was shaky, but that the tracks implicated Thomset.

We found the tracks of two persons. I began by first testing David Lowder's shoes and discovered at once that they did not compare with either of the two tracks by making impressions beside the tracks in the snow and comparing the tracks in that way and also by in some instances fitting the shoe in the original track. I made impressions beside the original track with the boots I had taken from Thomset and found that they compared exactly with the track of one of the persons. We found a point of separation of the two tracks in the vicinity of Johnson's island. One track proceeded right on towards Tubbs Island and the other track proceeded in a direction towards the Lowder place. I made further tests after the point of separation and found that the boots I had received from Thomset made identical tracks and fitted identically to the tracks that were pointed out to me leading in a direction past Johnson's Island off in the direction of Tubbs Island. The two tracks were not at all alike and there was no difficulty in distinguishing them. I did not proceed very far beyond the point of separation.

McKinnon decided that if David Lowder's boots had not left the tracks, another member of the Lowder family must have been implicated in the crime. He returned to Bloomfield and directed George Lowder's arrest. Although the same evidence of the tracks that provided the basis for arresting George appeared to exclude David Lowder, David remained in custody charged with murder.

More Tracking

The tracks McKinnon investigated on Saturday were at about the midpoint between the Jones farm and Thomset's house. Tracks in the snow are quickly lost or transformed with wind and changing weather conditions. Given the importance the tracks almost immediately assumed in identifying the alleged murderers, it seems odd that McKinnon did no further investigation of any other tracks that day. It was hardly surprising that there would be tracks in the snow leading to both the Lowder and Thomset residences. Unless those tracks could be traced from the Jones farm, they proved nothing.

The tracking efforts had continued the morning after the murder and after the arrest of Thomset and David Lowder. Abram Saylor, Charles Saylor, Constable Babbitt, Constable Bedell, and Stephen Bowerman all set out at various times. All agreed that there was nothing to indicate where Lazier's killers had come from, but there were tracks leading away from the Jones farmhouse. One track, made by a boot that had a patch-bottom, went through the yard. The other, made by a smooth bottomed boot with a 'rounding toe,' led down the driveway from the kitchen door. This was the path Gilbert Jones had seen the man who shot Peter Lazier take, and it meant that the killer was wearing a smooth-bottomed boot with a rounded toe, the style of boot worn by Joseph Thomset.

The recollections of the trackers about exactly when and with whom they went varied considerably, but they did claim, with varying degrees of certainty and precision, that one could follow two tracks as far as Springbrook, where they separated. One went south across West Lake and then south along the sand bar from Tubbs Island. The track was then lost, but similar tracks were found outside Thomset's house.

Alfred and Delia Hicks reported that Joseph Thomset had come to their door at about 11 p.m. the night of the murder to ask for a ride to Picton the next day. Charles Saylor and Stephen Bowerman carefully timed the walk from the Jones farmhouse to the Hicks residence. It took precisely one hour and six minutes, according to Charles Saylor, 'at a good walk.' Stephen Bowerman agreed on the time, but described the pace differently: 'we walked as fast as we could – a good rapid walk.'

Abram Saylor provided the most coherent explanation of the trail that led from the Jones house to the Thomset and Lowder residences. At the road in front of the Jones farm, both tracks turned west 'six or seven or eight rods' and then south and into Saylor's orchard. The tracks went through the orchard, and then through a brickyard to the railway track. The brickyard was very rough where Saylor had been digging clay, and it was not possible to see distinctive features of the boots. The tracks then turned west on the railway track 'for eight or ten rods,' then south at a gate at Bowerman's, and over a bridge and across a marsh to a point of land, and then to the other side of the marsh to the point called Springbrook, where the tracks separated, one going in the direction of Lowder's home and one going in the direction of Thomset's. On the lake, the tracks had blown away in places, but the trackers now had little doubt that they could trace the paths taken by Lazier's killers.

The traffic along this trail was considerable, and there were many tracks in the snow along the route left by other trackers. Abram Saylor himself insisted that he covered the track two or three times before eight o'clock in the morning. Despite all the traffic, he and the other trackers insisted they could distinguish the culprits' tracks from the others by the amount of snow that had drifted into the former. The tracks thought to be those of the two culprits had distinct features – one had a rounded toe and the other had a patch-bottom – although those features were not observed by all the trackers.

Before McKinnon's arrival, efforts were made to measure the size of the suspicious tracks. Abram Saylor initially used a stick and then cut a paper model of the tracks in the marsh. Saylor used the paper model to compare the tracks in the swamp with the tracks near Thomset's house and found them to be the same. However, both the stick and the paper model were lost by the time of the trial months later, and Saylor admitted that the paper was 'not cut very nice – it was just cut out with a jack-knife.'

Hugh McKinnon resumed his work on Sunday morning. He went with George Pope to Bloomfield, where he met Chief Constable Babbitt from Picton, Edmund Bedell, and Magistrate Adam Saylor, who handed McKinnon the boots he had seized at the Lowder farm. The boots had been patched on the bottom and had a narrow leather strip that ran around the outside of the bottom of the boot. McKinnon noticed an irregularity – the distance between the heel and the patch on the sole on one of the boots was about a quarter of an inch more than on the other. Both the patch-bottom boots and Thomset's boots had the appearance of having been in wet snow and slush.

Although McKinnon had learned of the tracks near the windows at the Jones farm when he arrived there on Saturday morning, it was not until Sunday that he investigated them. McKinnon took the boots Saylor had given him to the Jones farm and tested several of the tracks behind the house.

There were a number of tracks covered up with dishes and boxes and one thing and another, perhaps a dozen. I made impressions beside the tracks and compared them and in some of the tracks fitted the boots right and left and found that they fitted exactly and that the impressions were exactly those made by these boots. I came to the conclusion that the boots which I received from Mr. Saylor were on the feet of the person who left those tracks behind the house.

McKinnon's Investigative Techniques

Despite his reputation as an expert in crime detection, McKinnon's method was open to question. He did not use calipers or even a ruler to measure the tracks and had no note or precise record to support his contention that the tracks matched. When testing the tracks near the Lowder house, he used bellows to blow fresh snow out of the tracks. He also placed the boots in the tracks, as did several other trackers who measured the boots with the impressions in the snow. This was contrary to the advice offered in a standard manual used at the time for the investigation of footprint evidence:

Foot-prints near the body should be guarded from obliteration. The method usually recommended for ascertaining if a foot-print was made with a particular boot is to make an impression with the boot near the one found, and compare the two. Placing the boot into the impression is not advisable, as doing so may destroy the print without giving any satisfactory evidence, and will not afford any means of comparing the nails, patches &c., on the sole with the original impression. Some writers assert that the foot-print on the ground is generally smaller than the foot which made it, owing to the consistence of the soil, the shape of the foot, or the boot or shoe covering it, or the manner in which the foot was placed in walking. Sometimes it is said to be larger if on a light soil.[30]

For some unexplained reason, McKinnon appears not to have measured Thomset's boots in any of the tracks at the rear of the house. That was not done until four or five days later, when Constable Bedell returned with Thomset's boots to test the imprints.

After examining the tracks behind the Jones house, McKinnon proceeded to the Lowder residence to examine tracks left by the patch-bottom boots. He found tracks leading from the lake to the house, but the trail from the point where the two tracks separated at Springbrook was broken and could not be traced.

McKinnon then entered the Lowder house, where he saw two dou-ble-barrelled shotguns and a musket or single-barrel shotgun in a bed-room. One of the double-barrelled guns was loaded and the other had an exploded cap. He also went to Thomset's house. He did not himself search the premises, but gave directions to have such a search done. Constable Babbitt did a thorough sweep of the house top to bottom. Nothing was found – in particular, there was no sign of a pistol or of a hood or mask of the kind worn by Peter Lazier's killer.

McKinnon then returned to Picton without making any further tests, apparently confident that the true culprits had been identified. He made no attempt to follow the tracks from the Jones farmhouse to-wards the Lowder and Thomset houses and he did not test Thomset's boots against the footprints near the windows at the back of the Jones house or the tracks that were thought to be those of the man who fired the fatal shot. At the jail, the bootless prisoners, Joseph Thomset and David Lowder, had their footwear restored, despite the fact that the boots were crucial pieces of real evidence allegedly linking the prison-ers to the crime.

Right to Silence

Neither McKinnon nor any other constable made any attempt to ques-tion the three prisoners. The right to silence was an established prin-ciple of law in the nineteenth century, a product of the common law's revulsion against forcing accused persons to condemn themselves and the discredited inquisitorial practices of the infamous Star Chamber. In the nineteenth century, the right to silence was seen to preclude ques-tioning a person who had been arrested and accused of a serious crime. A suspect could be questioned before arrest, but as an 1885 English decision explained: 'When a prisoner is in custody, the police have no right to ask him questions … A prisoner's mouth is closed after he is once given in charge, and he ought not to be asked anything.'[31] While some judges took a different view,[32] that case also held that if a prisoner was questioned, evidence of what he or she said would not be admis-sible at trial.

Trickery and Deceit

McKinnon respected the rule that precluded questioning the accused, but to bolster his case he decided to resort to trickery and deceit. He knew that the case would be much stronger if the murder weapon could be found and he was prepared to use devious tactics to find it. He made no secret of what he had done.

I went to Mrs. Thomset to discover if a revolver was to be found in the house and I took the only possible way I thought of getting it at the time. I went there for the purpose of deceiving Mrs. Thomset. If I could so deceive her and succeed in getting that revolver, my object would have been accomplished. I told her that her husband had confessed and had given directions for me to get the pistol. She first said she would send for Delia Hicks, a friend of hers living near there. I repeated to her a story manufactured for the occasion. I told her in a sympathetic way that I regretted very much the position she was in and her trouble. I told her that Thomset had made a confession I then repeated to her the confession.

Mrs Thomset either had nothing to reveal or, if she did, she was not fooled by McKinnon's ruse. No murder weapon was produced. Apparently not satisfied, McKinnon decided to test her again. A day or so later, he sent her a forged letter, said to be from her husband, confessing. But this too failed to uncover the murder weapon.

4

A Place Apart

The Lazier murder case was widely covered in the press across the province. The *Intelligencer*, a daily newspaper published in Belleville, immediately dispatched reporter J.L. Mills to Prince Edward County when it learned that one of its residents had been murdered. Mills and his journalist colleagues from Belleville's *Daily Ontario*, Kingston's *British Whig*, Toronto's *Globe*, and Picton's own *Gazette* covered the case from the day after the murder. Mills advised his readers that the murder of Peter Lazier provoked 'intense' excitement in Prince Edward County, where the people are 'law abiding and peaceable,' making it 'a poor field for litigation.'[1] As we shall see, the reaction of the citizens of Prince Edward County to the murder of Peter Lazier and the mood of the community at the time of the trial had a powerful influence on the fate of the accused men. To fully understand how the legal process was played out, we need to understand the particularities of the place and its people.

Peter Lazier was well known in Prince Edward County. The Laziers were Huguenots who came to America in 1708 to escape religious persecution in France. Peter's grandfather, Nicolas Lazier, was a United Empire Loyalist who had fled New York – bringing his slaves with him – during the American revolution to remain loyal to the British crown.[2] The United Empire Loyalists were the first European settlers to put down roots in the County.[3] For generations to come they held elevated status as the founders of a new land and pillars of the community committed to traditional British values. The murder of a 'U.E.L.' descendant represented a serious blow to the County's self-image as a tranquil and peaceful place.

Peter Lazier was born in Picton and lived near the town until he moved to Belleville some five years before his death. He was married, had one son, and had travelled to Prince Edward County in late December in the employ of Patterson and Company, for whom he sold farm implements. A newspaper account of the crime described him in glowing terms: 'A man of excellent habits, undemonstrative, temperate, sociable and gentlemanly, and had not an enemy. His quiet bearing, gentlemanly demeanour and cheerful manner of address won him a wide circle of friends who deeply regret his untimely demise.'[4] Another report described Lazier as 'well known in this and surrounding counties for his upright dealing and a manly, straightforward manner of doing business.'[5]

The County

Despite the proximity of Belleville to Bloomfield and Prince Edward County, the *Intelligencer*'s reporter described his journey in terms that suggested he was travelling to a distant and foreign land: 'Prince Edward is a strange county, and strange indeed are the majority of people who dwell therein.' Although it was said to be 'the wealthiest county in the province,' the reporter complained that its roads were in a deplorable state, making his journey even more arduous.[6]

Prince Edward County has always been a place apart.[7] 'The County,' as it has long been known to its inhabitants, is an irregularly shaped peninsula of some 241,500 acres – approximately 380 square miles – that juts out into Lake Ontario south of Belleville and west of Kingston. The only point that joins the County by land to the rest of Ontario is a narrow isthmus at Carrying Place near Trenton, and even that connection was severed in the late 1880s by the construction of the Murray Canal. The physical separation from the mainland of Ontario has encouraged the County's strong sense of being a distinctive community.

Because of its irregular shape and a coastline disproportionately long in relation to its area, no place in the County is far from the waters of Lake Ontario. There are few lakes or streams, but the County enjoys a richness of bays and inlets along its shores on the Bay of Quinte to the north, Long Reach and Adolphous Reach to the west, Weller's Bay to the east, and West Lake, Athol Bay, Soup Harbour, and Lake Ontario to the south. In addition to their natural beauty, these shores provided the County's farmers with excellent access to shipping.

In the 1880s, Prince Edward County's economy was primarily agricultural. The main crop was barley and the principal market was in the United States. Farmers shipped their barley across Lake Ontario to New York State, where it was used to make beer. In 1881, barley was grown in 40,000 acres, nearly one-third of the County's cultivated land. Hops was also a major crop, and the soil and climate in the Bloomfield area where Gilbert and Margaret Jones farmed was conducive to its cultivation. Fortunes were made on barley and hops. Gracious homes were built and frugal farmers, who knew that their bounty depended upon unpredictable weather and changing market conditions, carefully saved fearing less prosperous times could come. Shipbuilding thrived. In the late autumn, ports at Big Island, Northport, Milford, Cressy, Waupoos, Rednersville, Consecon, and Wellington were crammed with schooners, barques, and barges loading barley to be shipped across the lake before winter. It was during the 1880s that the County reached the height of its prosperity and that era is still nostalgically remembered as the 'Barley Days.'[8] As the compilers of a historical atlas published in 1879 observed, 'Compared in size and population, there are among its inhabitants a greater number of comfortably situated *owners* of the soil they till, than any other section we have ever visited.'[9]

The County also had a successful fishing industry. Large catches of whitefish, lake herring, lake trout, and great northern pike taken by fishers such as Joseph Thomset and John Lowder from Lake Ontario were shipped to the United States by rail or boat.[10]

With prosperity came innovation. The introduction of the telegraph in the 1870s permitted effective communications, and a fledgling telephone system was established in 1883. Horse and buggy remained the only available mode of transportation until 1878, when Picton was linked to the Grand Trunk Railway line and service was provided between Picton, Bloomfield, and Wellington. By 1880, grammar schools were built throughout the rural areas and a high school was established in Picton.

The dominant religion was Methodist, but there were many other Protestant churches, a significant Roman Catholic presence, and, particularly in the area near Bloomfield and West Lake, a vibrant community of Quakers. The Quakers formed a distinctive religious group, but with their 'quiet independence, conservatism, strength, faith and loyalty'[11] they were entirely in tune with the prevailing mores of the County.

The County's population of some 19,000 souls lived a relatively tranquil, isolated, and prosperous life. An element of smugness and a sense of self-satisfaction mingled with contentment. Although no doubt prone to exaggeration and flattery to secure sales and to please the 'patrons' who had paid to have their names included, the compilers of an 1879 historical atlas probably reflected the self-image of the County's residents:

We may truthfully say that as to varied and delightful scenery, magnificent roads, pleasant drives, interesting natural and historical landmarks, and an intelligent, refined, and hospitable people, Prince Edward beyond question claims a foremost position; while in everything which tends to make a country prosperous, its people contented with their lot, and others contented with them, it occupies no second-place.[12]

Picton, the largest town and the county seat, lies at the head of Picton Bay. The second largest community, Wellington, sits ten miles west on Lake Ontario and midway between the two is Bloomfield, the County's third largest community, which lies just beyond the head of West Lake.

In the 1880s Picton was the bustling and prosperous centre of the County. It had two newspapers, the *Gazette* and the *New Nation and Times*. The Bank of Montreal and the Standard Bank boasted imposing buildings on Main Street. The town had six lawyers, seven doctors, two photographers, four drugstores, and three jewellery stores. There were numerous grocery stores, confectioners, bakeries, butcher shops, a dozen dry goods stores, five merchant tailors, and seven boot and shoe stores. The town was amply supplied with hotels, eight in total, one of which was a temperance hotel and seven where one could enjoy a drink at the bar.[13]

The 'Barley Days,' and the County's prosperity, came to a crashing halt in 1890, six years after the murder of Peter Lazier. At the insistence of American farmers, the United States introduced the McKinley tariff in 1890 to protect barley and many other agricultural products. It would take the County more than one hundred years to recover something approaching the economic power of the three decades from 1860 to 1890 during the glorious barley boom.

Sir John A. and County Politics

County residents have always been proud of the fact that Canada's first prime minister, Sir John A. Macdonald, practised as a young lawyer in the County for four years in the 1830s. Macdonald articled with his uncle, Lowther Macpherson, and became active in local politics. He felt 'instantly and easily at home' in the County.[14] One of the first cases he argued in Picton's new courthouse was his own. When a political argument became heated, blows were exchanged and Macdonald was charged with assault. The young lawyer convinced the jury to enter an acquittal.[15] Counter-charges against the complainant, tried the next day, resulted in conviction and a fine of six pence.[16]

Whenever Macdonald returned to the County he was treated like a long-lost son.[17] In 1861 a large contingent of the 'most respectable of our farmers and their families' travelled by steamer to Kingston to collect Macdonald, then attorney general for Canada West. He returned to greet a large crowd in front of the courthouse, where, he reminded the audience, '[I] earned my first fee and made my first speech to a jury … at the first Quarter Sessions that were held in it.' Macdonald spoke nostalgically of 'the good old county' where he cut his professional teeth and 'spent some of the happiest days of my life.'[18]

But despite Macdonald's flattery of the County and the pride its residents took in claiming him as a favourite son, the riding of Prince Edward was predominantly Liberal in the early years of Confederation. Walter Ross, a prominent Picton businessman who operated a general store, owned a steamship, and served several terms as the town's mayor, was elected as a Liberal member of parliament in the first three federal elections. He sat as an opposition member following the 1867 and 1872 elections that returned Macdonald as prime minister and then as a government member under Liberal prime minister Alexander Mackenzie in 1874. Conservative businessman James Simeon McQuaig finally succeeded on his fourth attempt to defeat Ross in 1878, when Macdonald returned to office. Given McQuaig's support for Macdonald, who did not hide his love of drink, it is perhaps ironic that McQuaig won the election on a temperance ticket.[19] However, McQuaig lost by 19 votes in the 1882 election to Liberal John M. Platt, physician and editor and publisher of Picton's *New Nation*, and once again, the member for Prince Edward sat in the opposition benches as Macdonald retained office.[20]

Crime in the County

There was little serious crime in Prince Edward County in the late nineteenth century. The records of the Picton Jail reveal that most of the individuals incarcerated there were charged with drunkenness and that few spent more than a day or two in the jail's tiny cells.[21] There were relatively few of the more exotic or serious offences – the occasional forgery, bigamy, malicious wounding, threatening to commit arson and 'wife beating.' Most were cases of vagrancy, assault, non-payment of fines, larceny, sheep or horse stealing, abusive language, contempt of court, indecent exposure, 'insanity,' want of sureties to keep the peace, or 'fighting in the street.' In an 1877 province-wide survey of the number of committals for trial for indictable offences, Prince Edward County reported the lowest number of any county.[22]

Almost all inmates held in Picton's jail were men described to be 'white,' although there was the occasional inmate said to be 'Indian.' There had been only one execution in the history of Prince Edward County – a black man named Hightower was hanged for rape at the Picton Jail on 12 May 1837.

The Lazier murder was the third County homicide in a period of just over twenty years. The tranquil pattern of the past had been broken. The first homicide was the grisly murder of Abraham Peterson, aged 48, and his wife Sarah, aged 60, at their home between Picton and Demorestville on 12 October 1860.[23] Seth Smart, an Aboriginal man from the village of Shannonville, north of the County and adjacent to the Tyendinaga Mohawk reserve, was arrested within days of the murders. Smart was said to have confessed to the crime and to have been extremely remorseful. His victims had suffered a cruel death. Smart had burst into their home during the evening and demanded money. He struck Sarah Paterson on the head with piece of wood, knocking her unconscious. He proceeded to the bedroom, where he did the same to Abraham Peterson before killing him with a blow to the head with a pick axe. After ransacking the house to find close to $200, Smart lit a fire near the bodies of his victims and fled. While awaiting his trial, Smart hanged himself with his suspenders in the Picton Jail on 3 May 1861.

The second homicide to shock the usually tranquil County occurred at Pleasant Bay near Consecon on 16 May 1880. John Amans was shot and killed at the farm of James Pierson. Thomas Thompson, a labourer from Hillier, was charged with murder; James Pierson was charged with being an accessory to murder. Their trial proceeded at the Picton fall assizes before Mr Justice Burton in October 1880. The key Crown witness was Catherine Vincent, a woman in her early twenties, who had come to reside with James Pierson and his wife after bearing a child. John Amans, the deceased, was the father. Amans, said to be 'dissipated and generally loose in his habits,' had studied at Albert College and the University of Toronto and had been left a substantial legacy shortly before his death.[24] He had been drinking the night he died and went to the Pierson residence, where he made a noise at Catherine Vincent's bedroom window. Vincent wanted nothing to do with him and asked him to leave. When Amans persisted, Thompson, who was also staying at the house, and Pierson were summoned for help. Thompson and Pierson had been drinking together earlier at Wellington. Thompson suspected Amans to be the intruder and asked him to leave. Pierson went to get a gun for protection. When Amans refused to leave, Thompson took the gun, fired a shot, and Amans was fatally wounded. Catherine Vincent testified that the killing had been deliberate, but Pierson's wife disputed Vincent's version and suggested that the killing had been accidental.

In the end, the Crown's case was inconclusive. The trial judge directed the jury to acquit James Pierson. George Dickson, the Belleville lawyer who would defend George Lowder three years later, argued that Thompson's gun had discharged accidentally. Crown counsel fairly conceded that the evidence did not support a murder conviction and urged the jury to find Thompson guilty of manslaughter. After deliberating for half an hour, the jury returned a verdict of manslaughter. Justice Burton clearly saw the case as borderline and imposed a lenient sentence of six months' imprisonment.

Less than two weeks after the Amans homicide, John Terry, described as a thirty-five-year-old labourer, was arrested on a charge of wounding with intent to murder. Terry, who had previously served three years in the penitentiary for larceny, had been on a drinking binge. His wife threw him out of the house. He confronted her with a butcher knife at the store and telegraph office at Roblin's Mills, Ameliasburgh. Both the female telegraph operator and Mrs Terry were wounded fending off his slashing blows. Terry ran off, but was quickly arrested and brought before the magistrates.

The Belleville *Intelligencer's* report of the incident noted: 'The usually quiet County of Prince Edward, which has long enjoyed immunity from crimes of violence, is having a plethora of that class of crime at present.'[25] Still, Terry did not kill his victims and while the Thompson and Amans case was a serious one, it was the product of an unfortunate coincidence of passion, alcohol, and accident, the culprits were easily identified, and the crime did not unsettle the community the way the Lazier murder did four years later.

Until the Lazier murder in 1883, the residents of Prince Edward County still believed that they lived in a relatively tranquil place free from the threat of serious crime. Two years before the Lazier murder, when asked by the province's deputy attorney general about the adequacy of resources for detecting crime and bringing offenders to justice, the local county court judge, Robert Jellett, pronounced Prince Edward County to be 'comparatively free from crime.' Sheriff James Gillespie described the people of the County as 'generally law abiding' and Chief Constable H.N. Babbitt proudly proclaimed Prince Edward to be 'more free from crime now, and for many previous years, than any other county in the province.'[26]

5

Coroner's Inquest

The legal process began to unfold within hours of Peter Lazier's death. Dr Alan Noxon, who had been called to attend to Lazier, also happened to be the local coroner. As required by law,[1] he convened an inquest as soon as practicable on Saturday morning, the day after the murder. The inquest opened at the Jones residence before Lazier's body had been removed.

The Coroner as the Front Line of Criminal Investigation

In the nineteenth century, the coroner played a central role in the investigation of suspicious deaths. Together with the justices of the peace and constables, coroners were an integral element of Ontario's nineteenth-century community-based scheme for the administration of justice, a scheme that reflected a predominantly 'Tory' view of the world that relied on local elites to maintain order and shape values.[2] Coroners were appointed by the lieutenant-governor in council. The office of coroner carried prestige and was a sought-after position. An 1878 manual describing the duties of Ontario coroners frankly admitted that political connections counted: 'Appointments are generally made upon the recommendation of a member of Parliament, or other person possessing influence with the Executive.'[3] In a sarcastic aside, the author added that there was no limit on the number of coroners that could be appointed except 'possibly ... the energy shewn by those seeking office.'[4] He was not the only commentator to complain that 'these positions were bestowed by the party for the time being in power on political partisans only, the question of capacity or fitness being considered, apparently, of secondary importance.'[5]

The coroner was under a statutory duty to investigate deaths caused by violence, unfair means, or culpable or negligent conduct, as well as any death of a prison inmate.[6] The circumstances of Peter Lazier's death clearly called for a coroner's inquest. Coroners were required to act with the efficiency and dispatch to be expected of a public officer who bore primary responsibility for the investigation of a serious crime. The process began with the coroner's warrant, directed to the constable, to summon a jury of no fewer than twelve men. Qualification for service on a coroner's jury was minimal: jurors were expected to be impartial, to reside in the township where the death occurred, to be 'lawful and honest men' and to be able to write their own names.[7] Dr Noxon issued his warrant and, with the local community in an uproar over the news of the previous evening's events, the constables had no difficulty in convening a jury.

There was no right to a public inquest, but the coroner was advised to 'err on the side of publicity' and to avoid 'conducting his proceedings too secretly.' It would have been very difficult for Dr Noxon not to follow this sage advice with all the neighbours and concerned citizens milling about the Jones farm. The right to counsel stood on the same footing as the right to a public hearing: there was no right to counsel, but coroners were advised that the better course was to permit counsel to attend and to participate in the examination of witnesses.

George Lowder had gone to Picton as soon as his brother David was arrested to retain Nehemiah Gilbert, a young lawyer who had been called to the bar in the spring of 1882 and who carried on a quiet country practice. When George himself was arrested later that day, Gilbert acquired a third client, and he attended the coroner's inquest to represent Thomset as well as the Lowder brothers.

It was a legal requirement that the coroner and the jury view the body together. If possible, the body was to be examined immediately and exactly at the place where the death occurred. Instructions to coroners made it clear that viewing the body by the coroner and the jury were vital aspects of homicide investigations:

When viewing the body, its position and appearance, its dress and marks of violence, blood spots and marks of mud thereon, and the appearance of the surrounding earth or objects, should all be most minutely noticed. The skill and intelligence of the Coroner and jury can here be shewn more than in the performance of any other part of their duties.

Especially in rural areas where there were no full-time or professional police resources available, the coroner's inquest was the front line of criminal investigation. The coroner was directed to make careful investigation of the crime scene. Of particular relevance to the Lazier inquest was the injunction to guard against 'prejudice' and keep from moving too quickly from 'mere suspicion' to belief.

The coroner was further instructed to be on the lookout for things that might not be obvious and that he 'should not ... confine himself to mere inspection or what actually presents itself to his eyes.' He was to 'conduct his search with great caution, if not scepticism, always remembering that hasty conclusions or thoughtless omissions may both endanger his won reputation and the lives of his fellow creatures.' Careful observation of the parties in attendance was advised as 'the culprit is apt to betray himself by an excess of caution, or by numerous and improbable suggestions as to the cause of death. An intelligent observation of the surrounding persons, then, may sometimes be of use.'

By the 1880s, there was a growing sense of unease with the degree of reliance placed upon the coroner to investigate homicides. In 1882, future Supreme Court of Canada justice John Iddington, then Perth County's crown attorney, urged the attorney general to reform the office of coroner. 'I am sure,' Iddington wrote, 'that many a murderer thanks, or ought to thank, the coroner's inquest for saving him from his fate.' Decrying the lack of skill of 'a country physician' who 'knows little, and can tell less' about the detection of crime, Iddington recommended the appointment of police magistrates to the office of coroner to ensure proper homicide investigation and the appointment 'of a public officer, possessed of the highest skill as a physician and chemist, to make all *post mortem* examinations.'[8]

Bloomfield Town Hall

Once the body had been viewed, the inquest could be adjourned to another place. Dr Noxon decided to move the inquest to the Bloomfield town hall on Saturday evening. The hall was crammed with people anxious to follow the proceedings. The evidence at the inquest was relatively straightforward and was summarized by the *Intelligencer* reporter in a manner that portrayed Peter Lazier as the courageous victim of desperate thieves:

One of the murderers beat him with a gun about the head, and as he was a strong, active and well preserved man ... it was resolved by his adversary ... to get away ... After Lazier's antagonist had freed himself from him, the murdered man was even then loath to give up the battle. Pursuing his assailant, a shot was fired to frighten him, but he was not of the timorous order. Another shot followed, which struck him in the breast and killed him. As he fell with his feet outside the door he exclaimed 'I am shot.' These were the last words uttered by Peter Lazier.[9]

Dr Noxon instructed Dr Charles Wright and Dr J.M. Platt, both Picton doctors, to conduct a post-mortem examination. There was no question as to the cause of death – Lazier was killed by a .32 calibre bullet which had entered the middle of the chest and penetrated the right lung and right cavity of the heart. The path of the bullet was tracked through the sternum or breastbone, the right auricle of the heart and the right lung.[10]

By the time Dr Noxon had moved the proceedings to the town hall in Bloomfield, word had spread that Edmund Bedell and Aaron Macdonald had traced footprints in the snow from the Jones farm to the homes of Joseph Thomset and the Lowder family. It was believed that the intended robbery was well planned, but that the killers were unaware of Peter Lazier's presence at the Jones farmhouse the night he met his death.

David Lowder and Joseph Thomset were present at the town hall for the inquest and George Lowder was taken there upon his arrest. David Lowder and Thomset were handcuffed together, but all three men were allowed to roam about the room at their will. The *Intelligencer* reporter milled with the crowd at the inquest, listened to the talk and discerned that the local community was satisfied that the culprits had been found. He described Thomset as being about thirty-eight years old, 'medium build, ... plainly dressed and his face was adorned with heavy whiskers. He has a wife and one child.' The reporter added that Thomset was a fisherman who plied his calling on the beach between Wellington and West Lake.[11]

Where the evidence pointed to a suspect, the coroner had the power to commit for trial.[12] If the evidence did point to a suspect, that individual was not competent to testify as a witness, but if he wished to make an unsworn statement, the coroner could permit him to do so after administering a caution: 'Having heard the evidence, do you wish to say anything in answer to the charge? You are not obliged to say anything unless you desire to do so; but what you say will be taken down in writing, and may be given in evidence against you at your trial.'[13]

Dr Noxon had no occasion to ask the three accused men if they wished to make a statement. They had been arrested for the crime and were present and represented by counsel. The boots that would incriminate Thomset were placed ominously on the platform at the front of the town hall. But no evidence was introduced at the inquest as to their involvement in the murder. As the inquest did not reveal evidence incriminating any particular culprit, the jury could only return a verdict of homicide by persons unknown. The verdict, delivered Saturday evening, was anti-climatic. The jury sagely concluded that 'the deceased came to his death at the hands of some parties unknown to the jury.'[14] As the inquest had been concluded, Dr Noxon was able to authorize Peter Lazier's burial two days later in Picton on Monday, 24 December 1893.

Assumed Guilt and a Threat of Lynching

Although the coroner's jury was not asked to assign blame or responsibility for the crime, the crowd attending the proceedings more or less took it for granted that Joseph Thomset and at least one of the Lowder brothers were the killers. Magistrate Adam Saylor went to the town hall and discovered that Thomset was anxious to talk. Saylor heard Thomset state:

If I had wanted money, I would not have went to Mr. Jones's. I would have went for Ward [another local farmer]. I am told he had a thousand dollars. I would not have went to Mr. Jones's. There is plenty of other places in Bloomfield that, if I had wanted money, I could have went for. If I had, I would not leave any to tell the story.

Thomset's statement was crude and ill advised. He did not enjoy a good reputation in the community. He had a history of conflict with Aaron McDonald that had led to criminal charges and, rightly or wrongly, was suspected of several recent larcenies. The Lowders, by contrast, were described as being the sons of 'an industrious farmer who owns a large farm near West Lake,' and little was said against them except for their association with Thomset.

The lax security arrangements at the town hall were initially no cause for concern, but as the inquest proceeded, the atmosphere became ominous and threatening. The *Intelligencer* reporter observed that 'the general opinion in Bloomfield is that the authorities have hit on the right men,' and there was speculation that David Lowder would 'turn Queen's evidence' and disclose the whole plot. The accused men 'protested their innocence and stoutly affirmed that they could prove an alibi,' but the crowd was not persuaded and the talk turned to lynching the culprits. To get them out of harm's way, McKinnon ordered them taken to the Picton jail before the inquest concluded, but even then, a gang in Wellington threatened to go to Picton to stage a lynching.[15] The Trenton *Courier Advocate* credited the actions of the police with saving the lives of the prisoners: 'The strongest expressions of a determination to lynch the men arrested prevail and nothing but the prudence of the police in hurrying the men off to gaol, saved the people from taking the law into their own hands and perpetrating a grievous crime.'[16]

While Dr Noxon appears to have conducted the coroner's inquest in exemplary fashion, it accomplished very little. The jury's verdict was inevitable and vague. The Lazier murder inquest shows how the role of the coroner in the investigation of crime had diminished. Once one of the cornerstones of the community-based model for the administration of criminal justice, the coroner's inquest had become a routine procedure that the law said had to be followed. The real work of investigating the crime would be left to Hugh McKinnon, the man with no roots in the community but reputed to be a skilled detective. Still, the coroner's inquest had exposed to public view at a very early stage what was known about the murder, and that exposure contributed to something approaching a lynch-mob mentality.

6

Committal Proceedings

The committal proceedings before police magistrate George C. Curry of Picton, and justices of the peace Adam Saylor and John H. Allan commenced on Friday, 28 December 1883. Philip Low, QC, a prominent Picton lawyer who served as the local crown attorney, appeared for the Crown. Nehemiah Gilbert appeared for the prisoners.

Committal proceedings, like the coroner's inquest, originally had an investigative function. The justices of the peace could examine witnesses, even the accused, to obtain evidence that could be used to secure a conviction.[1] By the mid-nineteenth century, committal proceedings had lost their investigative function and acquired a more judicial purpose. Committal proceedings served to screen cases to ensure that there was sufficient evidence to warrant putting accused persons to their trial.

The Crown Attorney

Philip Low combined his duties as the local crown attorney with a lucrative business career and commercial law practice. Low was born in Jersey, one of the Channel Islands, and came to Canada as a child. He read law in Toronto and was called to the bar in 1836. As a loyal volunteer in the 1837 rebellion, Low saw action at Montgomery Hill. He was one of Picton's first lawyers, and he practised there for more than fifty years until his death in 1892 at the age of 81. As president of the

Grand Trunk Telegraph Company, he was responsible for the laying of the submarine cable across the Bay of Quinte to give Picton telegraphic communication with the outside world. Low was also instrumental in establishing a branch of the Bank of Montreal in Picton and proudly proclaimed on his letterhead that he served as the bank's solicitor. He promoted the Prince Edward County railway and served as chairman of the Board of Police and as Picton's mayor in the 1850s.[2] Low was a respected member of the legal profession, serving as a bencher of the Law Society of Upper Canada (the governing body of the legal profession in Ontario) from 1859 to 1871.[3]

The office Philip Low held reflected an important reform in the administration of justice that was instituted in 1857.[4] The establishment of local crown attorneys was intended to introduce some measure of professionalism and central control to the administration of justice. Local justices of the peace and constables understood their communities, but they generally lacked legal expertise. The establishment of local crown attorneys, appointed and paid by the province to take control of the conduct of criminal matters, represented a bridge between the model of community-based and locally controlled administration of justice and the more centralized, professional regime that was steadily emerging in the late nineteenth century.

To be appointed crown attorney, a lawyer had to reside in the county, but he was selected and paid by the province. Crown attorneys had to be lawyers of three years' standing, and as the job was part-time, they were free to maintain a practice provided neither they nor their partners acted as defence counsel in any criminal case. The crown attorney's duties included reviewing papers arising from proceedings before coroners and magistrates, subpoenaing witnesses, directing further investigations, and instituting proceedings before the magistrates and at quarter sessions. Crown attorneys prepared matters for the assizes – serious criminal charges such as murder and rape to be tried before a high court judge and jury. The conduct of trials at assizes, however, was left to a provincial crown law officer or his substitute. The local crown attorney acted if no substitute was appointed and assisted if one was.

The appointment of crown attorneys limited the right and displaced the need for victims and their families to retain counsel to prosecute offenders. Allowing private citizens to prosecute crimes 'allowed personal vindictiveness to be gratified by frivolous or unconscionable proceedings' – one of the evils the institution of crown attorneys was meant to remedy.[5] Yet for some unexplained reason, at the Lazier committal proceedings, his family retained S.B. Burdett to act as private prosecutor. No doubt still traumatized by the murder, the members of Peter Lazier's family probably wanted to be certain that no stone was unturned in prosecuting the men they believed were responsible for their terrible loss. Gilbert objected, but the magistrates disagreed and permitted Burdett to represent the Lazier family. In the end, Burdett appears not to have taken an active role in the proceedings and he did not reappear at the trial, fading from the case just as private prosecutors had faded from view with the establishment of the regime of crown attorneys.

'Feloniously and with malice aforethought'

The committal proceedings in the Lazier murder case attracted intense community interest. Picton's hotels were filled with visitors and there was much talk about the murder. A large crowd wended its way to the courthouse, where the proceedings began at 10 a.m. A number of Quakers in the audience, there to support Gilbert and Margaret Jones, followed the custom of wearing their distinctive black hats. The prisoners were brought in, George Lowder first, followed by his brother David and then Thomset. 'They appeared quite cheerful and exchanged smiling glances of recognition with their friends.'[6]

In the late nineteenth century, a person accused of a serious offence was taken before the justices of the peace as soon as practicable so that the prosecution's case could be assessed. The accused was presented with the charge and the Crown's witnesses were sworn and testified. The accused had the right to cross-examine and to be represented by counsel. The justices of the peace decided whether to commit the accused for trial with or without bail. However, as Joseph Thomset and the Lowders faced the death sentence, only a superior court judge could admit them to bail.[7] The only issue for the justices of the peace was whether the Crown's evidence was sufficient 'to put the accused parties upon their trial.' The prosecution did not have to prove its case at this stage. It merely had to make out a prima facie case for the prisoner to answer at his trial – in other words, the prosecution had to provide some evidence on all the necessary elements that, if believed, could sustain a conviction.[8]

The formal charge was read by Mr Taylor, the court clerk, alleging that the accused 'feloniously, wilfully and with malice aforethought, did on the night of the 21st of December, in the Township of Hallowell, kill and murder Peter Lazier.' All three accused pleaded not guilty.

Nehemiah Gilbert was concerned by the level of interest in the proceedings and no doubt feared that as community opinion was swinging strongly against his clients, it would be difficult to select an impartial jury when it came to the trial. He asked that the public be excluded. By statute, the justices had the power to exclude the public 'if it appear to him or them that the ends of justice will be best answered by so doing.'[9] Orders banning the publication of pre-trial proceedings are now routinely given to protect the fair-trial rights of the accused, but an order excluding the public would today be exceptional. Certainly in the Lazier case, the justices could not resist the pressure of the intense community interest in the proceedings, and they dismissed Gilbert's request for an in camera hearing. Gilbert's request for an order excluding witnesses until they testified to ensure that they gave an independent account was routine. Yet that request was also summarily dismissed.

Gilbert Jones, the first witness, followed the Quaker custom of affirming rather than taking the oath. Gilbert and Margaret Jones were very familiar with legal proceedings. Gilbert was named as the principal defendant in an action tried in Belleville in October 1883, just over two months before the murder. That case arose out of a split in the Quaker movement that divided the West Lake Monthly Meeting of Friends. Gilbert adhered to the traditionalist Discipline of 1859. Their adversaries, the plaintiffs in the lawsuit, adhered to a progressive and evangelical branch of Quakerism – identified as 'New Lights,' 'Fast Quakers,' or 'Progressives' – that emerged as a Discipline in 1880. They advocated a paid clergy and innovations in worship that adherents to the Discipline of 1859 rejected. The plaintiffs were in the majority and held title to the church property as trustees. They alleged that in December 1882, the defendants, including Gilbert Jones, had stormed the meeting house and attempted to exclude the plaintiffs by force. The dispute was difficult for Margaret Jones, as her daughter had married a Quaker minister who belonged to the rival faction.[10] The plaintiffs retained possession of the property and sued for a declaration and an injunction to secure their title.

Gilbert and Margaret Jones were anxiously awaiting the judgment of Justice William Proudfoot of the Chancery Division at the time of Peter Lazier's murder. Within a few days after they gave their evidence before the justices at the committal proceedings in January 1884, they learned to their enormous relief that they had prevailed in the Quaker litigation.[11]

Their victory was short lived. The Court of Appeal reversed the trial judgment in 1886[12] and the Court of Appeal's judgment was upheld by the Supreme Court of Canada in 1887.[13] Roger Clute, the prosecutor who would lead them through their evidence at the Lazier murder trial, had acted as junior counsel for their opponents in the Quaker litigation. Justice Christopher Patterson, who would preside at the murder trial, would later write one of the judgments that rejected their claims in the Court of Appeal.

At the committal proceedings, Gilbert and Margaret Jones described the events leading to the death of Peter Lazier. Margaret described the two intruders, one wearing a linen hood or mask and holding a pistol in his left hand and the other with what appeared to be a dark beard and holding a shotgun with his right hand. Gilbert explained that he had seen only one of the intruders as he emerged from the bedroom with his shotgun. That man, wearing a mask or hood, had shot Lazier with a pistol and then fled, running away with an awkward gait.

When Margaret Jones was testifying, Joseph Thomset and George Lowder were asked to stand up. A mask fitting the description of the mask worn the night of the murder was put on Thomset. To the consternation of the prosecution, Mrs Jones testified that Lazier's assailants looked taller than the prisoners and that the general appearance of the murderers was not that of these men. She thought that Thomset's clothes corresponded with those worn by the masked man that night, but the man who shot Peter Lazier looked larger than Thomset.

McKinnon, in court to watch the proceedings, decided to intervene. He thought that perhaps Mrs Jones's perspective was distorted as she stood in the elevated witness box and, perhaps also hoping that if she were given another chance her story might improve, asked her to step down at the same level as the prisoner. She did so, but repeated her earlier evidence that the intruder was a taller man than Thomset.

Nehemiah Gilbert hammered home the point in cross-examination that strongly favoured the defence: Mrs Jones confirmed that the men who came to the house that night looked taller and larger than the prisoners. This appeared to open a serious hole in the prosecution case. It was not just that Mrs Jones could not identify the prisoners; according to her, the robbers had distinctive features that would exclude the prisoners.

Thomset had another identifying feature – his heavy dark beard that

completely covered the lower part of his face. If he was one of the culprits, was it not more likely that he was the man with the shotgun,
described by Mrs Jones as appearing to have a heavy dark beard? But
the prosecution was bound to insist that Thomset was the masked man
who had fired the fatal shot with the pistol, as the boot marks left by
the fleeing shooter matched Thomset's boots. If Thomset was the man
with the mask and the pistol, the prosecution had to prove that George
Lowder was the man with the shotgun and what Margaret Jones
thought was a beard. This left the prosecution with another problem –
both Lowders were clean-shaven. It was likely McKinnon who eventually came up with an answer to solve this conundrum – the suggestion
that Margaret Jones would adopt at the trial, namely, that what she
thought was a beard must have been a false beard worn as a disguise.

'Such an eager crowd'

When the committal proceedings resumed after a short break for lunch,
the courtroom was even fuller, with anxious spectators clamouring for
every inch of space. As J.L. Mills reported in the Belleville *Intelligencer*,
there was a 'dense mass of people representing almost all sections of
the county.' The jury box was occupied by mostly female spectators
who, 'notwithstanding the ill ventilated state of the building and the
crowding, … remained while that the enquiry lasted.' An old man who
served as court officer 'remarked that in his experience such an eager
crowd had never congregated within the building.' Mills described the
prisoners:

David Lowder looked paler than usual, but otherwise was cheerful. His face
was frequently wreathed with smiles, and twice he joined in the outbursts of
laughter that occurred during the hearing of the case. Thomset, who sat next
to him, affected a nonchalant air for a time, but after a while exhibited a great
interest during the hearing of the testimony. George Lowder watched the face
of each witness with eagerness, and paid the closest attention to the evidence.[14]

Low called Albert Spencer, the station master at Bloomfield, who testified that on the day of the murder, Thomset was at the station. He
explained that Thomset came to his office to inquire about an express
parcel, but there was nothing there for him. Spencer saw Gilbert Jones
get paid for his hops. Although Spencer could not say that Thomset
had witnessed the transaction, Thomset could well have seen Gilbert

Jones at the station, and Spencer's evidence provided some support for the prosecution's theory that Thomset knew that Jones had received a large sum of money on the day of the murder. Herbert S. Miller, the man who paid Jones for his hops at the station, testified that he saw Thomset in the freight shed a short time before the money was paid, although he could not say that Thomset saw Jones get the money.

Jesse Miller explained how he had seen Thomset on the day of the murder at about five o'clock in the afternoon on the road between Bloomfield and West Lake and had offered him a ride. Thomset jumped on, then he got off at the Lowder residence at about dusk.

The next witness to take the stand was the imposing chief constable Hugh McKinnon, who confidently testified that he had considerable experience tracking footprints and footmarks and explained to the justices how he had investigated the tracks in the snow near the Jones residence. After arresting George Lowder, he took the boots Magistrate Saylor had seized from the Lowder residence and matched them to the footprints in the marsh. McKinnon had to admit, however, that those boots were not claimed by any of the Lowder family and that 'of my own knowledge I do not know to whom the boots belong.' On cross-examination, he agreed that Thomset and David Lowder showed no hesitation in surrendering their boots at the town hall. McKinnon was a confident witness prepared to spar with Nehemiah Gilbert, and during the examination there were 'several colloquial sallies which created laughter quite frequently.'[15]

George Pope explained that he had accompanied McKinnon when he examined the tracks in the snow. Pope boasted that he had been engaged in lumbering for many years and had frequently followed tracks and trails in the woods. Like McKinnon, Pope was a confident witness who, in the opinion of the *Intelligencer* reporter, got the better of Gilbert. The reaction of the audience foreshadowed the partisan pro-prosecution outbursts that would mar the trial.

It became apparent which way the crowd watching the proceedings was leaning.

While Mr. Pope was giving his evidence he and Mr. Gilbert, the prisoners' counsel, had several set to's in which the former had decidedly the better of the argument. These séances led the audience to cheer and laugh immoderately and added greatly to the lawyer's chagrin. At this stage the chairman of the presiding justices stated that if the noise would continue he would call upon the officers to stop it. After that better order prevailed.[16]

Chief constable Horatio N. Babbitt explained the efforts he had made to investigate the murder and John Fralick testified that George Lowder had stated that the boots seized from the Lowder home were his and that he wanted them back so he could do his chores.

The proceedings resumed on Saturday, 31 December, but a tremendous snowstorm caused difficulties for several witnesses and other interested parties wishing to attend. Fewer spectators attended when proceedings commenced, but as the morning wore on, the courtroom filled and by the afternoon session, the room was again crowded and overflowing. Abram Saylor, Edmund Bedell, and Aaron McDonald explained their tracking efforts on the night of the murder, and Bedell described the circumstances of Thomset's arrest. There was evidence that Thomset had called at the home of Alfred and Delia Hicks, located on the road between the Lowder residence and Thomset's home, some time before 11 p.m. on the night of the murder.

By mid-afternoon, the prosecutor, Philip Low, asked for an adjournment to Friday, 4 January, when he expected to be in a position to produce further evidence. Gilbert asked that the prisoners be released on bail, but only a superior court judge could grant bail to those charged with murder. After a brief conference, the justices remanded the prisoners in custody and adjourned the inquiry to the next Friday at 10 a.m.

The Justices Commit for Trial

A week later, the inquiry resumed, the evidence was completed[17] and Low asked the justices of the peace to commit all three prisoners for trial for the murder of Peter Lazier. Given the mood in the community and the atmosphere in the courtroom, it probably came as no surprise to Nehemiah Gilbert that his three clients were committed for trial. The evidence of the footprints in the snow leading away from the Jones farmhouse in the direction of the Lowder and Thomset homes and the evidence that the imprints matched the boots worn by Thomset and those said to belong to George Lowder was some indication of their involvement in the crime.

On the other hand, the case was far from open and shut. There was really no evidence against David Lowder, whose boots the authorities admitted did not match the tracks. The inability of either Gilbert or Margaret Jones to identify any of the accused also represented a serious hole in the prosecution's case. The prosecution theory that the clean-shaven George Lowder was the man who appeared to have a beard was problematic. Of even greater concern was the fact that Margaret Jones thought that the man who had the pistol and who had fired the fatal shot was taller than either Thomset or George Lowder. There was also other evidence that could either implicate or exclude the accused as the perpetrators. Gilbert Jones had watched the shooter flee the house and escape through the yard. He testified that 'the man who shot had an awkward way of running' and that he 'could recognize that particular gait.' Mrs Jones testified that the shooter had held the pistol in his left hand. Were any of the accused left-handed? Did any of them have an injury or condition that caused them to run with an awkward gait? There is nothing in the records or reports of the case to indicate that these questions were ever asked or answered. Was the Hicks' evidence that Thomset called on them before 11 p.m. on the night of the murder consistent with the tracking evidence that he had gone from the crime scene across the frozen lake to his own home? Or did the Hicks' story support what Thomset had told Bedell – that he had spent the evening at the Lowders' and stopped by at the Hicks house as he made his way home?

7

Picton Spring Assizes, 1884

The judge assigned to sit in Picton for the 1884 spring assizes was Mr Justice Christopher Salmon Patterson.[1] Born in England and educated at the Royal Belfast Academical Institution, Patterson was intimately familiar with Picton and Prince Edward County. He came to Canada in 1844 at the age of twenty-one and settled in Picton, where he embarked on his legal career, serving as Philip Low's articling student. Patterson was called to the bar in 1851. He was married two years later and eventually had five children. After working for five years as Philip Low's partner, Patterson moved in 1856 to Toronto, where he practised with the firm Wilson, Patterson & Beatty – from 1862 Patterson, Beatty and Hamilton – until his appointment to the bench eighteen years later. He 'secured a name for accurate knowledge of law, affability, and high personal character' and was considered to be a well-read man, 'familiar with the choicest productions of our best writers, especially in poetry.'[2]

Patterson took an active role as a Presbyterian in the affairs of his church and served as chair of the board of the Toronto General Hospital. He was appointed a bencher of the Law Society of Upper Canada in 1866 and succeeded in being elected by his peers in the first bencher election in 1871. His appointment that same year as a member of an important commission to consider the key law-reform issue of the day, the fusion of law and equity, was warmly applauded. Patterson was described as standing 'very high' at the bar 'without the showy qualities of some others ... known to be a man with broad views of things, and of much learning and industry.'[3] Patterson was made a Queen's Counsel in 1872 and was appointed to the Court of Error and Appeal in 1874 (called the Court of Appeal after 1876)[4] at the age of fifty-one by Liberal justice minister Edward Blake. He ended his career at the top. Although Patterson was reported to be reluctant to move to Ottawa, in 1888 he accepted Prime Minister Sir John A. Macdonald's offer of a seat on the Supreme Court of Canada, where he served until his death at the age of seventy in 1893.

The Court of Appeal was not a particularly busy court in the 1880s. Its judges were authorized to sit in any superior court and as they were not fully occupied hearing appeals, they regularly took on additional duties as trial judges. An additional incentive was financial. Court of Appeal judges were only paid $5000 a year – more than ten times the average annual wage for a tradesman,[5] but a sum low enough to prompt a legal editorial writer to complain that 'the occupants of the Bench in Ontario are more inadequately paid than any other class of public officials,' and that while good men were appointed, those in the 'front rank' of the profession could not 'afford to give up their large incomes for the miserable salaries' they would receive as judges.[6] The 'circuit allowance' Justice Patterson received for each assize he covered produced a surplus over actual travel expenses to augment his modest salary.[7] Justice Patterson spent a good deal of his time travelling around the province presiding as a trial judge at the assizes. In the spring of 1884, he sat in Lindsay in March, in Brockville and Belleville in April, and finally in Picton, where he opened the spring assizes on the afternoon of Tuesday, 6 May.[8]

'The Great Murder Trial'

The Lazier trial was a major event in the life of the town. It attracted a crowd similar to the throng that had attended the running of the Queen's Plate at the Picton Driving Park five years earlier on Victoria Day, 1879.

The Picton *Gazette* announced that it would publish a daily edition to provide details of the trial.

DON'T FAIL
To secure a copy of the
'Daily Gazette'

During the Great Murder trial now in progress. It will contain
full particulars and be published each day as long as the trial
lasts. 3 cents a copy.

The trial attracted the interest of several Ontario newspapers. Reporters
from Belleville's *Intelligencer* and *Daily Ontario* and Toronto's *Globe* all
provided detailed daily accounts of the proceedings. The Trenton *Courier Advocate* and Kingston *British Whig* also followed the case closely.
Of these the *Gazette* was clearly the most partisan. For the most part,
the out-of-town press revealed no discernable bias either in favour of
or against the accused, although many of the reports hinted that they
were likely to be convicted. Picton's own *Gazette*, however, more or less
assumed the guilt of the accused men, and its reports likely contributed
to the hostile local mood that prevailed throughout the trial.

People started arriving as early as 6 a.m., and 'the hotel yards were
filled with rigs and the public houses with people – all come to hear the
trial.'9 All the talk was of the murder, how it had been committed, how
the culprits had been tracked down, and how the trial was likely to unfold. A steady crowd wended its way down the hill from Main Street,
along the tip of Picton Bay, and then up Union Street to the courthouse.

Prince Edward had become a separate judicial district in 1831 and
work commenced on a courthouse. The first quarter sessions were held
in the late-Georgian domestic-style courthouse in 1834, although the
completion of its construction was delayed by financial issues until
1840. Handsomely built in fine, squared, cut limestone, the courthouse
sits on a rise as if to dominate the town. It has a Greek-inspired por-
tico on four plain Doric columns that were added in the 1840s as well
as a cupola, also added later to improve ventilation. The doors have
moulded fan-transoms. The courtroom sits on the second floor and has
magnificent windows overlooking the front lawn on which the spectators gathered in May 1884 to await the trial of Thomset and Lowder.
The royal coat of arms of William IV, which hangs behind the judge's
dais and the prisoner's dock where Thomset and the Lowder brothers
sat, remains to this day. Although there have been many changes over
the years, the courtroom and its furnishings retain much of their original feel and elegance.10 The adjoining jail and jail yard, added in the
1860s, also retains its original feel – chilling and harsh.

The seating area in the courtroom is large and could accommodate a
public audience of about 120 seated and another 50 standing.11 Many
more than that wanted to watch the trial, and many disappointed spec-

tators were left to wait on the courthouse lawn, hoping to gain entry as the day wore on. Reporters complained that spectators had taken spaces at the table reserved for the press and behaved in a manner that 'interfered with their easy performance of the difficult task of taking a faithful report of the proceedings.'[12]

The bustle of the overcrowded courtroom hushed as Sheriff James Gillespie, 'a tall man with a ruddy face and prominent nose,'[13] escorted Justice Patterson to the dais to open the assizes on the morning of Tuesday, 6 May 1884. The judge dealt with some routine business before starting the only significant case on his list, the trial of Joseph Thomset and George and David Lowder for murder.

Philip Low, QC, the local crown attorney and prominent local lawyer with whom Justice Patterson had articled, had taken the case through the committal proceedings, but trials at the assizes were routinely prosecuted by a provincial Crown law officer or counsel retained to act in that capacity.[14] Low was in court to assist Roger Conger Clute, a rising star in his mid-thirties who had been retained by the Crown for the trial. Clute was born near Picton in 1848. Like Peter Lazier, Clute had United Empire Loyalist roots. 'A bright curly-haired young lad from Belleville,'[15] he was called to the bar in 1873 after articling with Christopher Patterson's Toronto firm. Clute practised in Belleville, where he quickly established his reputation as an excellent trial lawyer. Starting in 1881, when he successfully prosecuted a man named Lee for murder in Napanee,[16] Clute was retained over thirty times by the Crown to conduct difficult murder trials. He was an unsuccessful Liberal candidate for parliament in 1891, and went on to a very successful career as a lawyer in Toronto as the senior partner of Clute, Macdonald, MacIntosh and Hay. He would later preside over a commission of inquiry regarding mining (1899) and another regarding Chinese and Japanese Immigration (1900), and was appointed as a high court judge in 1905 and then to the Exchequer Division in 1913. He was known as a 'lawyer who has a heart as well as a mind.'[17]

Nehemiah Gilbert, the very junior Picton lawyer called to the bar only two years earlier, appeared for all three prisoners.

The Grand Jury

Shortly after 11 a.m., the grand jury returned a 'true bill' against the three accused. The grand jury was an ancient English institution (now abolished in Canada, England, and most common-law jurisdictions outside the United States) composed of at least twelve and fewer than twenty-four citizens. In early times, the grand jury was an organ of local government with investigative powers and was charged with the general responsibility of surveying and reporting on criminal behaviour in the community.[18]

In nineteenth-century Ontario, judges regularly used the traditional grand jury address as a platform to express their opinions on general matters of judicial policy, law enforcement, public morality, and the state of public institutions.[19] By the 1880s, most judges had become more cautious and restrained and avoided discussion of issues of social and judicial policy. Ontario grand juries still had a significant 'presentment' function of reporting on the condition of jails, insane asylums, and other public institutions,[20] but that role was fading as public institutions were more effectively supervised by government inspectors.[21]

The primary function of the grand jury was to decide whether a bill of indictment was justified before a case could proceed to trial. In an earlier era, the grand jury had served as an important check on the arbitrary exercise of executive and judicial power. By the nineteenth century, the risk of arbitrary exercise of power had diminished. Prosecutions were screened at the committal stage and the grand jury's screening function was being displaced by committal proceedings and professional crown attorneys. Moreover, shortcomings in grand jury procedure undermined confidence that the institution was capable of performing an effective screening role. The presiding judge still delivered a general instruction to the grand jury at the opening of the assizes, but he did not preside over the grand jury's deliberations on indictments, and those deliberations were not open to the public or to the accused. The grand jury decided whether or not to return a 'true bill' after hearing from only the prosecutor and any witnesses deemed necessary.

By the time of the Thomset-Lowder case, abolition of the grand jury was a matter of lively debate.[22] Grand jury procedures so clearly favoured the prosecution that the institution was incapable of offering any meaningful protection for the rights of accused persons. While some members of the judiciary cherished the tradition of the grand jury and the involvement of ordinary citizens in the justice system, others were openly critical of the institution and saw it as costly and useless. Two years after Confederation, a future member of the Supreme Court of Canada and a leading grand jury critic, Justice John Wellington Gwynne, addressed the grand jury at the autumn assizes in Kingston and, in the spirit of the times, publicly stated his own doubt about the future of the institution of the grand jury. He explained that there had already been a preliminary examination of the evidence before the magistrates and that the need for a second preliminary review was questionable: 'It is a matter worthy of consideration whether relief might not without danger to the liberty of the subject be extended to the gentlemen who are called upon to discharge the duties of grand jurors to their own great inconvenience, and with so little practical benefit.'[23]

By the time of the Thomset-Lowder trial, such attacks on the grand jury had rendered it a 'mortally wounded ... institution.'[24] If Philip Low and Roger Clute had thought there was any chance that the grand jury would not agree that the trial should proceed, they would not have waited until the very morning the trial was to begin to present their case. At the opening of the Picton spring assizes on 6 May 1884, it came as no surprise when, after a brief meeting with prosecutors Low and Clute, the grand jury returned a 'true bill' against all three accused so that the trial could proceed.

The Prisoners Appear

The prisoners were brought from the adjacent county jail and the formal indictment charging them with the murder of Peter Lazier was read. All three accused pleaded not guilty. The *Intelligencer* reporter, who had followed the case from the start, thought that the accused had 'become fleshy during their incarceration,' and they 'showed by their actions an air that manifested indifference: they did not seem to realize by their conduct that they were on trial for murder.'[25] The Lowder brothers were described by the *Globe* reporter as being 'of low stature, but of stout build' with clean-shaven faces except for David's bushy sideburns,[26] and by another observer as 'fair haired boyish-looking fellows' who 'look as little as possible like the conventional murderer.'[27] They were seen to be 'twisting about, glancing here and there among the crowd ... and seemingly passing remarks on various persons they recognized ... accompanied with broad smiles and jaunty tosses of the head though they seemed at the same time to be under the influence of considerable nervous excitement.' At one point 'their apparent merriment found expression in an audible laugh.'[28]

Thomset was more sombre, although when he recognized a friend in the crowd, he too smiled through his thick dark beard. One reporter described him as having 'a dogged appearance' and a 'sneaking look' with a thin projecting chin and an extended nose, yet not one to be 'singled out as a man likely to be guilty of such an atrocious crime.'[29]

After the pleas were taken, the prisoners' counsel Nehemiah Gilbert advised Justice Patterson that Thomset had retained D'Alton McCarthy, QC, member of parliament and one of the leading counsel in the country. McCarthy was detained on other business in Ottawa and could not arrive in Picton until the next day. Gilbert also explained that he had just retained George D. Dickson, QC, of Belleville to assist him with the defence of the Lowder brothers and asked for 'a sufficient delay to enable him to consult with that gentleman.'[30] Justice Patterson agreed to adjourn the court, but only briefly until 2 p.m., when the trial would proceed.

Jury Selection

The jury was selected when court resumed for the afternoon. The cards with the names, addresses, and occupations[31] of the jury panel summonsed for the assizes were randomly drawn. To be eligible to serve on a jury, a person had to be a resident of the county, over twenty-one years old, 'in the possession of his natural faculties, and not infirm or decrepit [sic],' and the owner or tenant of property assessed at not less than $400.[32] The statute did not explicitly define 'person' as being 'a male person,' but women were certainly excluded from jury duty. The law of the day reflected widely held and deeply rooted sexist attitudes and it was simply taken for granted that when a statute, like the Juries Act, set out the qualifications of a 'person' for any public duty or office, only male persons were included.[33] Twelve men and no women would decide the fate of the prisoners.

As the accused were charged with a 'felony punishable with death,' they each had the right to challenge up to twenty prospective jurors peremptorily, that is, without any cause or explanation.[34] The Crown was afforded only four peremptory challenges, but also had the right 'to cause any juror to stand aside until the rest of the panel had been gone through,'[35] at which point the jurors temporarily 'stood aside' would be recalled. Roger Clute exhausted his rights of peremptory challenge and eliminated four prospective jurors.[36] There is nothing to indicate that he also exercised the Crown's right to stand additional jurors aside. The accused challenged five prospective jurors, some of whom were farmers living near Bloomfield.[37]

Both sides also had the right to challenge any prospective juror for cause, in other words, to convince the court that the juror should not sit on the case on account of bias or some infirmity. However, in practical terms this right could rarely be exercised, as the judiciary steadfastly resisted the American practice of allowing prospective jurors to be questioned.[38] Parties could only hope to challenge a juror for cause if they already had proof of some fact that would preclude the juror from sitting. In the Thomset-Lowder case, this meant that any concerns the accused men or their counsel may have had about the effects of pre-trial publicity could not be explored.

Selecting a jury in the United States, where the lawyers were allowed to question prospective jurors about what they knew of the case, often took several days.[39] While modern Canadian practice has resisted this open-ended type of questioning, selecting a jury in a high-profile homicide case to screen out jurors who would be unduly influenced by pre-trial publicity[40] or racial bias[41] can also be a lengthy procedure. But in 1884, Gilbert did not even attempt to question the jurors, and it took only a few minutes to empanel twelve Prince Edward County citizens to try the case.[42]

The twelve men selected to serve on the jury came from all corners of the County. However, the County community was close-knit and legal qualifications for jury service ensured that although randomly selected, the jury would represent the attitudes of the propertied, professional, and merchant classes. The occupation of over half the jury was described as 'yeoman,' a man who owned and cultivated a small estate. One juryman was a grocer and another was described as a 'clerk.' The occupations of two jury members gave them some standing in the community; one was a dentist, and J.W. Fegan, described as a 'merchant from South Marysburg,' was a prominent County citizen and reputed master builder. Fegan had recently constructed the magnificent Victorian Gothic home of Edwards Merrill, Picton's mayor and a prominent lawyer. Fegan was selected by the jury to act as foreman.

Given the serious charges the accused men faced, the members of the jury were sequestered and not allowed to separate from the time they were sworn until they rendered their verdict.[43] This meant that until the trial concluded, they would eat their meals together, be taken to a hotel at the end of court each day, and brought back in the morning by a sheriff's officer.

Justice Patterson had mastered the art of shorthand and, although a court reporter recorded the evidence, the judge kept his own detailed shorthand account of exactly what each witness said.[44]

Clute Calls the Crown's Case

Roger Clute opened the case for the Crown by presenting a brief outline of the evidence he intended to present. Clute had been retained to prosecute the case in February 1884[45] and, unlike D'Alton McCarthy and George Dickson who had yet to arrive, he was well prepared. He explained that 'it was his desire to approach the case dispassionately, and with every due consideration for the prisoners at the bar.'[46] Clute told the jury he would lead evidence that boot marks left around the Jones residence matched the boots worn by Thomset and George Lowder and that he would prove that 'Thomset knew that Mr. Jones was a man of means and told a person how easy it would be to scare money out of him.' Evidence would be led of a horse and conveyance being driven very rapidly towards Bloomfield on the evening of the murder along the road leading from the direction of where Thomset and the Lowders lived. As the Crown's theory relied heavily on the tracks of two men leading back to the Thomset and the Lowder homes, the use of a horse and conveyance suggested that three men were involved in the crime.

Clute then called Gilbert and Margaret Jones, dressed in traditional Quaker garb, to the stand to describe in detail the horrifying events that took place at their home almost six months earlier on the night of 21 December 1883, when Peter Lazier was murdered before their eyes by the unidentified intruders.

As at the committal proceedings, neither Gilbert nor Margaret Jones could identify the accused men as being the intruders who killed Peter Lazier. Clute and McKinnon both knew that this represented a potentially serious weakness in their case. Clute carefully avoided the problem that arose at the committal proceedings, when Mrs Jones testified that the man who fired the fatal shot appeared taller than Thomset, by not repeating the error of asking her to compare Thomset's height and appearance to that of the killer. Nehemiah Gilbert failed to bring out in cross-examination the fact Mrs Jones had sworn at the preliminary inquiry that the intruder with the mask and pistol was taller than Thomset. This was a serious error, one more experienced counsel like McCarthy would not have made had he been in court when the trial began.

Mrs Jones described the man who had attempted to strike Lazier on the head with a gun as appearing to be wearing a false beard, although she could not see his face clearly. Clute had George Lowder stand up, and he asked Mrs Jones how George compared in size to the man who attempted to strike Lazier over the head with his gun: 'It is my impression that the man I saw with the gun was about his size,' she replied.

Gilbert Jones had only seen the man wearing the mask, the man who fired the fatal shot – on the Crown's theory, Thomset. Jones conceded that he thought the killer was taller than Thomset, but he attempted to explain away the significance of that fact by stating that 'the man had such a mask up on him that he would naturally appear taller to me.'

Clute's theory of the case was that Thomset was the man with the pistol who had shot Lazier. The fact that, on the Crown's theory, neither of the Lowders had fired the fatal shot did not mean that they could not be convicted of murder. The law provided that if two or more people form a common criminal purpose, they were all guilty of every crime committed by any one of them in the execution of that purpose. It was only where one of them committed a crime 'foreign to the common criminal purpose' that the others would not be guilty of that crime.[47] Clute argued that the object of the men who went to the Jones' house with two weapons, at least one of which was loaded, was to commit robbery and, if necessary, to use violence to accomplish that purpose. The fact that the man with the shotgun had clubbed Lazier indicated his preparedness to use violence.

Clute followed with Hugh McKinnon, who came across as an imposing witness. Detailed evidence of the tracking by the neighbours followed. By having McKinnon, the confident and reputed detective and professional police officer, describe his investigations first, Clute was able to present the tracking evidence in its best light. McKinnon explained to the jury the steps he had taken to investigate the murder and to track down the killers. On the morning following the murder, he had gone to the Jones farmhouse, and from there to the town hall in Bloomfield, taken Joseph Thomset's and David Lowder's boots, and then proceeded to the marsh to test the boots in the tracks. Thomset's boots matched the tracks, but David Lowder's did not. McKinnon then decided to have George Lowder arrested and, the next day, he took the patch-bottom boots seized by Adam Saylor from the Lowder residence to test them against the tracks left at the Jones residence and on the marsh leading towards Lowder's home. McKinnon's evidence was clear and certain: 'I found that they fitted exactly, and that the impressions were exactly those made by these boots.'

The defence would seize on McKinnon's deceptive tactics and argue that the jury could not trust anything he said. But he was unshaken when confronted in cross-examination with his attempt to trick Mrs

Thomset into thinking her husband had confessed to the crime. McKinnon appeared to see nothing wrong with what he had done. He freely admitted the lies he had used as the lead investigator for this serious crime in his unsuccessful attempt to find the murder weapon.

The first day of the trial ended with medical evidence to establish the cause of Peter Lazier's death. Dr Allen Noxon explained how he pronounced Peter Lazier dead when he examined the body lying on the floor sometime after 10 p.m. on the night of 21 December. Noxon also described the tracks he and Mrs Jones found at the rear of the house. Late in the afternoon, Dr Charles Wright and Dr J.M. Platt, both Picton physicians, told the jury that they had performed a post-mortem examination on Saturday, 22 December and concluded that Peter Lazier had died from a bullet wound that had penetrated the right auricle of his heart, his right lung and fractured his seventh rib. Dr Platt, who had been well acquainted with Lazier, produced the fatal bullet, 'a number 32.'

Court adjourned at 6:30 in the evening. Many of the spectators and newspaper reporters walked from the courthouse past the town's harbour and up the town hill to seek food and drink in one of the hotels. The members of the jury were sequestered to ensure that their consideration of the evidence would not be contaminated by any discussion of the case outside the confines of the jury room. But as men who knew their community, they were well aware of its mood.

D'Alton McCarthy Jr for the Defence

D'Alton McCarthy Jr, the man retained to defend Joseph Thomset, arrived in Picton the evening of the first day of the trial. McCarthy was without question one of Canada's leading litigators.[48] Seven years earlier, in 1877, he had established a partnership in Toronto with B.B. Osler. Their practice steadily grew to be one of the largest and most significant firms in Canada, the precursor of two modern legal giants – McCarthy Tétrault and Osler, Hoskin & Harcourt. McCarthy was the son of a lawyer and his own son, D'Alton Lally McCarthy, also became a leading counsel, ensuring the continued association of the family name with excellence in advocacy.

Born in Ireland in 1836, D'Alton McCarthy immigrated to Canada ten years later. He was called to the bar in 1859 and joined his father's Barrie firm in 1860. He quickly rose as a leader of the bar, with a huge practice in the courts, and was appointed a bencher of the Law Society in 1871, a post he retained until his death in 1898.[49] McCarthy was deeply involved in Conservative politics. He lost his first three bids for parliament starting in 1872, but was elected in 1876 and continued to gain re-election and serve as an MP until his death.

There is no indication of who paid McCarthy's retainer to defend Thomset, but there can be little doubt that his fee was substantial and well beyond the modest means of his client. It was likely Sarah Poland, Thomset's sister and the wife of a Rochester, New York doctor, who came up with the money for her brother's defence. McCarthy would not have taken the case without a substantial fee. At the time, he was desperate for money and very much in demand by wealthy corporate clients who were prepared to pay his huge fees. He had invested heavily in the lumber trade and lost a fortune in the depression of 1870, leaving him with debts that he still had not managed to clear by 1884. In a letter he wrote a few weeks after the trial to Prime Minister Sir John A. Macdonald turning down the offer of appointment to the cabinet as minister of justice (McCarthy had turned down a judicial appointment six years earlier), McCarthy explained: 'The amount I still owe the bank is very large, so large that it would be simply madness in me to give up my profession ... I must work away as I am doing for three or four years, when perhaps I may have relieved myself from the burden that has weighed down the best years of my life.'[50]

McCarthy enjoyed a close relationship with Sir John A. Macdonald, both personal and political. He married the widow of Macdonald's brother-in-law and, although he never entered the cabinet, he was a key adviser to Macdonald on legal, constitutional, and election law issues in an era when contested elections were a major area of political and legal activity. During the 1880s, the Dominion government retained McCarthy to argue a string of important and still studied constitutional cases before the Supreme Court of Canada and the Judicial Committee of the Privy Council advocating for an expansive federal power. Despite McCarthy's skill as an advocate, these arguments fell on deaf ears, especially at the Privy Council.[51]

McCarthy blamed the influence of Quebec for the failure of his ideal of a strong and centralized Canada.[52] He held strong views on language and culture that were popular in rural Ontario and he would have been well known in Prince Edward County. 'His vision of the Canadian nation was unitary and British: there would be one culture, one language, one set of laws and one national government uniting all Canadians.'[53] He became a fiercely partisan anti-French advocate, and campaigned for a unilingual Canada. At one time touted as a future leader of the Conservative Party, McCarthy's political influence diminished in direct proportion to the growing extremity and ferocity of his views. His reputation as a racial and religious bigot and his unwillingness to participate in the give and take of political dealing necessary to navigate the French-English linguistic and religious divide eventually rendered him a marginal political figure.

But McCarthy's political shortcomings did nothing to prevent his law practice from flourishing, fuelled by his fierce intelligence and his passionate advocacy. He had a lean and athletic build, dark piercing eyes, an aura of austere determination and a reputation as Canada's finest jury lawyer.[54] Two years before the Picton trial, in one of his best-known trials as a criminal defence lawyer, McCarthy's eloquent and impassioned plea won a widely publicized acquittal for William Ney, accused of murder at Barrie.[55] In 1883, McCarthy earned the appreciation of Justice Patterson and his judicial colleagues by urging higher salaries for judges.[56]

Sarah Poland could not have found a better advocate to defend her brother. On the other hand, McCarthy had little or no time to prepare for Thomset's defence. He arrived during the evening after the first day of trial, never having met with his client and after three crucial Crown witnesses – Gilbert and Margaret Jones and Hugh McKinnon – had testified. McCarthy was going to have to rely upon the briefing he received from Nehemiah Gilbert and his own natural talents as a cross-examiner and advocate.

McCarthy stayed at the Royal Hotel, the best the town had to offer. Several townsfolk lingered near the hotel to catch a glimpse of this well-known political fighter as he left to make his way to the courthouse to take his place as Thomset's counsel before the start of the second day of the trial.

The Trial: Day 2

The jury members were escorted to breakfast by the bailiffs. 'They appeared cheerful and laughed and talked as they went on their way to the courthouse.'[57] By nine o'clock, the courthouse was crowded and there were officers at the front door to control the crowd. Hundreds were turned away and many who gained entry had no seat and were left standing and clamouring to gain a perch on the window sills. The courtroom was silent as Justice Patterson took his place on the dais and the members of the jury were asked to respond as their names were called.

From this point, George D. Dickson, QC, an experienced counsel from Belleville, is listed in the transcript as counsel for the two Lowders, while Nehemiah Gilbert is shown as junior counsel to both McCarthy and Dickson. This indicated that although the accused had retained separate counsel, they intended to present a common front and that there was nothing to the rumours that David Lowder would turn on his brother and Thomset and testify for the Crown.

Justice Patterson had made an order excluding witnesses from observing the proceedings until they had testified, a routine procedure designed to ensure that witnesses give their own independent recollections untainted by what they might hear from other witnesses. As McCarthy and Dickson intended to call several members of the Lowder family as defence witnesses, the only Lowder in court apart from George and David was their sister. The Lowders' mother, father, and brothers, who would later be called to the stand to present an alibi defence for all three accused, had to absent themselves from the courtroom.

Thomset's wife, child, and sister arrived after the first witness of the day had started to testify, but they were permitted to shake the prisoner's hand and to sit immediately behind the dock where he sat. Mrs Thomset looked more nervous and worried than her husband. Thomset's sister Sarah Poland greeted her brother with obvious emotion and sat down with tears streaming down her cheeks. Thomset was also tearful and he seemed particularly moved when his daughter proudly presented him with an orange.[58] The Thomset women knew they would be on display and they were well turned out for the trial. Mrs Thomset was described by a reporter as 'a woman of fine appearance: she was dressed in black.' His sister wore 'a black velvet dress and a violet coloured jacket ... a black hat adorned with a fringed white feather covered her head ... and rings were upon her fingers.'[59] Thomset's daughter wore a blue dress and a gold chain with a cross around her neck. His sister took notes of the evidence with a pencil and wept at one point when McCarthy pressed a witness in cross-examination: 'Three men's lives are at stake!'[60]

Tracking Evidence

For the next two days, Clute called a succession of witnesses who explained their efforts to trace the tracks in the snow from the Jones farm in Bloomfield to the homes of Thomset and the two Lowders at West Lake – Abram and Charles Saylor, Stephen Bowerman, Frank McDonald, Nathaniel B. Cole, James W. Talcott, Constable Edmund Bedell, and Chief Constable Horatio N. Babbitt. In response to Clute's careful and detailed questions, they told the jury of each step they had taken the night of the murder and the next day in their determined effort to track down Peter Lazier's killers. These solid Prince Edward County citizens, doing their best to solve a shocking crime, likely made a good impression on the jury.

McCarthy and Dickson fired their questions with the confidence of skilled cross-examiners. For the most part, the witnesses stood their ground. But with their detailed probing questions, McCarthy and Dickson tested the trackers' evidence, suggesting that their efforts, however well intended, were amateurish and uncoordinated and that the possibility for confusion increased each time a different man or team traversed the same ground. The descriptions of where the tracks could be seen and followed were not altogether consistent. Some witnesses could find only one track at crucial points, particularly leading from the Jones farmhouse. At other points along the trail, there were accounts of three or four tracks, likely left by other trackers. At the point where McKinnon tested Thomset's and David Lowder's boots in the swamp, there were as many as twelve to fifteen different sets of impressions. Most important, the defence established that no one had been able to follow the tracks all the way from the Jones farm near Bloomfield to the Lowder and Thomset homes at West Lake, and some witnesses described gaps in the trail of up to a mile.

For the most part, the three accused paid close attention to the evidence. But at times their attention seemed to wander. Thomset exchanged words with his family, seated behind the prisoners' box. David Lowder frequently looked about the courtroom for his friends to exchange a wave or bow. Of the three, George Lowder was most attentive.

An Unruly Crowd

One of the most disturbing aspects of the trial was the boorish, partisan, and unruly behaviour of most of the spectators in the courtroom. The deplorable conduct of the audience riled Justice Patterson, rattled D'Alton McCarthy, and profoundly disturbed Picton's mayor Edwards Merrill, a lawyer who observed the case from start to finish. The spectators made it clear that they did not need to hear the evidence. Already

convinced of the prisoners' guilt, they were out for blood. Their frequent outbursts of approval when the prosecution scored points and
mocking jeers when McCarthy or Dickson challenged a prosecution
witness prompted Sheriff Gillespie to threaten to put them out. The
noisy demonstrations continued and, obviously irritated by the lack of
decorum, Justice Patterson ordered the courtroom to be cleared shortly
before lunch. Those excluded yelled at the hopeful spectators waiting
on the street that it was pointless to go to the courthouse as the public
had been excluded, but Justice Patterson's order was only temporary
and, shortly after court resumed at 1:30 p.m., the courtroom was again
filled with spectators.

D'Alton McCarthy Attacks

McCarthy was particularly forceful when he cross-examined Aaron
McDonald, the man enlisted by Constable Bedell on the night of the
murder after Bedell had lost the trail. One reporter described the cross-
examination as 'long-continued and severe.' There was an element of
spectacle and sport as the famous lawyer tangled with the local boy.
McDonald remained cool and confident and 'his composure under the
fire attracted considerable attention.'[61]

It was McDonald who had led Bedell to Joseph Thomset. McCarthy
attacked McDonald for his enmity towards Thomset and for being a
man with a violent criminal record. McDonald admitted that there was
a history of 'bad feeling' between him and Thomset that had existed for
several years and that had led to violent confrontations, one of which
had led to McDonald being charged and fined.

Q: So that you have not any very kindly feeling towards him?
A: I have not.
Q: Perhaps you would like to be at the hanging?
A: No, I do not.
Q: Have you been prosecuted for other matters?
A: Yes.
Q: How long ago since you have been prosecuted?
A: Last fall.
Q: What was that for?
A: Putting a man off my property.
Q: Were you convicted of that too?
A: Yes.

Q: Then you are a man of violence?
A: I do not think so.

McDonald admitted to McCarthy that he and Bedell lost the track around Springbrook, as at that point the lake was glare ice. He conceded that the track could have gone in any direction at all, but that he and Bedell decided to see if they could pick the track up on the mainland. They proceeded to Tubbs Island.

Q: Had you any thought of Thomset before you got to Tubbs Island?
A: Yes
Q: Had you made up your mind then that he had made the tracks?
A: No.
Q: Who was it, you or Bedell?
A: I cannot tell which of us spoke of it first.
Q: But he was spoken of by you or Bedell?
A: Not until we got on Tubbs Island.
Q: When you saw the tracks on Tubbs Island either one of you suggested that it was Thomset?
A: Yes.

McDonald agreed that they had not followed the track on Tubbs Island but had gone to the house of William Leader to ask 'if he had seen anyone about or not.' Leader was not at home and McDonald explained that they then went on to the road, where they followed a track to Thomset's house.

McDonald stood with his elbow on the edge of the stand, his head resting on his hand. As McCarthy pressed on with questions about matching the tracks in the marsh later in the day with McKinnon and his entourage, McDonald's confidence cracked and he collapsed under the strain. 'Suddenly his arm quivered, he turned pale, and would have fallen had not someone supported him.'[62] The trial transcript indicates: 'At this point the witness becomes ill and has to be removed from the witness box.' Justice Patterson recorded in his bench book 'Witness fainting.'[63] Reporters for both the *Globe* and the *Intelligencer* attributed McDonald's collapse to the vigour of McCarthy's cross-examination. 'The witness was undergoing very severe cross-examination when he fainted and was about to fall when he was caught by friends. He was then removed to the Grand Jury room, apparently to the gratification of the prisoner Thomset.'[64]

Despite the fact that Justice Patterson was suffering from a severe cold, he allowed the proceedings to go on until 7 p.m., when he finally called it a day and ordered the tired looking jury to be back in court to start again at 9:30 the next morning. No doubt acting under the judge's direction, Sheriff Gillespie and the court officers took a firm hand with the audience. They announced that tomorrow no spectators would be admitted beyond the number that could be comfortably seated in the courtroom. The sheriff also prevented the Thomset family and Miss Lowder from conversing with the prisoners after the court rose.

The rumour mill reported talk of another thirty Crown witnesses and as many as eighteen defence witnesses, and speculation that the case would not be completed before Saturday. But Justice Patterson was determined to complete the case within the week he had planned for the Picton Spring assizes.

The tone of the trial had been set. Justice Patterson would try to ensure that it be conducted efficiently and according to the letter of the law, and Clute, McCarthy, and Dickson would display their impressive skills as advocates. But this murder had shaken the community, and the crowd that had clamoured for seats in the courtroom was not interested in forensic precision. In the eyes of the law, the jury reflected the values of the community, but at the trial of Joseph Thomset and the Lowder brothers, the community would insist on making all aware that it had already arrived at its own verdict as to their guilt.

8

Surprise Evidence

Cool weather and drizzling rain did not discourage a large crowd from gathering at the courthouse on Thursday morning. The jury was brought in promptly at 9:20 as the courtroom again filled with spectators. The crier's 'Keep silence!' announced the arrival of Justice Patterson and, after he was seated, Sheriff Gillespie commanded, 'Bring up the prisoners.' The Thomset ladies took their usual place behind the prisoners' box and shook Joseph's hand when he entered. The Picton *Gazette* reported that W.H. Vantassel, Peter Lazier's employer, was in attendance. This gentleman clearly shared the prevailing view that the accused were guilty. He told the reporter that his 'only desire is ... that the guilty ones may receive that just punishment which their base and bloodthirsty conduct so richly deserves.'[1]

The first order of business was to recall Aaron McDonald, who had fainted the day before. McDonald was nowhere to be found. Clute proceeded to complete the tracking evidence. He then spent the rest of the day leading evidence further implicating Joseph Thomset in the murder.

Thomset's Call on Alfred Hicks

Alfred Hicks lived on West Lake Road north of Thomset in the direction of the Lowder house and Bloomfield. He testified that on the night of the murder, right after he had gone to bed, and shortly before 11 p.m., Joseph Thomset knocked at his kitchen door.

I heard him when he came in. I was partly in a doze, just going to sleep and his coming in woke me up. I heard him talking to my wife. He stepped to the bedroom door and asked me if I was going to Picton on Saturday. I said I did not know whether I should or not. He said 'If you go down can I ride down with you.' I told him he could.

Delia Hicks, Alfred's wife, testified that Thomset was wearing a cap, a dark coat, and no overcoat. This description did not correspond with the clothing Margaret Jones described the intruder wearing – grey, not dark, and a hood rather than a cap on his head. Delia Hicks gave what she believed to be the precise time of Thomset's visit:

He rapped at the door and I went and opened the door. He asked if my husband was at home and I told him, yes, he had gone to bed. He says 'I think it is nearly bedtime' and he asked what time it was. We both looked at the clock and I said it was 10 minutes to 11. He said he did not think it was so late. He passed on to the bedroom and spoke to my husband about going in the morning to Picton. And then he went out.

The effect of this evidence was equivocal. Other witnesses had testified that it took just over an hour to walk from the Jones farmhouse to the Hicks residence walking at a good pace. Lazier had been shot just before 10 p.m. If Thomset was one of the intruders, it would be very difficult for him to have arrived at the Hicks home before 11. On the other hand, the alibi evidence the defence would call had Thomset leaving the Lowder home just before 10 p.m. The Hicks home was only a short distance away, easily reached in far less than an hour. Another complicating factor was that the various clocks and watches used by the witnesses to determine the time were not synchronized and the evidence indicated considerable variations. Abram Saylor testified that when he arrived at the Hicks home the next day, he noticed that the clock was running 20 minutes fast, a difference that would be more consistent with Thomset leaving the Lowders' than the Jones' at 10 p.m.

The picture was further clouded by the evidence of witnesses who testified to a single set of tracks between the Hicks house and Thom-

set's. That supported the defence contention, based on Thomset's statement to Bedell upon arrest as well as the alibi evidence described in the
next chapter, that Thomset had walked from the Lowder house to his
own, stopping by at the Hicks home. However, Chief Constable Babbitt
testified that he had examined the footprints and concluded that the
individual who had left them was walking from the direction of Thomset's home towards the Hicks residence. That undermined the defence
position, but left the unanswered question of how Thomset got back
home without leaving any track.

McCarthy seized on two points in cross-examination that would help
with Thomset's alibi defence that he had spent the entire evening at the
Lowders' before returning home before eleven o'clock.

Q: Did you notice anything in his appearance excited, or as if he had run
    three or four miles?
A: I did not notice anything particular.
Q: Coming from Lowder's house he would necessarily pass by your
    house?
A: Yes to go to his own.

Alfred Hicks confirmed that Thomset appeared to be in a normal state,
not 'blown or excited,' and that the tone of his voice was natural.

McCarthy's effort to use Hicks to bolster his client's reputation was
less successful. Alfred Hicks told McCarthy: 'Personally I cannot say
anything against the man. He has always dealt with me honestly as
far as we have had any dealings. He has bought some grain of me and
he has bought wood of me and that was the principal dealings we
had. Personally I can speak well of him, he always used me well.' This
opened the door for Clute's damaging re-examination:

Q: What was the reputation of Thomset apart from your personal knowledge?
A: Well some do not give him a very good name.
Q: In what way?
A: Well that he is not a very honest man.
Q: What do you mean by that?
A: That if he wanted chicken and he would go and take it or watermelons or
    anything like that. I never heard of anything more than that. I never heard
    of his taking money or anything like that.

McCarthy did his best to salvage the situation:

Q: He might take a chicken or watermelon. He might perhaps take an apple out of an orchard, perhaps two. You never heard anything more than that at him?

A: No, I never heard of him taking any money, anything further than that.

Patch-bottom Boots and a Pistol

Clute then called Abram Saylor and John and Emma Fralick to establish the seizure of the patch-bottom boots from the Lowder house on Saturday, 22 December, and to introduce the statements made by Thomset at the town hall and by George Lowder before his arrest asking about the whereabouts of his boots.

Despite his best efforts, McKinnon was never able to find the murder weapon. However, on 24 April 1884, a few days before the trial, a Bloomfield schoolboy found parts of a .32 calibre pistol near a small bridge in a field close by the Bloomfield schoolhouse. The frame was found in water and the cylinder was found on land a few feet away near a tree. Ernest Cooper, his friend John Mitchell, who was with him when he found the weapon, and William Brown, the boys' teacher, to whom they had given it, were called to the stand by Clute. If this was the best the Crown had to offer in relation to what had become of the murder weapon, it was hardly compelling evidence against the prisoners, as the weapon was not found on the route between the Jones residence and West Lake.

But Clute had more to offer on the subject of pistols. He led the first of several pieces of evidence that would take the defence by surprise, evidence no doubt that was uncovered by the diligent Hugh McKinnon. William Peters, who lived near Rednersville in Ameliasburg, testified that he had met Thomset at the Grand Trunk Station in Kingston a little over a month before the murder. While travelling by train to Belleville, Thomset showed Peters a .32 calibre pistol. The two men took the streetcar together from the station to the ferry house to cross to Prince Edward County some time after eight in the evening. The ferry had stopped running for the day and they called on the ferryman to see if he would take them across. A dog came out and barked and Thomset took out his pistol. The dog got away, but according to Peters, Thomset said that if he had got the chance he would have put a hole through the dog. It is difficult to see the relevance of the evidence regarding the dog's near miss, except that it cast Thomset in a negative light, but McCarthy made no effort to have it excluded.

Peters was asked to compare the pistol he saw with that found by the schoolboys: 'It was a good deal brighter that that. It was a very nice revolver. I should judge it was about the size of that revolver ... It was very nicely finished.'

'Evidence which fairly staggers the Court'

McCarthy complained that he was taken by surprise by this evidence, a complaint he would soon repeat. He approached the prisoners' dock to speak to Thomset. While he did so, Thomset's sister, who had had several tearful moments during the trial, fainted and had to be taken from the courtroom.

After a hurried, whispered discussion with Thomset, McCarthy launched into his cross-examination. He suggested that Peters was prompted by McKinnon to say that Thomset described his pistol as a .32 calibre. Peters agreed that McKinnon had mentioned a .32 calibre, but insisted that he had an independent recollection of Thomset telling him his was a .32 pistol. When McCarthy pressed the witness, he drew a hostile reaction from the partisan audience, and again the sheriff had to warn those present that they would be removed if the noise did not cease.

Clute surprised McCarthy again with evidence of two witnesses indicating that Thomset regarded Jones as a wealthy man who could easily be robbed and that he had been planning the robbery for some time. James Hicks, of West Lake, testified that at some unspecified time the previous year he had given Thomset a ride to Wellington. On the way, in Bloomfield at Cooper's sawmill, they met Gilbert Jones. 'I said "That old gentleman drives a better horse than I do." Thomset said "Yes," and said he, "He knows how to make money a little better than you do." We rode a little bit farther and he said it would be no knack at all to scare that old man out of his money. No knack or something to that effect.'

Clute did mention in his opening that he would lead evidence to this effect, but McCarthy had not yet arrived at that point and Gilbert must not have warned him that it was coming. Some nineteenth-century English judges insisted that the Crown had a duty to disclose its case and anything helpful to the defence[2] and many prosecutors made a practice of disclosing their case before trial. However, the doctrine did not fully take hold in Canada until after the Charter of Rights and Freedoms.[3] Although Clute's tactics may now seem unfair, 'the element of surprise was one of the accepted weapons in the arsenal of the adversaries,'[4] and there was nothing McCarthy could do about it. Obviously unprepared for this evidence, he asked a few perfunctory questions about the Lowder family.

Clute's next bombshell witness was Phoebe Cunningham, who lived in Hillier, about fourteen or fifteen miles from Bloomfield. She had only surfaced as a potential witness a week or so before the trial, when McKinnon heard a story she had told to her brother Abram Huyck and her neighbour David Spencer. In mid-September or early October, Thomset was with Cunningham at her home in Hillier and, according to her, talked openly about robbing Jones. Cunningham claimed that Thomset told her that Jones had plenty of money and 'how easily a fellow could get some of it when they knew they had it in the house.' When she said that Jones 'was a pretty gritty old fellow,' Thomset replied: 'Let a couple of masked men go in there and put a couple of revolvers up to their faces and they would give it up.' To that he added: 'If I should get in such a scrape as that I would shoot a man so dead he would never say anything about it.' When Cunningham's daughter said, 'Why, Joe, you would be hung,' Thomset replied, 'I do not care how quick.'

Phoebe Cunningham's testimony provoked another strong reaction from the spectators in the courtroom, who clearly regarded it as devastating evidence against Thomset. The Picton *Gazette* described it as 'evidence which fairly staggers the Court as well as Counsel for the prisoners' and 'created a great sensation' and that 'was listened to with breathless attention by those assembled.'[5]

Again, McCarthy had to confer hurriedly with Thomset. His cross-examination implied that Cunningham was motivated to lie by reason of her disappointment over a romantic relationship with Thomset. The whole scene was extremely difficult for Mrs Thomset to sit through, especially as Phoebe Cunningham had sworn that Thomset complained that he did not understand why his wife had married him, as she did not seem to care for him. As McCarthy conferred with Thomset, Mrs Thomset was 'overcome with emotion' and fainted. Efforts were made to revive her, and she was led out of the courtroom 'muttering in a half audible voice "oh! dear; oh! dear."'[6]

McCarthy suggested in cross-examination that Jones's name came up in their conversation in relation to the recent Quaker trial in which Jones had been involved and that story about robbing a Quaker came from a discussion that she, her husband, her son-in-law, and Thomset had had about how the notorious robber Jesse James had made 'some Quaker give up his grist to a poor man.' As the Quaker trial occurred after the Lazier murder, McCarthy seemed to be treading dangerous ground. Cunningham recalled a conversation about Jesse James, but insisted that her story of what Thomset had said to her was true. McCarthy then suggested that the devious hand of Hugh McKinnon was at work. The witness agreed that she had spoken to McKinnon, and that both her brother and McKinnon had taken down what she said in writing. When McCarthy asked her to repeat what Thomset had said, she did so more or less verbatim, leading McCarthy to suggest that her story was rehearsed and unreliable.

Clute was nearly ready to close the Crown's case. He called evidence to establish that Thomset had been at the Bloomfield station the day of the murder when Jones was paid $555 for his load of hops. Alfred Spencer, the station master, testified that he knew Thomset and saw him at the station that day. Thomset asked if there was an express parcel for him and Spencer told him there was not, and indeed none had arrived since. Another witness, Gregory Dougall, testified that he had seen Thomset at the station at the same time that Jones was being paid for his hops.

In cross-examination, McCarthy established through Spencer that there had been a number of strangers at the station that day, men engaged in putting in a telegraph line, idle on account of the storm. However, Spencer thought that all these men had left on a west-bound train at four in the afternoon.

Jesse Miller testified that at about four o'clock the day of the murder, he had been driving from Bloomfield towards where the Lowders and Thomset lived. He overtook Thomset who was walking in the same direction and gave him a ride to the Lowders', where he got off.

Mysterious Night Riders

To complete the Crown's picture implicating Thomset and the Lowder brothers, Clute called Sandford White and his son George, who testified that a little after 8 o'clock on the night of the murder, while going from Bloomfield to West Lake, they met a horse-drawn conveyance coming from the direction of the Lowders' towards Bloomfield. Sandford White's description was vague.

Q: What kind of conveyance was it?

A: I could not tell you, because I did not discover it sufficient.

Q: Did you see anything?

A: I did. I saw a rig of some kind. I could not tell you whether it was a single or a double rig.

Q: Can you tell me how many were in the rig?

A: I could not.

Q: How fast were they driving?

A: The rig was going very fast … a fast trotting gait.

The ominous suggestion of a horse-drawn carriage racing in the night from West Lake in the direction of the Jones farm probably helped the prosecution. On the other hand, this evidence also raised questions. If the murderers had gone from the Lowders' to the Jones' farmhouse by sleigh, why was there no evidence of sleigh tracks or footprints leading up to the Jones house? More puzzling, why would the culprits abandon the sleigh and walk back, making for a slower and more arduous escape and leaving tell-tale tracks in the snow? Could it be that there were initially three culprits, one of whom had abandoned the scheme with the horse-drawn conveyance long before the crime was committed?

Aaron McDonald finally reappeared just as the Crown's case was winding to a close, and after he answered a few perfunctory questions, Clute announced that the Crown's case had been completed.

Directed Verdict

Dickson rose to argue that Justice Patterson should direct the jury to return acquittals in favour of both David and George Lowder on the ground that the evidence against them was not sufficient to warrant leaving the case with the jury. If Patterson was satisfied that no reasonable jury could convict on the evidence led by the prosecution, he was entitled to direct the jury to return a verdict of not guilty.

Dickson easily succeeded in having the case against David Lowder withdrawn from the jury. Justice Patterson immediately told Dickson that he need say no more about David Lowder, indicating that he agreed there was no case against him. Justice Patterson invited Dickson to make his argument that George should also be discharged.

Dickson submitted that there were five people in the Lowder house and the boots did not point to George any more than any other member of the family. There was no evidence that George actually saw the boots that Saylor had seized, and the evidence failed to show that the boots were his. Moreover, even if there was some evidence that George was the man who went with Thomset to the Jones' house, the purpose was burglary, not murder, and he had abandoned the criminal enterprise by fleeing the scene before the fatal shot was fired by the other man.

Justice Patterson took no time to deliberate and delivered his ruling on Dickson's motions from the bench. As he had previously indicated, there was no evidence to implicate David Lowder. The Crown's case against the Lowder brothers depended entirely on the tracks in the snow, and no one suggested that the tracks could have been left by David Lowder's boots. There is no record of Justice Patterson's reasons apart from this notation in his bench book: 'Dickson submits that there is no evidence as to David Lowder and no sufficient evidence as to George Lowder. I direct acquittal of David.'[7]

Justice Patterson ruled that there was enough evidence against George Lowder to warrant putting the matter to the jury for its decision. He thought that the jury could find the evidence of the patch-bottom boots and the tracks in the snow that appeared to match those boots sufficient to prove that George was the second intruder. Although the man the Crown alleged was George Lowder had fled the scene before the fatal shot was fired, there was evidence that minutes earlier, that man had attempted to strike Lazier with the gun. This occurred when both assailants were present. It indicated a common intention to rob and to use violence and, ruled the judge, it would be open to the jury to conclude that the participation of the man with the gun was enough to support a conviction for murder.

The jury acquitted David without leaving the jury box and he was immediately released. His friends and family greeted him as a free man at the courtroom door.

McCarthy asked for an early adjournment at 6:00 p.m., and Justice Patterson adjourned the court until 9:30 the next morning.

That evening, David Lowder wandered the streets of Picton as a free man, accompanied by his sister Hannah and his brother Christopher and greeted by his friends, who were clearly delighted by his acquittal. George Lowder and Joseph Thomset returned to their cells in a gloomy mood, realizing that their fate likely turned on whether the jury would accept the alibi evidence to be presented the next day.

Home of Gilbert and Margaret Jones
(Peter Lockyer)

Patch-bottom boots
(Peter Lockyer)

Hugh McKinnon

Justice Christopher Patterson
(Library and Archives Canada)

Philip Low, QC
(*Illustrated Historical Atlas of the Counties of Hastings and Prince Edward*,
Toronto: H. Beldon & Co., 1878)

D'Alton McCarthy Jr, QC
(Library and Archives Canada)

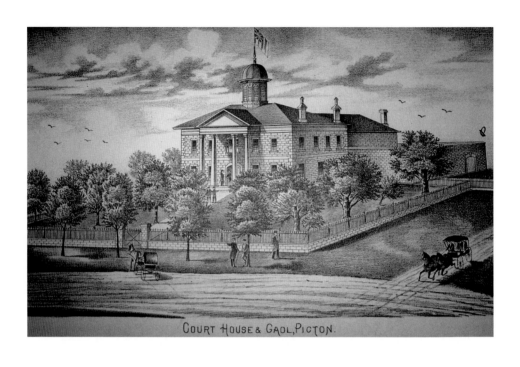

COURT HOUSE & GAOL, PICTON.

Prince Edward County Courthouse
(*Illustrated Historical Atlas of the Counties of Hastings and Prince Edward*,
Toronto: H. Beldon & Co., 1878)

Edwards Merrill

(Illustrated Historical Atlas of the Counties of Hastings and Prince Edward,
Toronto: H. Beldon & Co., 1878)

Sir John A. Macdonald
(Library and Archives Canada)

Alexander Campbell
(Library and Archives Canada)

Note written by Sir John A. Macdonald rejecting pleas for clemency
(Capital Case File, LAC, RG 13, vol. 1420, file 184A)

Gallows, Prince Edward County Jail
(Sandra Foreman Photography)

George Louder's Gravestone, Glenwood Cemetery, Picton
(Author photo)

9

The Defence

All 120 seats in the courtroom were filled by 9:00 am on Friday, 9 May for the fourth day of the trial. Again a disappointed crowd of people outside pleaded unsuccessfully with Sheriff Gillespie to allow more spectators to enter. The jury filed in showing signs of weariness after four days in court and three nights sequestered away from home. The prisoners, also showing signs of strain and fatigue, took their places in the dock.

Compelled Silence

The jury carefully scrutinized the demeanour and the behaviour of Thomset and Lowder for any signs that might indicate either guilt or innocence. But the law of the day did not allow the jury to hear either accused man give his version of what happened on the night of 21 December 1883. An accused person was not allowed to testify in his or her own defence. Even spouses of accused persons were excluded as witnesses, and so Thomset's wife, who might have testified as to his whereabouts at the time the murder was committed, could not take the stand in her husband's defence. The very people who almost always knew the most about the case – the plaintiff and the defendant in civil cases and the accused in criminal cases – were prevented by law from testifying on the ground that given their direct interest in the outcome, they could not be trusted to tell the truth. By 1884, parties to civil suits could testify, but the common law rule prevailed in criminal cases and posed a serious problem for an accused person who wanted to proclaim his or her innocence.

There were essentially two arguments advanced to support the rule in criminàl cases. One rested on the rights of the accused, while the other rested on the very different value of crime control and the community's interest in convicting the guilty. The historic common-law rights against self-incrimination and to the presumption of innocence were derived from resistance to the discredited coercive and inquisitorial practices of the infamous Star Chamber. The prevailing view of the legal profession was that these were important rights that had to be preserved at all costs. Allowing the accused to testify, it was feared, would introduce, through the back door, the dreaded French inquisitorial system of justice. It was argued that if an accused were *allowed* to testify, he or she would effectively be forced to do so as the jury would assume guilt from silence. In other words, as a practical matter, any accused who did not take the stand would be presumed to be guilty. As an 1867 article published in the *Upper Canada Law Journal* put it, making the accused competent to testify would amount to a 'revolution' that would 'destroy ... the presumption of innocence; and ... compel ... an accused party to furnish evidence which may be used against himself.'[1] This lamentable result, argued the opponents of change, could only be avoided if the accused were prevented by law from taking the stand.

The second argument was that the accused's evidence was inherently suspect. An accused person would say anything to escape punishment, especially when the sentence was death. As an early English text on the law of evidence stated, the evidence of an accused person would be more 'cause for distrust than any just cause of belief' and the law prevents a person with such a strong interest in the outcome from testifying 'to prevent them sliding into perjury.'[2] A correspondent to the *Canada Law Journal* expressed a similar view in 1868: 'Interests and passions will bias the oaths of a large majority of men. Why put this new temptation in their way?'[3]

Traditionalists argued that to allow the accused to testify would, as a practical matter, 'compel the guilty to either criminate themselves, or rely upon perjury for their protection.'[4] The fundamental common-law principles of the right to silence and the presumption of innocence would be undermined and the trial process would be overwhelmed with tainted and unreliable evidence. As a supporter of the traditional rule put it: 'There are but two words which a person accused of serious crime, should, if he is well advised, say ... from the hour of arrest to the rendition of the verdict, and those two words are "not guilty."'[5]

But banning the accused from the witness stand exacted a heavy price. The rule was unfair to an accused willing to explain his side of the story and the rule certainly deprived the jury of some vitally important information. In England, an accused person could sometimes make an unsworn statement to the jury. This practice developed before accused persons acquired the right to counsel.[6] At the end of the Crown's case the accused was permitted to state his defence. Some judges continued to allow the accused to make an unsworn statement even when defended or even to allow counsel to tell the jury what the accused would say if he were allowed to testify. However, there was considerable debate on the issue. It seemed odd to allow the accused to make an unsworn statement when he could not offer his story under oath. Until the 1880s, there appear to have been no clear rules, and the practice varied from judge to judge.[7]

By 1884, the general consensus was that counsel could not tell the jury what the accused would say, but that the accused could make an unsworn statement at the end of the case, subject to the Crown's right of reply.[8] This practice mitigated the disadvantages of the common-law rule, but often backfired when the accused rambled on or made statements that undermined the arguments defence counsel had presented. The defence bar tended to be very wary of allowing a client to offer unsworn statements, fearing that the client would make an unwise statement at a very crucial point in the case and preferring to put the defence in their own terms.[9]

By the mid-nineteenth century the rule that an accused person was incompetent to testify was under severe attack in the United States and in England from law reformers such as Jeremy Bentham, Sir James Fitzjames Stephen, and the Criminal Code Commissioners who pushed for a prisoner's evidence clause in their proposed Criminal Code.[10] Reformers argued that there were other ways to satisfy the concerns underlying the rule without imposing such a heavy cost on a party who wanted to take the stand on his own behalf. The judge could caution the jury about the inherent danger posed by the self-interested witness and if the accused did choose not to testify, the prosecutor could be barred from commenting on the fact or inviting the jury to infer guilt from the accused's silence.

The testimonial incompetence of the accused was removed by statute for certain criminal cases in 1886,[11] then for all cases in 1893,[12] five years before reform came in England,[13] but nine years too late for Thomset and Lowder. It is impossible to say what effect this change in the law might have had on the Thomset-Lowder case. Would any of the three accused have taken the stand if they had the right to do so? Would one or more of the accused have tried to escape the gallows by pointing the finger at the co-accused? There were certainly rumours at the time that David Lowder was trying to find a way to do just that. The fact that both Thomset and George Lowder protested their innocence from the moment they were arrested suggests that they almost certainly would have wanted to testify. On the other hand, McCarthy and Dickson might have advised them not to risk what was almost certain to be a fierce cross-examination by the skilful prosecutor, Roger Clute, particularly if they thought the Crown's case was weak.

A Common Defence

Defence counsel called a number of witnesses in an attempt to poke holes in the Crown's case, but the central defence was alibi. McCarthy and Dickson led evidence from several individuals related to the accused men in an attempt to prove that both Thomset and George Lowder spent the evening of 21 December at the Lowder residence. Thomset, McCarthy argued, left the Lowders' for home shortly before ten o'clock and went home after stopping by the Hicks' house to arrange a ride to Picton the next day. Dickson submitted that George Lowder never left the house except to feed the horses at about the time Thomset left, and he slept the entire night in the same bed as his brother David.

McCarthy and Dickson presented what amounted to a common defence, and they took turns calling their witnesses. Constable Edmund Bedell was recalled to the stand as the first witness for the defence. This provides further indication that defence counsel, who arrived in Picton after the trial had started, were not well prepared. Had the defence been better prepared for the trial, anything the defence hoped to elicit from Bedell would have been brought out in cross-examination. That said, McCarthy quickly established two points. First, when Bedell arrested Thomset early on the morning following the murder, the shotgun or rifle that he saw in Thomset's house was dusty and had not been used recently. Second, Thomset was undressed when arrested and the clothes he had been wearing were in the kitchen. Thomset started to put those clothes on, but his wife got him another suit, 'in a better state of preservation' and lighter in colour than the suit lying in the kitchen.

As Bedell stood down, Thomset's wife, child, and sister, clad in purple, entered the courtroom, shook hands with Thomset, and took their usual places behind the dock. McCarthy announced his next witness, H.S. Miller, the agent for the man who bought Jones's hops on 21 December. McCarthy established that when Jones was paid for his hops at the Bloomfield station, the door to the room was closed before the money was counted out and handed to Jones. McCarthy also established that while Thomset was at the station shortly before the money was paid, there were two or three other men present whom Miller did not know.

Q: Was there any whose conduct excited your suspicion?

A: There was one man. He was trying to weigh a bale of hops that lay on the scales, and I had my book and pencil figuring it up; and I was trying to weigh, and he was joggling the scales, and I wondered what he was doing there.

McCarthy was hoping to show that there was a suspicious man – identity unknown – who knew about the $555 Jones had received and who might have been responsible for the crime.

Patch-bottom Boots

Charles E. Watson, a Bloomfield shoemaker, was the first witness Dickson called on behalf of George Lowder. Both Dickson and McCarthy would try to show through Watson that there was nothing at all distinctive about either pair of boots that had left the tracks in the snow the night of Peter Lazier's murder. Watson testified that he often made patch-bottom boots and that it was usual to find the patches at different distances from the heels.

Q: Is it usual that the patch on either the right or the left boot would be a different distance from the heel from that on the other boot?

A: Yes, either one or the other. The length of the shank would sometimes not show any difference to the eye, but you would find it when you came to measure.

Q: What would be the usual amount of variance?

A: From a quarter to three-eighths of an inch.

Watson explained that he had never noticed that sort of variation until last Friday, when George's brother Sylvanus had come to his shop to ask him to measure his stock.

I did so and found what I have stated about the difference in length in patch-bottom boots.

Justice Patterson, who had asked very few questions during the trial, wanted to know a little more about the patch-bottom boots.

Q: Are those half soles put on to mend the boots, or are they put on originally?
A: I think they were put on to mend the boots.
Q: What you mean to say is that if you are putting on half-soles, you are not careful to make the half-soles exactly the same length?
A: Yes.

Watson estimated Thomset's round-toed boots to be a size 8. McCarthy established that size 8 was the most common. Watson explained that about half the boots he sold were size 8 and that round-toe boots, like those belonging to Thomset, had been in ordinary use for some years. He thought the boots seized from the Lowders' were size 6 and a half, and estimated that one-third of the boots he made would be that size.

Q: Do you make many of that kind of [patch-bottom] boot?
A: Yes.
Q: And very much worn about the section of the county where you live?
A: Yes.

Dickson called another shoemaker, Walter Tully from Picton, who confirmed that patch-bottom boots are a 'common article ... for country wear' and 'very much preferred to the double sole.' The boots seized from the Lowder farm were size 6 and hand made. Tully regarded the counter, the back part of the boot around the heel, as being a little out of the ordinary, but he agreed that there was nothing else unusual about these boots. He testified that if the boots were made by hand, there is likely to be some variation in the length of the shank. McCarthy hammered home the point that size 8 was the most common and that round-toed boots had been in common use for years.

The defence next tried to show that just as there was nothing distinctive about the boots, there was nothing unusual about a .32 calibre revolver. H. Wellbanks, a Picton hardware merchant, testified that he had sold revolvers since he started business five or six years earlier. Wellbanks was shown the weapon found by the Bloomfield schoolboys and stated that it was an ordinary 'Blue Jacket' revolver that would sell for about $5. When Clute suggested that it might be a 'Smith and Wesson,' the ever-observant Justice Patterson examined the weapon and pointed out that it was stamped 'Hopkins & Allen Manufacturing Company.'

A Question of Height

McCarthy then took the unusual step of recalling Margaret Jones to the stand. He wanted the jury to know a fact crucial to the defence, namely, that at her examination at the committal proceedings, a few days after the crime, Mrs Jones had testified that the man who fired the fatal shot was taller than Thomset. At the committal proceedings, Margaret Jones testified that she thought the man with the pistol and the mask was about the height of her husband, who stood 5 feet 9 inches. The defence later called one of the jailers who had measured both Thomset and George Lowder – Thomset was 5 feet 5 and ¾ inches and George Lowder was 5 feet 4 and ¾ inches.

Again, this reveals the defence's lack of preparation when the trial began. McCarthy's belated effort to score the potentially vital point as to Mrs Jones's estimation of the height of the shooter was less successful than it might have been had he been there to cross-examine her when she testified on the first day of the trial. Despite her clear statement before the justices at the committal proceedings, by the time of the trial Mrs Jones had become convinced – the defence insisted that she had had considerable coaching from Hugh McKinnon – that any difference between Thomset's height and that of the man she saw the night of 21 December was attributable to the linen mask the intruder was wearing. She now swore that the man with the mask was only 'a trifle taller' than the other robber and that although at the time she thought he was a tall man, she was now convinced that 'the mask made him appear a tall man.'

The second problem was that as McCarthy had called Mrs Jones as his own witness, he was not entitled to cross-examine her. When he confronted her with her testimony at the committal proceedings, Clute objected that McCarthy was cross-examining his own witness. Justice

Patterson hesitated but, perhaps sensing the importance of the point for the defence, decided to allow McCarthy to proceed. Justice Patterson's rather generous ruling allowed McCarthy to press on.

Q: You saw these men for the first time [before the justices]?
A: One I had seen before. Thomset lived in our neighbourhood. I had never seen the others to know them.
Q: Were you asked about them at that time, whether you could identify them or not?
A: I think I was asked the same questions – if I knew them – and I gave the same answer, that I had never seen the Lowders before to know them, but that Thomset, I was acquainted with him.
Q: Did you say the others were the men that were at your house that night?
A: I do not remember.
Q: Do I understand you to say that you then said that your impression was that the men who were at your door that night were taller than any of the three prisoners?
A: I said it was my impression that he was taller. I had reference to the one with the mask; that was the only one referred to when I made the reply that he was taller – Thomset as he stood there before me.

Mrs Jones agreed that she had been asked to stand down from the witness box level with Thomset to assess his height, that a mask had been put over Thomset's head, but that even then, she had said then that he did not seem to be as tall as the intruder.

McCarthy suspected that Hugh McKinnon likely tried to influence the witness.

Q: Do you remember McKinnon saying to you, 'Mrs. Jones, you were frightened then, and that is the reason'?
A: I do not remember it.
Q: You do not remember McKinnon saying you were scared, and therefore you thought they were bigger than they really were?
A: I do not remember that.

McCarthy sensed that Mrs Jones was equivocating and managed to extract a grudging admission that McKinnon's devious hand might been at work to repair this serious hole in the prosecution's case.

Q: I would just ask you again whether you do not remember McKinnon trying to coax you to say that Thomset was not any shorter than the man you saw?

A: I do not remember.

Q: But you would not say that it did not take place?

A: No.

Throughout the rest of the day McCarthy returned to the issue of Mrs Jones's identification evidence before the justices that the intruders were taller than Thomset or Lowder. Several witnesses who had attended the committal proceedings were asked to recount her failure to identify the accused and her statement then that the shooter appeared to be taller than either accused.

Alibi

Margaret Lowder, George's mother, was the first witness called in support of the alibi defence. Mrs Lowder testified that the night of the murder she was at home with her husband John, her sons George, David, and Christopher, and her father-in-law, whom she described as being 'very poorly, … very much crippled up … very old' and unable to get around. Her youngest son, Allan, was not home that night. She stated that on the day of the murder George had drawn saw logs with Chris. She thought that David had gone to the family's fishing beach on the sandbanks near Wellington. Her husband had been setting nets in West Lake during the day with one of his fishing partners, Cornelius Mastin. He came back for his mid-day meal and returned again at about three or four o'clock. Later in the evening, he went down to Horse Point with his 'car,' a vessel 12 feet long, 6 feet wide, and 3 feet deep, used to contain live fish from the nets until they were shipped. After John Lowder came back home, Thomset arrived and stayed with the family for tea. She testified that Thomset was a frequent visitor: 'If he is going that way, he is apt to stop.' Another neighbour, Thomas Street, Thomset's father-in-law, dropped in just as they sat down to their meal.

Q: How long did Thomset remain?

A: He stayed all the evening talking.

Q: And did all your sons that you have named stay there?

A: Yes.

Q: Did any person of those you have named leave?

A: No.

Q: Who was the first to go away?
A: Mr. Thomset.

Mrs Lowder testified that she recalled winding the clock a minute or two before Thomset left at twenty minutes to ten, but the clock was 'slow about ten minutes by the other time piece, Picton time.' She recalled one of the boys telling her to 'set the clock on.' George went to the barn to feed the horses just before Thomset left and returned to the house. Street was still there when George returned from the barn. After Street left, everyone retired for the night. Mrs Lowder testified that she first heard of the murder the next morning at breakfast when Babbitt came and arrested David. Only Christopher had left the house that morning to feed the horses. He did so before Babbitt arrived.

Clute rose to cross-examine and, knowing that other members of the family would also be called in support of the alibi defence, he grilled Mrs Lowder – as he would the other alibi witnesses – on the specific details of precisely what happened that evening, hoping that the others would give different versions. After supper, Mrs Lowder said, she washed her dishes, and then sat down to her knitting while the rest of them talked about fishing and hunting. Thomset said he wanted to bring his nets to the Lowders for the winter, where any required repairs could be done.

Clute thought that 10 o'clock was late to be feeding the horses. Mrs Lowder explained: 'George asked Chris, who usually fed the horses, if he had fed them yet, and Chris said no. "Well" said George, "You go and feed them." Chris said, "I have got my boots off, and I don't want to go out."'

Clute questioned Mrs Lowder's precise recollection of the time:

Q: I ask you whether you always look at the clock when you wind it to see what time it is?
A: I generally do.
Q: Could you tell me what time it was the night before that?
A: I do not know as I could exactly.
Q: Could you tell me what time it was the night before that?
A: No.
Q: Or at any time that week?
A: No.

She testified that after George went to bed, David sat by the stove until shortly before eleven. She sat up knitting and retired at about eleven after covering her father-in-law, who slept on the ground floor.

McKinnon the Trickster?

Clute suggested to Mrs Lowder that she had told McKinnon that George and Thomset had gone out together much earlier than 10 o'clock. Her answer indicated that McKinnon may have tried to trick her by suggesting that the prisoners had made statements that contradicted her story. Clute suggested that she told McKinnon that George and Thomset left together:

A: I did not. I said 'Who says they went out to the barn together?' 'Why' he said. 'George said so.' I said, 'George said so eh?'

But under sustained pressure from Clute, Mrs Lowder was driven to reveal some serious confusion as to what she told McKinnon about the time that George and then Thomset had left the house. Again, she tried to cover any inconsistency with the suggestion that McKinnon had lied to her or tried to trick her:

A: I said somewheres between nine and ten or somewheres along there, or eight or half past nine, or something like that.
Q: Which did you say, nine or eight?
A: There were people came there and tried to make me tell things and I made up my mind I was not going to tell. They came there and tried to make me say things.

She insisted that she did not say that Thomset left at eight o'clock, but Clute pressed on:

Q: Did you mention any other hour than eight as the time that Thomset left?
A: I think I did.
Q: What other hour did you mention as the hour Thomset left?
A: About half past eight or nine.
Q: I want you to tell me what time you told McKinnon that Thomset left?
A: I can't exactly tell.
Q: Do you remember mentioning eight o'clock as the time that Thomset left?
A: I might have. I do not know whether I did or not.
Q: Did you know at that time the hour that Thomset left?

A: All I know is by the clock when I wound it.
Q: Did you know that when you were talking to McKinnon?
A: I did.
Q: Why didn't you tell him?
A: Because they came with falsehoods in their mouth, and I thought that
    when I was called here to give my affidavit, I would give it exactly.
Q: Did you think of the time Thomset left when you were talking to McKin-
    non?
A: Yes, but I thought I would tell it when I came to court.

She insisted, 'They bewildered me so much I hardly knew what I was
saying.' She admitted again that she might have told McKinnon that
Thomset had left at half past eight or nine, but denied that she had lied
or attempted to mislead McKinnon and insisted that Thomset left at
twenty to ten.

McCarthy did his best to salvage Thomset's alibi in re-examination,
reverting to the theme that Margaret Lowder was distressed at the time
and that McKinnon was not a man who could be trusted. He established that McKinnon came together with Babbitt, Bedell, and Pope and
that before questioning her, they had done a thorough search of the
house with which she and her husband John had cooperated.

Q: Would you say your mind was distracted?
A: I was so bewildered I hardly knew.

McKinnon had admitted that he had lied to and tried to trick Mrs
Thomset and McCarthy did what he could to suggest that McKinnon's
tactics had also been used on Mrs Lowder.

Q: You say that they came there with lies in their mouth. How did you know
    they came with lies in their mouth at that time?
A: Because it sounded like it.
Q: Did you think that McKinnon was lying to you?
A: I thought that it did not look reasonable, what he told me.
Q: What did he tell you that you thought did not look reasonable?
A: He said about George going out, and saying he went out with Thomset.
Q: You knew where George was that night?
A: I knew he was at home that night.
Q: And because you thought he was lying to you, how did you feel about
    answering him?

A: I felt just as if I did not care whether I answered him or not, to think that anyone would come and try to deceive me. That was what I thought at the time.

As Mrs Lowder prepared to leave the stand, Justice Patterson asked for clarification about the time the horses were fed. It seemed odd to him that the horses would not be fed until 10 o'clock.

Q: I would like her explanation as to whether the horses were fed at the usual time.
A: It was later than usual.

McCarthy interjected to ask why.

A: On account that they had been at work drawing saw logs out and skidding them, and the horses were warm, and they did not feed them on account of their being warm. They had their tea and kind of forgot it; they got talking and it kind of slipped their mind.

Mrs Lowder knew that her son's life depended upon her evidence and she clearly felt the strain, as did George. He openly wept while she was being grilled in the stand. One reporter observed that the latter part of her evidence under Clute's cross-examination 'was extracted with great difficulty' and that 'she hesitated a great deal.'[14] When her ordeal was finally over, Mrs Lowder broke down completely.[15]

John Lowder's Story

George's father John Lowder then took the stand. After the trial, John Lowder was suspected by many to have been implicated in the crime,[16] but there was no hint of that when he testified in his son's defence. He explained to the jury that he worked as a fisherman in separate partnerships on fishing leases with both Cornelius Mastin and Joseph Thomset. He had worked with Thomset for eight or ten years. Both leases were along Lake Ontario and West Lake from Horse Point to Johnston Island. He claimed to have a large fishing business. The fish were mostly sold 'to the other side' and shipped by rail or boat.

John Lowder's explanation of what he had done on the day of the murder corresponded closely with Mrs Lowder's evidence. In the morning and early afternoon, Lowder was setting nets with Mastin between his own property and Johnston Island. There was drifting snow on the lake in the afternoon. Lowder went home for his dinner and then back out in the evening with his car or fish box. When he returned home, Thomset was there together with his family, George, Chris, David, his father, and his wife. They ate supper together and were joined as they sat down by Thomas Street. During the evening, he had discussed fishing arrangements with Thomset, who wanted to use Lowder's team of horses to bring some nets in for repairs.

John Lowder swore that George was the first to leave the house to feed the horses. Thomset left while George was in the barn and George came back in within minutes of Thomset's departure. Street left shortly after George returned from the barn. Lowder fixed the time of Thomset's departure at ten minutes to ten:

As Thomset got ready to leave, he asked Chris what time it was, and Chris pulled out his watch, and said, 'It is ten minutes to ten.' I saw the watch; he pulled it right out before me, and he said it was ten minutes to ten, and I saw it was. Chris said, 'You had better stay all night and sleep with me and help me to build fires.' Thomset said he would not. George came in from the barn then right straight. I thought George met Thomset, but I do not know whether he did or not.

Lowder described how McKinnon, Babbitt, and Pope had searched his house the day after the murder 'from top to bottom ... up the garret and down the cellar.' Lowder tried to follow them down to the lake when they measured the tracks, but McKinnon ordered him back: 'He said he did not wish me to see that part of it.' Lowder did, however, observe the track they followed and suggested that it was the very track he had made when tending to his fishing on the afternoon before the murder.

Q: Can you say how the track they followed compared with the track you had made on the way you had come home on Friday night?
A: I think they probably took my track. They went on the same path down to the lake, over the same place in the wire fence, and after they left the road they went over the same rail. There was a willow bush standing in the marsh, and I almost ran into it before I saw the bush, and I turned around it. The pathway they followed was the same, around the willow bush.

Lowder swore that on Sunday he could see the track he had left on Friday.

Q: What kind of boots were you wearing [on Friday]?
A: I was wearing a pair of coarse boots, patch-bottomed.
Q: How does your boot compare with George's boot?
A: Him and I wear the same sized boots.
Q: Is there any other member of your family that wears the same sized boot?
A: Yes
Q: Who is it?
A: Sylvanus.
Q: Can you wear one another's boots?
A: Yes.

Lowder thought that his son Christopher also wore size 6 boots. This made four members of the Lowder family who wore the same size boots. John Lowder also explained that he had bought his boots at Hart's in Picton and he thought George had purchased his there as well.

Justice Patterson, clearly anxious to complete the trial within the week, allowed only a short break for lunch, adjourning at 1 p.m. and resuming at 1:30. As he had done with Margaret Lowder, Clute attacked John Lowder's evidence as to the time Thomset left the house. Clute confronted John Lowder with the suggestion that on Saturday morning, after Thomset's arrest, he had told Cornelius Mastin and Frank McDonald that Thomset left the Lowder house at around eight o'clock the night of the murder. Lowder denied the statement. He also denied hearing his wife tell McKinnon that Thomset had left at about eight o'clock, but when pressed he conceded that he could not swear that she had not done so. Lowder could not recall if McKinnon had asked for George's boots or that he had told McKinnon that he had George's boots.

David Lowder Takes the Stand

The parade of Lowders taking the stand to establish the alibi defence continued. David, now a free man, testified in his brother's defence. The constables had been told by Margaret Jones that the man with the gun was tall. David said that he was 5 feet 7 and ¼ inches while George was under 5 feet 5 inches. He believed that he had been arrested because of his height.

David stated that he had spent the day of the murder in the swamp hunting rabbits. On his way home just before dusk, he visited his brother Sylvanus, who lived a short distance away in the direction of Thomset's house. Sylvanus asked him to stay for supper, but his boots were wet and he decided to go home, where he found Thomset and Street. David testified that he heard his brother Chris 'say by the watch' that it was ten minutes to ten just before Thomset left: 'Thomset says, "Well, it must be getting pretty late. I guess I will go for home." And some of us says, I know I did, I says "Joe, you had better stay all night; it will be late, and your wife will be to bed" and he said "No."' David did not look at the watch, but he did look at the clock and it was ten minutes to ten. That night, he slept upstairs in the same bed as George, who retired first. He swore that George did not get up in the night.

In cross-examination, David introduced an entirely new and surprising element to the case. Thomset, he stated, had come that evening from Bloomfield, where he had bought a place where he was planning to put up some shelves to keep bees.

Q: Had Thomset's coming to your place that night any connection with his coming from his place at Bloomfield?
A: Well, he came there to know was there some of us could go and take a load of bees out to his place, as he had been out there and fixed up some shelves – wanted to know if we could take him out there the first week.
Q: That is what he came to your place that night for?
A: Yes.

The story of Thomset's place in Bloomfield for bees was problematic. David did not mention it until cross-examination and none of the other alibi witnesses had said that was why Thomset had stopped by. Was the alibi unravelling?

Thomas Street's Version

Thomset's father-in-law Thomas Street lived alone about a quarter of a mile from the Lowders in the direction of Bloomfield. He testified that it was his habit to pass by the Lowders on Friday evenings to read the newspapers they took. He went there on the night of the murder. Thomset, whom he had seen earlier in the day walking towards Bloomfield, was there having supper with the family. Street testified that he stayed 'until pretty nigh ten o'clock.' Thomset left a few minutes before he did, and just before Thomset left, George Lowder had gone to the barn to feed the horses. Street fixed the time of Thomset's departure recalling that his son-in-law had asked Christopher the time: 'Says he, "It wants ten minutes of ten." Thomset said, "I must be going."'

Street conceded in cross-examination that although the paper was there, he did not read it at the Lowders' that evening. Street's evidence varied from that of the Lowders on two points. First, he described Christopher's gold watch as being silver. Second, his evidence as to where people were sitting was at odds with what others had described.

More Lowders Testify

Sylvanus Lowder lived about a quarter of a mile from his father's house, away from Bloomfield and in the direction of where Thomset lived. He was called to support Thomset's alibi. He testified that on the night of the murder, the clock struck ten o'clock. He put down the book he was reading and before going to bed, went outside to get some kindling for the morning. He saw Thomset passing by on his way home and the two men exchanged greetings. This evidence supported Thomset's presence at the Lowders until nearly ten o'clock, but was it consistent with the suggestion that he then stopped at the Hicks' home closer to 11:00?

Christopher Lowder explained that he and George had drawn saw logs during the day. They took one load to Bloomfield and returned home together. He fed the horses some hay when they returned to the barn at about four o'clock, but they were too warm to be fed grain. His father went down to the lake late in the afternoon, and Thomset came in just before his father returned, followed by Street as they sat down to tea. Christopher's version of who left when was consistent with that of the others: George went out to feed the horses, then Thomset left, followed by Street. It was Christopher's job to feed the horses, but he told George he had his boots off and asked him if he would go. Just before Thomset left, he asked the time and Christopher took out his watch and told him it was ten to ten. Christopher slept by the stove and testified that to leave the house, one would have to pass by where he slept. No one left the house that night.

Hannah Way, Margaret and John Lowder's daughter, was present at the Lowder farm on Sunday when McKinnon, Babbitt, and Bedell came to search the premises. She was present when McKinnon questioned her mother about the time Thomset left.

A: He asked Mother where George and Thomset went at night when they went out together. She said, 'Who told you they went out?' He says,

'George told me that he and Thomset went out at night about half past nine.' She says, 'George told you, eh?' I said, 'Mother, don't you tell anything until you come to court.'

Q: Did he try to pump her?

A: He asked several questions. They were all questioning her.

Q: Did your mother make any answers?

A: I do not remember hearing her make any answers.

The Defence Closes

The defence closed its case and Dickson renewed his plea for a directed verdict of acquittal in favour of George Lowder on the basis that all the evidence indicated that only one man was present at the scene when the fatal shot was fired. This was a difficult argument to sustain. As already explained, if two people form a common criminal purpose, they are liable for each other's acts done in pursuit of that purpose. The two intruders went to rob and, as their possession of weapons indicated, to use violence if necessary to accomplish that purpose. The man the Crown alleged was George Lowder had clubbed or attempted to club Lazier with his shotgun and had fled the scene only seconds before the fatal shot was fired. Ordinarily, there must be timely communication of the intention to abandon the common purpose from the party dissociating himself from the contemplated crime so that the remaining party knows that from that point he is acting on his own.[17]

Justice Patterson ruled that as there was some evidence from which the jury could conclude that the intruder with the gun had assaulted the deceased in furtherance of the common purpose, the case should be left with the jury.

Clute's Reply Evidence

Clute attempted to call reply evidence to prove a crucial point, namely, that the patch-bottom boots seized at the Lowders' belonged to George. Clute asked George Pope about what transpired when he went to the Lowders' on Sunday with Babbitt, Bedell, and McKinnon:

Q: What was said there by McKinnon in the presence of these persons [the Lowders]?

A: McKinnon asked for George Lowder's boots.

McCarthy immediately objected that this was not proper reply evidence which can be called to meet a point that arises from the defence case that the Crown could not have anticipated. Otherwise, the Crown would be allowed to 'split' its case and this would be unfair to the accused, who are entitled to know the full case against them before calling their defence. Justice Patterson agreed and ruled: 'About taking the boots there is no evidence ... I do not know that anything that was said by McKinnon is evidence in rebuttal.'

Clute did succeed, however, in having Pope, Babbitt, and Bedell state that Margaret Lowder had said that George Lowder and Thomset went to the barn not later than eight o'clock. George went to feed the horses as Christopher had taken his boots off and asked George to do the chore. George returned to the house alone in twenty minutes, and remained at home for the rest of the evening.

To counter this extremely damaging evidence, McCarthy got Babbitt to agree that there was some 'funny talk' and some 'queer talk' by McKinnon. McCarthy also gained grudging admissions from all three witnesses that they had recently discussed what Mrs Lowder had said with McKinnon, suggesting that McKinnon had coached them on what to say. When Babbitt was on the stand, the audience ridiculed McCarthy's efforts in this regard, once again leading Justice Patterson to rebuke them for 'conducting themselves as though at a circus rather than attending a trial where the lives of their fellows were at stake.'[18]

Bedell admitted that on Tuesday evening, after the trial started, McKinnon had discussed the matter with him. McCarthy tasted blood when Bedell was rattled and confused in response to McCarthy's cross-examination. Bedell was unable to give a coherent explanation of how the conversation between McKinnon and Mrs Lowder had gone.

Q: Will you just tell me what [McKinnon's] question was?
A: Yes. He said, 'What time did Thomset and George go out of the house that evening?'
Q: Was that all he said in the question that led to that answer?
A: No.
Q: Was it a longer question?
A: That was about the question at that time.
Q: Then in answer to that question Mrs. Lowder said what?
A: The family said no.
Q: Did they all speak with one voice?

A: It was a general consent like.
Q: You swore that Mrs. John Lowder made a certain answer; then I asked you
what the question was to that answer, and now you profess to say that the
answer to that question was no?
A: Well, it was the same question exactly.

Clute did not recall McKinnon, despite the central role he played in
eliciting whatever it was that Mrs Lowder had said, no doubt fearing
that this would only invite a renewed attack by McCarthy on McKinnon's devious investigative methods.

Frank McDonald was recalled to testify that on the day after the murder, John Lowder told him and Cornelius Mastin that 'Thomset left his
place the night before, about eight o'clock, or half past eight, or not later
than nine anyway.' But again, McCarthy succeeded in showing that the
hand of Hugh McKinnon seemed to be at work. McDonald conceded in
cross-examination that he had made no mention of this statement when
he was examined before the justices, but had spoken of it since 'to the
man that runs the billiard table up at the Royal,' and that he had told
McKinnon about John Lowder's statement after the trial began.

George Pope, recalled a second time, now stated that John Lowder
had also spoken of George and Thomset going out at eight o'clock the
night of the murder. Why he would not have given this evidence previously or why he was allowed to give it in reply is a mystery.

Justice Patterson allowed the defence to recall Christopher Lowder
in 'sur-rebuttal.' Christopher swore that he was there when McKinnon,
Pope, Bedell, and Babbitt came to the house the Sunday following the
murder, and that he could not recall his mother saying anything about
the hour Thomset and George left the house. The Crown did not cross-
examine on this evidence.

The unruly and partisan courtroom spectators had openly derided
the defence alibi and cheered the prosecution's efforts to debunk it. Justice Patterson expressed his displeasure and warned that if there were
similar disturbances the next day, he would clear the courtroom.

Court finally adjourned at 6:15 p.m. after a long day of sitting. Mc-
Carthy and Dickson were no doubt distressed to see the headline in
the Picton *Gazette* the next day proclaiming: 'THE GREAT MURDER TRIAL:
THE DEFENCE WEAK!'[19] The local press was certainly contributing to the
lynch-mob mentality of the courtroom spectators.

10

Verdict

By Friday night, everyone expected that the case would be completed on Saturday with the drama of counsel's closing submissions, the trial judge's charge to the jury, and the jury's verdict. The Picton *Gazette* reported that 'the interest in the trial has daily increased, and this community was never so stirred up with excitement.'[1] Picton's hotels were filled with visitors. The town's atmosphere was carnival-like. A band played music from the balcony of the Royal Hotel and more music could be heard in the other hotels and public houses.

But the gaiety of the music did not reflect the more sinister mood among some townsfolk. The *Intelligencer's* reporter observed: 'Music it is alleged, hath charms to soothe the savage beast, but the people of this town were not soothed, and may, therefore, be considered ferocious, as they cared little for the music and preferred to talk about the trial.'[2]

The prevailing view expressed in hotel barrooms and pubs was that both George Lowder and Joseph Thomset deserved to hang. The town would be upset if tomorrow did not end with two death sentences. The jury was sequestered throughout the trial to ensure that the verdict would be based upon the evidence and not tainted by any outside influence. But the twelve men who would decide the prisoners' fate had been exposed throughout the trial to the partisan outbursts of the spectators, and they were almost certainly keenly aware of the mood of the town. Indeed, a Picton *Gazette* report suggests that the sequestration was far from perfect. That evening, as the town was abuzz with talk of the trial, one of the constables 'had the jurymen out for an airing, and they paraded the streets for a considerable length of time in order to shake off the feeling of weariness which had come over them in consequence of their long and close confinement during the progress of the trial. The kindness thus shown them was very much appreciated.'[3]

Interest in the proceedings had intensified as the case wound its way to a verdict. More visitors, hoping to be in court for the trial's finale, arrived on Saturday morning. The day was cold and wet, with intermittent showers and drizzle. Hotel yards were filled with horses and carriages by 8 a.m. There was a steady stream of traffic on the streets leading to the courthouse. Once again, many were disappointed not to gain admission. The *Gazette* reported that 'several hundreds more than could gain admission to the courtroom were on the jail grounds and in the street surrounding ... Seats were at a high premium and it taxed all the patience and tact of the constables to guard the entrances to the courtroom against the surging crowd who sought admittance.'[4] Some resorted to subterfuge, representing themselves to be reporters, family members, or even justices of the peace.

Justice Patterson entered the court promptly at 9:30 a.m. and the prisoners were brought in. Thomset's sister, wife, and daughter took their usual place behind the dock. The sheriff, undoubtedly at Justice Patterson's direction, warned the crowd that if they did not behave themselves the courtroom would be cleared. The jury, realizing that if they were able to reach a verdict at the end of the day, they would be able to return home that evening, looked fresher and brighter than they had the previous day.

The evidence was quickly completed with the testimony of Sylvanus Lowder's wife Lucinda, who had been ill and unable to attend court the day before. She supported her husband's evidence that Joseph Thomset had passed by their house at about 10 p.m. the night of the murder. She swore that Sylvanus had been reading until about ten, when he went outside and she heard a voice she did not recognize call 'Holla.'

The rest of the day was taken up with counsel's closing arguments, Justice Patterson's instructions to the jury and the wait for the jury to decide.

D'Alton McCarthy's Plea

As Justice Patterson noted with precision in his bench book, D'Alton McCarthy started his closing address[5] on behalf of Thomset at 9:44

a.m. and concluded at 12:22 p.m.[6] McCarthy congratulated the jury on reaching the end of the trial and indicated that the jury's task was one of tribulation. He complimented them for having paid close attention to the evidence but, knowing that he was fighting the mood of the community as well as the case the Crown had presented, he warned the jury about being swayed by the hostile mood of the community and 'the magnetic influence of public opinion.'

McCarthy noted that the large audiences assembled in the courtroom had shown strong feeling against the prisoners throughout the trial and that there had not been one indication of sympathy in their favour. 'You, gentlemen, are to try this case according to the evidence and get a verdict accordingly. If any of you have a prejudice you should endeavour to cast it away. The lives of two men are at stake.' This reduced Thomset's wife and sister to tears and Justice Patterson ordered them to be taken from the courtroom.

McCarthy conceded that the murder was foul, but cautioned the jury to be wary of the cry for vengeance. There was little if any direct evidence against the prisoners. The Crown had endeavoured to show a chain of circumstantial evidence linking them to the crime. McCarthy suggested that it would be criminal to jump hastily to a conclusion based on the kind of circumstantial evidence the Crown had presented when the penalty these men faced was the loss of their lives. He referred to cases where men had been wrongfully convicted, and submitted to the jury that the case against the prisoners was based on rumour, speculation, and the community's rush to judgment. 'People talk and start believing things they did not see.'

One of the men who entered the Jones house that night was tall. The prosecution claimed that man was Thomset, yet Mrs Jones had testified at the committal proceedings that none of the three prisoners seemed to be as tall as the man she saw in her house. She testified that Thomset was not tall enough to be the man she saw. The man Mrs Jones saw was wearing grey clothing, not the dark clothing Thomset was wearing less than an hour later when he visited Alfred and Delia Hicks.

McCarthy emphasized that the distance between the Jones and Hicks houses was four miles by the most direct route and five miles by the route traced by the trackers. Could a man walk that distance in the snow in one hour and six minutes as claimed by the prosecution witnesses? If he could, he would have been pretty well 'blown' by the time he arrived at the Hicks residence. Yet according to the Crown's own evidence, Thomset arrived at the Hicks house calm and collected and not tired from a rapid walk of four or five miles. He wore a hat and he was dressed in dark clothes that did not match the description of grey clothing Mrs Jones said the robber was wearing.

Thomset's size did not correspond to that of the intruder and his appearance and demeanour at the Hicks residence was not that of a man who had just rushed away from committing a murder. When he was arrested by Bedell, Thomset was perfectly calm and he quickly told the constable where he had been the previous evening when the crime was committed.

The Crown, McCarthy argued, had 'overworked' its case. He reminded the jury that under the law, if a doubt existed that doubt must favour the prisoners. 'You, gentlemen of the jury, have to answer to your God for the verdict you may render and do justice to these men in the box.'

The tracking evidence, McCarthy argued, depended on whether or not the tracks were actually made by Thomset's boots. He urged the jury to scrutinize the evidence in this area with the greatest of care. Aaron McDonald was the only man to say he had followed the track to Thomset's house, and as 'there was a feud existing between McDonald and Thomset,' he urged them to dismiss McDonald's evidence 'with the contempt it deserved.'

Throughout his address, McCarthy returned to his passionate attack on the popular prejudice that seemed to surround the case. He urged the jury not to hesitate to stand out against such heated public opinion: 'Our reputation for honest trials is well known. The administration of the law is fairly above suspicion. The purity of the bench is not to be assaulted. There is a belief that a man will not be hanged first and tried afterwards.'

McCarthy strongly attacked McKinnon's integrity and urged the jury to reject the detective's efforts to build a case against the accused. 'On the evidence of the detective I would not hang a dog. This man McKinnon committed a forgery in Her Majesty's name ... and he was not fit to live among civilized beings.' Despite all McKinnon's efforts – even the attempt to deceive Mrs Thomset – no pistol and no mask had been found. And why, asked McCarthy, had the detective, who was paid to do such things, not attempted to follow the tracks from one end to another? McCarthy derided McKinnon's attempt to browbeat the Lowders into giving evidence against their sons, and he urged the jury not to believe a word of his testimony.

McCarthy was equally scathing about the evidence of William Peters, the man who claimed to have seen Thomset with a pistol on the train. Surprise evidence, he argued, was unfair and should not be admissible. Here, evidence had been sprung on the defence at that last minute and was probably manufactured 'out of whole cloth.'

McCarthy then turned to the evidence of Phoebe Cunningham. Her dramatic evidence late in the trial that Thomset had hatched a plot to threaten and rob Jones months earlier had clearly made a strong impact on the trial. McCarthy described 'a romantic story which has been sprung upon us.' Her evidence was good for newspaper reporters and newsboys, but he asked the jurors to consider her demeanour in the witness box and the way she told her story. McCarthy asked rhetorically: 'Was there not a mountain of perjury piled up here?'

As for the defence evidence, McCarthy conceded that there were possibly discrepancies in the alibi evidence. But these inconsistencies, he submitted, were no more than would be shown by the recollections of honest people. 'It is rarely that people remember small occurrences that take place during the evening assembly of neighbours.'

In the end, McCarthy stated, the Crown had not succeeded in attacking the credibility of the alibi evidence. Christopher Lowder's evidence that his mother and father had not given McKinnon an earlier time of Thomset's departure had not been cross-examined, which McCarthy urged the jury to take as an 'admission by the Crown that the testimony was unimpeachable.' He suggested that George Pope's evidence was the product of the strong feelings of a relative and that McKinnon was an admitted deceiver.

McCarthy reached the conclusion of his impassioned address. He pleaded that the jury were being asked to sacrifice a human life on 'slipshod evidence, shifting as the sands.' Pointing to where Mrs Thomset and her daughter had sat, he stated: 'On this uncertain evidence, if your minds are free from bias you jurymen will not make that woman a widow and that child fatherless and the father drop from the gallows at the hands of the clumsy hangman. Do not allow your minds to be swayed. The responsibility is yours not mine.' Conviction could only rest on solid evidence, not doubt, and he urged the jury to acquit.

The *Intelligencer*'s reporter was impressed by McCarthy's eloquence: 'Mr. McCarthy's peroration was considered one of his finest efforts. It was grand. The language was plain and touching. The address was a perfect appeal to the sympathy of the jury. It was considered the best ever made here. It brought tears to the eyes of a large number of those present and the prisoners as well.'[7]

Thomset's sister was overcome with tears and she had to leave the courtroom with Mrs Thomset and her daughter. The *Gazette* reporter observed that 'during the delivery of Mr. McCarthy's address, the prisoners Thomset and George Lowder, as well as many of the ladies who were in the court room were frequently affected to tears.'[8]

Justice Patterson, anxious to complete the case by the end of the day, called a short luncheon recess of half an hour. Many spectators decided to forgo lunch so as not to lose their places for the afternoon. McCarthy's powerful oratory had not changed the prevailing view of the crowd. The noisy spectators remained convinced that the prisoners were guilty, and they looked forward to the verdict they were so confident would come. It remained to be seen whether McCarthy's skill and eloquence would carry the day with the jury.

George Dickson's Plea for George Lowder

The proceedings resumed promptly at 1:05 p.m., when George Dickson arose to address the jury on behalf of George Lowder. Again the courtroom was crowded to overflowing and the constables had difficulty restraining those who clamoured at the courthouse door for admission, some even offering to pay the constables one dollar to let them in. Mrs Thomset had returned to the courtroom with her child, but was asked to leave to avoid any further interruption. She stood in the hallway, where she could hear Dickson and Clute make their closing arguments.

Like McCarthy, Dickson questioned the strength of the circumstantial evidence. He emphasized the failure of Gilbert and Margret Jones to identify either of the two prisoners as the men who were in their house and reminded the jury that they had testified the assailants were taller men. Mrs Jones testified that the man whom the prosecution alleged to be George Lowder had a beard and that she could not tell whether it was real or false. The possibility that it was a real beard was enough to acquit his client. There was no evidence to show that the boots that made the tracks belonged to George Lowder. There simply were too many holes in the Crown's circumstantial case: no weapon, no mask, and no unbroken trail. No one had been able to trace the tracks all the way from the Jones' house to the Lowders'. The gaps in the evidence, Dickson suggested, deserved a great deal of weight and consideration.

The Crown's suggestion that the assailants had driven to the Jones farm in a rig made no sense – why would they abandon the rig and walk home? Dickson reminded the jury that one of the assailants had fled the scene before the fatal shot was fired. Even if the jury accepted the Crown's theory that that man was George Lowder, Dickson argued, George could not be responsible for the murder as he had abandoned any common criminal enterprise he might have had with the other assailant.

Dickson argued that quite apart from the weaknesses in the Crown's case, the alibi evidence alone was sufficient to acquit his client. Six witnesses had solemnly deposed that George Lowder was home all Friday night. The Picton *Gazette* described his argument in the following terms:

If the jury convicted the prisoners they would have to either set aside the evidence of five or six witnesses, who had deliberately taken the Bible in their hands – from a mere lad to the oldest man of upwards of 70 years of age, tottering almost to the grave – and sworn 'to tell the truth the whole truth and nothing but the truth', or pass their belief that these witnesses had drawn down upon themselves the sin of perjury.[9]

The circumstantial evidence was weak and there was positive evidence in George Lowder's favour. Dickson asked the jury for an acquittal. Dickson's closing address was competent, although less impassioned than that of McCarthy.

Roger Clute Closes for the Crown

Roger Clute rose to address the jury on behalf of the Crown at about 2:40 p.m. He had a full rich voice that penetrated every corner and commanded the full attention of the courtroom. He alluded to the wickedness of those who had committed this dastardly crime and commended Lazier for his courage to battle with his life to defend Gilbert and Margaret Jones. The men who went to the Jones house were there for the purpose of robbery, if not murder. They went there to commit a felony and they should be held accountable for the murder that followed from their actions. Clute relied on the tracking evidence from the Jones house to the point of separation at Springbrook and the trails leading to the Thomset and Lowder homes. He insisted that George Lowder's boots had made those tracks and that the man who wore the mask and who used the pistol was Joseph Thomset. Thomset, Clute argued, had formulated his plan to rob Jones months earlier. He was at the Bloomfield Station when Jones was paid for his hops and the footprints in the snow were traced directly to his house.

With respect to the alibi defence, Clute observed that counsel for the accused did not dare to ask any of the Lowders who owned the patch-bottom boots. He described an alibi as 'the last refuge of scoundrels' and this alibi evidence, he suggested, was inconsistent and should not be relied upon.

Clute praised Chief McKinnon as an effective detective, known to have solved previous crimes. Without commenting on McKinnon's methods, Clute appealed to the need for effective police work and praised McKinnon for some of his well-known exploits. 'It is such as he by whom society is protected.'

To counter the defence arguments about the lack of direct evidence, Clute pointed out that most cases rest on circumstantial evidence, which is often more trustworthy than direct evidence. If direct evidence were required in every case, the result would be anarchy. Here, the circumstantial evidence of the tracks directly implicated the prisoners. He concluded his address after an hour and a half:

Upon a covering which Heaven had sent, the criminals wrote out with their footprints the evidence of their own guilt. You have given your attention to this case and know how important it is that an impartial trial should be had, and the prisoners found guilty if proven so. This is a serious matter for you and for the prisoners. You have nothing to do with poor Lazier or his widow or Thomset's wife and child and in giving your verdict it will be to vindicate your own honour and that of the country.

Clute's address drew loud applause, no doubt to the consternation of Thomset, Lowder, their families, and their legal counsel. As the Toronto *Globe* reported: 'The popular feeling in the community in regard to the affair found expression at the end of Mr. Clute's address in a certain amount of handclapping.'[10]

Justice Patterson Instructs the Jury

Justice Patterson commenced his instructions to the jury at 4 p.m., shortly after Clute sat down.[11] He began by chastising the audience for the many partisan outbursts. These demonstrations, he said, were a disgrace to the administration of justice.

Justice Patterson explained that the main issue for the jury was the identity of those responsible for the crime and the tracing of the footprints of the men who had been at the Jones house on the night of 21

December. Justice Patterson left little doubt that his view of the tracking evidence favoured the Crown. The persons who committed the
crime were about the house for some time, as was shown by the tracks
that led around the premises. There was nothing to indicate what direction they came from. The tracks indicated that they were watching for
their opportunity to do their work after the hired man, Wallace, had
gone home. The evening was favourable to tracing footprints and the
tracks were traced with a promptness and vigour that showed care-
fulness and enterprise, which compared favourably with any similar
occurrence with which he was familiar. If the jurors were satisfied that
the tracks had been correctly traced to Thomset and Lowder, then the
one fact which is the foundation of the whole inquiry had been established. But if the tracks were not perfectly traced, the whole foundation
of the prosecution would be broken. The prisoners, he reminded the
jury, were entitled to the benefit of the doubt. The jury had to decide
if the tracks had been made by the boots of the prisoners and properly
traced to their doors.

The defence was not helped by the judge's treatment of Mrs Jones's
evidence that the assailants seemed taller than the prisoners. In the excitement of the moment, he asked, could she accurately tell the size
of the assailants? Justice Patterson's view of the alibi evidence also
favoured the Crown. He told the jury that there was always a strong
temptation for relatives to concoct a story to save a member of the family. He noted that there were discrepancies in the alibi evidence, particularly with respect to the time of Thomset's departure, but he allowed
that it was not uncommon for people to speak in different ways as to
the time of occurrences.

Justice Patterson instructed the jury that, as a matter of law, if two
people go together to accomplish a criminal purpose, they are guilty
together for each other's acts. The object of the men who went to the
Jones' house was to commit robbery and, if necessary, to use violence.
This meant that both the man who fired the fatal shot and his accom-
plice were criminally responsible for the death that ensued from their
common criminal enterprise. He reminded the jury that there was evidence that the man with the gun had clubbed Lazier, indicating his
preparedness to use violence.

Justice Patterson instructed the jury that to convict, they should be
satisfied that the Crown had established that Thomset had fired the
fatal shot.[12] He left with the jury the question of whether the man with
the gun had desisted and fled before the fatal shot was fired. Justice

Patterson also explained that it was open to the jury to find one of the accused men guilty and the other not guilty.

Justice Patterson concluded his charge after one hour and ten minutes at 5:10 p.m. The jury retired to consider its verdict. Few in the courtroom doubted that the judge had essentially invited them to convict the prisoners.

After the jury had retired to deliberate, Dickson objected that Justice Patterson had said nothing about circumstantial evidence. Justice Patterson's cool response was that if he had said anything, it would have been that circumstantial evidence is often stronger than direct evidence. This peremptory rejection of Dickson's argument is surprising. The law of the day required the trial judge to direct the jury in accordance with what was known as the 'rule in *Hodge's case*':[13] where the Crown's case depends exclusively on circumstantial evidence, the circumstances must be not only consistent with the guilt of the accused, but inconsistent with any other rational conclusion.[14] A direction to that effect would have favoured Thomset and Lowder.

Was Justice Patterson's charge to the jury fair to the accused men? It is difficult to get the full flavour of the charge and to assess its fairness without a transcript, but the newspaper accounts suggest that it strongly favoured the prosecution. Another difficulty in the way of assessing the charge is that the law of the day laid down very little in the way of guidance or minimum standards for jury charges. Jury charges were not transcribed and they were not subject to appellate review. Trial judges were essentially left to their own devices and free to charge the jury as they saw fit, and there was an enormous variation from case to case as a result.[15] It was certainly accepted, however, that the judge was entitled to convey his view of the case. Indeed, an eminent contemporary English judge wrote that while a judge should strive to be 'true and just,' 'he ought not to conceal his opinion from the jury.'[16]

This stands in marked contrast to the situation today. Judges are not precluded from expressing a view of the evidence, but one-sided charges that lean too far in the direction of the Crown can result in a successful appeal. Jury charges are now prepared with the assistance of elaborate model instructions and then carefully reviewed by appellate courts, and thus the practice is considerably more uniform than it was at the time of the Thomset-Lowder case.

The prisoners appeared to be quite despondent as they left the courtroom to await the jury's verdict. George Lowder, appearing to anticipate conviction, turned towards the man he blamed for his plight, Hugh McKinnon, and said bitterly: 'I hope your soul will rot in hell the way you have sent mine there.'[17]

Verdict

The jury reached its verdict quickly. After about an hour and a quarter, at 6:30 p.m., court was reconvened to hear the verdict. This was much sooner than expected. The eager crowd had gone for refreshments and the attendance in the courtroom was much smaller than it had been earlier in the day.

The jury was asked if it had reached a verdict. Foreman J.W. Fegan, in a voice trembling with emotion, said, 'We find the prisoners guilty with a recommendation for mercy.'

The verdict was devastating for the accused men and their families, although probably not unexpected given the hostile atmosphere that had prevailed in the courtroom. The jury's recommendation for mercy would not stand in the way of the imposition of the mandatory death sentence. But it gave Thomset and Lowder a glimmer of hope that they might escape the gallows by petitioning the federal cabinet for commutation of the death sentence. It is impossible to say why the jury recommended mercy. It may have revealed some doubt about the identity of the man who had fired the fatal shot or perhaps an uneasiness in seeing two men hang in a case where the Crown's evidence of guilt was far from overwhelming.[18] Still, the jury's rapid decision is difficult to reconcile with the existence of doubt, compromise, or even significant debate about the result.

Justice Patterson asked the prisoners if they had anything to say. Thomset said he was not guilty, but that he would 'die like a man.' George Lowder stated: 'I am not guilty. I'd rather go with Thomset than have my liberty taken from me for life.'

While there is nothing in the record of the case to indicate that Justice Patterson followed the practice, it was usual for the judge to retire briefly and then return wearing a black cap and gloves.[19] Justice Patterson certainly did not hesitate to impose the death sentence demanded by the law:

You and each of you have been found guilty of the wilful murder of Peter Lazier. I certainly concur in the verdict and I do not see how I can otherwise do so. The jury have recommended mercy but I have nothing to say in regard to that and nothing to do with it. I can hold out no promise or inducement that the mercy of the law will be extended to you.

The sentence of the court is that you Joseph Thomset and you George Lowder and each of you be confined in the Common Gaol of the County until the 10th day of June next, then to be hung by the neck until dead.[20]

George Lowder asked if he could address the audience, but Justice Patterson pointed out that he had already been given his chance before sentence was passed. The condemned men were taken from the courtroom.

The diligent Belleville *Intelligencer* reporter, J.L. Mills, claimed to have learned from a guard at the jail how the condemned men spent the night. 'They moaned and groaned during the night, wept piously and tossed about in the beds of their cells. They now fully realize the situation in which they are placed.'[21]

The Picton *Gazette*'s headline proclaimed triumphantly 'GUILTY!' adding 'Result not Unexpected.'[22]

11

Last Hope

The law did not afford Thomset and Lowder a right of appeal against their convictions for murder or their sentences of death.[1] The common-law remedy of writ of error was so narrow and circumscribed that it had become an obsolete relic by the 1880s.[2] A convicted person could only ask the trial judge to 'reserve the case' if it raised a difficult legal point.[3] Even this was not a right of appeal, as the matter was left to the discretion of the trial judge, although it was possible to have the judge's exercise of discretion reviewed.[4] If the trial judge agreed that the case involved a contentious point of law that he should not simply decide on his own, it would be sent to a panel of judges for consideration. Those judges would not sit on appeal from the verdict or conviction – they would merely decide the contested point of law and then remit the case to the trial court for final disposition. There is no indication that any of the three defence counsel thought the case against Thomset and Lowder raised a point of law that would merit a request to Justice Patterson that he reserve the case.

Any complaint the prisoners had with their convictions related to the facts and how the trial had been conducted. The legal remedies available at the time of the Thomset-Lowder case to safeguard against any miscarriage of justice on grounds such as these have been described as 'hopelessly inadequate'[5] and 'limited to a degree now hard to realize.'[6]

Whether appeals ought to have been available was certainly a subject of debate in the nineteenth century.[7] Efforts to reform the process began in England in the 1840s, but did not achieve success until many years after the Thomset-Lowder case.[8] In 1845, the eighth report of the Criminal Law Commissioners described the law as inadequate and wrongful convictions as not infrequent, and recommended appeals on fact in criminal cases.[9] While some members of the bar urged change, the legal establishment, in particular the judiciary, was opposed. The arguments against extending full rights of appeal essentially rested on a desire for the speedy and efficient disposition of criminal cases and an abiding confidence in the capacity of trial judges and juries to see that justice was done. Although there was a significant decline in the use of juries in the nineteenth century and the institution and the ideology that supported it was under attack,[10] an unquestioning confidence in juries remained an article of faith for most experienced lawyers and judges. They simply did not believe there was a problem of wrongful convictions.[11] Executive clemency, they thought, could be counted on to deal with any injustices that did occur. They feared that introducing appeals would undermine the process of executive clemency and create a floodgate of frivolous complaints from convicts having nothing to lose. This would bog down the system and undermine confidence in the integrity of the trial process. Appeals would also delay and thereby impair the deterrent effect of punishment, especially capital punishment. Somewhat inconsistent with the floodgates argument was the fear that allowing convictions to be appealed would introduce two laws: one for the rich and one for the poor. Those able to afford an appeal would postpone or even avoid punishments that would be immediately inflicted on the poor. Even the rights of the accused were invoked in support of the status quo. It was argued that juries would be more likely to convict in dubious cases if they knew the conviction could be appealed. If a convicted person were given the right to appeal, a similar right would have to be extended to the prosecution and this would undermine the finality of acquittals.

After almost seventy years of reform effort, the legal establishment finally relented in England in the face of two blatant cases of wrongful conviction.[12] In 1907, the Criminal Appeal Act conferred a right of appeal and created the Court of Criminal Appeal. Change came earlier in Canada with the adoption in 1892 of the Criminal Code,[13] which amplified the right of appeal by way of reservation of a point of law and introduced the possibility of moving for a new trial when the verdict was against the weight of the evidence.[14] Fuller rights of appeal, more or less as they exist today, were finally introduced in 1923.[15]

The Prerogative of Mercy

Condemned prisoners such as Thomset and Lowder were not, however, left to await their death with no hope of reprieve. The Governor General in Council – the cabinet – reviewed all cases in which the death sentence had been imposed. The trial judge prepared a report of the case giving his assessment of the evidence and the soundness of the verdict. A full transcript of the evidence was prepared,[16] and anyone, including the prisoners or their lawyers, could make written submissions to plead for mercy.

Capital cases often evoked strong feelings from the community. Petitions were frequently mounted in support of condemned prisoners pleading for mercy. Supporters frequently wrote letters to the minister of justice or the prime minister and editorial writers made known their views. All of this material was assembled in a 'Capital Case' file and considered by lawyers in the Department of Justice, who reviewed the case and prepared a report and a recommendation for the minister of justice to take to cabinet. The minister, and often the prime minister, took an active role in the consideration of these cases.[17]

In the Thomset and Lowder case, a transcript of the evidence was prepared and sent to the secretary of state on 22 May 1884, ten days after the verdict.[18] The transcript contained a complete record of the evidence given at the trial, but omitted several items that significantly limited the level of scrutiny that could be brought to bear on the fairness of the trial. Counsels' closing addresses to the jury were not transcribed, nor were any of Justice Patterson's rulings on points of evidence or his instructions to the jury. The closing addresses of counsel would provide a clear statement of the crucial points at issue and of the strengths and weaknesses of the case. The trial judge's rulings and instruction to the jury would provide a concise summary of the case from the judge's perspective and a record of the legal points he decided. Most important, a transcript of the jury instructions would allow for full consideration of any misstatements of fact and errors of law and the fairness of the way the case was left with the jury.

When full rights of appeal were accorded years later, the trial judge's rulings and jury instructions became a central feature of post-conviction review. But in the late nineteenth century, the trial judge's rulings and instructions were essentially immune from review. The trial judge was entrusted with virtually complete control over any consideration of the case following conviction. It was the trial judge who decided

whether to 'reserve' a point of law and it was the trial judge who provided the vital information used by the Department of Justice and the
cabinet in post-conviction review.

The 'Lottery of Death'

Many factors influenced the exercise of executive clemency – the personal views of the minister of justice and the cabinet, the gender of
the person convicted,[19] the jury's recommendation for mercy, and the
happenstance of political mood and exigency. Racialized individuals
sometimes benefited from paternalism, benign consideration of cultural
practices, and fear of race-fuelled reprisals,[20] but more often, racial discrimination was a factor in refusing clemency.[21] It was a discretionary
and largely undisciplined process,[22] labelled by a leading scholar as the
'Lottery of Death.'[23]

The odds Thomset and Lowder faced in the 'lottery' were about 50-
50. From 1867 until the abolition of capital punishment in 1976, 1532
individuals were sentenced to death. Of those, only 705, or slightly less
than half, were hanged. Eight died before being executed, eleven benefited from abolition, and the rest had their convictions set aside or
their sentences commuted through the exercise of the prerogative of
mercy.[24] The rate of those executed varied during this period from a
low of 12.5 per cent in the 1960s to a high of 74.9 per cent in the 1930s. In
the 1880s, the decade of the Thomset-Lowder case, the rate was margin-
ally above the average, at 57.9 per cent. The decade before, it was much
lower, at 28.9 per cent, but in the decade following, it was almost the
same, at 57.5 per cent.[25]

Thomset and Lowder's chances were somewhat reduced, however,
by the fact that Justice Minister Alexander Campbell[26] would marshal
their case through the process of executive review. Before confederation, Campbell practised law in Kingston with Sir John A. Macdonald
and future Ontario Liberal premier Oliver Mowat. Campbell was active
in municipal politics before Confederation and was twice elected to the
provincial legislative assembly. Despite an acrimonious breakup of
their law partnership and lack of personal friendship or warmth, Macdonald and Campbell enjoyed a long-standing and mutually beneficial
political relationship. Macdonald appointed Campbell to the Senate in
1867, and from his secure seat in the upper house, Campbell served
as a loyal and trusted confidant of the prime minister and as a political manager and 'fixer' within the Conservative party. Campbell was a

constant fixture in Macdonald's cabinet until his appointment as lieutenant governor of Ontario in 1887. He served as postmaster general on four occasions, superintendent general of Indian affairs and minister of the interior, receiver general, and minister of militia and defence. The *Canada Law Journal* applauded his appointment as minister of justice and attorney general in 1881, a post he filled until 1885: 'His extensive knowledge of constitutional and statute law, combined with the fact that he is a high minded courteous gentleman, will render his reign in his new Department very satisfactory to the public.'[27] Campbell also enjoyed an active business career in railways, banking, and insurance, and from 1861–4 he served as dean of the faculty of law at Queen's College in Kingston.

Campbell was a tough-minded minister. The year after the Thomset-Lowder case, he insisted that Métis leader Louis Riel be sent to Regina for trial before a six-person jury under the North West Territories Act rather than in Manitoba, where there would be risk of an acquittal by a jury that was likely to include sympathetic francophones. Campbell's administrative style has been described as 'cool, conscientious, conservative, legalistic, narrow, paternalistic, and frugal.'[28] These features are revealed by his treatment of capital cases. Campbell had the second lowest rate of commutation of all post-Confederation justice ministers who preceded him. His predecessors commuted 56.5 per cent of the time, while Campbell commuted 39.5 per cent of the capital cases considered during his tenure.[29] The jury's recommendation for mercy improved the odds, but only slightly. Of the fifteen cases Campbell commuted, only seven involved a recommendation from the jury, and Campbell refused commutation in four cases where the jury had recommended mercy.[30]

Thomset and Lowder were not going to benefit or suffer on account of racial or gender bias, but class might be a factor. Again, however, class appears to have cut both ways. Thomset and Lowder were rural, working-class individuals who had been convicted of a crime that threatened Prince Edward County's landed gentry and that involved a descendant of the revered United Empire Loyalists. However, the common folk who attended their trial and created the hostile atmosphere in the courtroom played a role in their condemnation and, as we will see in chapter 12, it was the clergy and the political elite who came to the men's aid in pushing for commutation of their sentences.

There were other factors that could tilt the odds in favour of commutation. The jury's recommendation for mercy and a growing sentiment in the community that an injustice had been done might influence a process that was in the hands of political men with an eye on popular opinion and the mood of the public. But those factors were unlikely to sway the precise and legally rigorous trial judge or the cool and calculating minister of justice.

Justice Patterson's Report

During his fourteen-year career as an Ontario judge, Justice Christopher Patterson passed the death sentence on eleven men, including Thomset and Lowder.[31] Patterson wrote detailed reports in all these cases to facilitate review by the minister of justice and the cabinet. In every case, Patterson's recommendation was followed. Of the eleven men Patterson condemned to death, only three were hanged. One escaped, and was never caught, and the seven others were reprieved, given life sentences, and eventually released. The fact that almost 80 per cent of the men and women Patterson felt compelled to sentence to death (almost 90 per cent if one excludes Thomset and Lowder) were commuted following his reports and recommendations might appear to have improved Thomset and Lowder's chances dramatically.

Indeed, given the central role played by the trial judge in the commutation process, this might have been the most important factor of all. The role of the trial judge did not end with the verdict and imposition of sentence. The trial judge, in effect, worked in partnership with the Department of Justice, the minister, and the cabinet, and a review of Justice Patterson's cases and the other capital cases considered in 1884 suggests that the trial judge's report usually controlled the outcome.[32]

But raw statistics are often a misleading guide, particularly where the numbers are so small and in areas where decisions and judgments turn on careful consideration of the particular facts of each case. A closer qualitative review of what considerations moved Justice Patterson and his contemporary judicial colleagues to recommend commutation reveals a much less promising picture for Thomset and Lowder.

The officials in the Department of Justice, who administered the process, and the minister of justice, who took the case to cabinet, did not conceive of commutation as a form of post-conviction review or a search for error in the trial process. Executive review served not to correct mistakes made at trial but rather as a means to accommodate considerations bearing upon the culpability of the accused and the justice of the death sentence. Patterson and his contemporary judicial colleagues saw the process in the same way. They regularly urged the reprieve of condemned individuals in cases where it seemed that the letter of the law failed to take into account facts bearing upon moral culpability or that the law was simply too harsh. But they were convinced of the capacity of the jury to come to the right result and naturally unwilling to consider that their own conduct of the trial could produce unfairness or injustice.

The Unfair Application of the Felony-murder Rule

Justice Patterson presided over the trial of Dr Eric Benzel Sparham and William H. Greaves, convicted by a jury of the murder of Sophia Elizabeth Burnham in Brockville on 30 March 1875.[33] The Crown's theory was that the victim died of blood poisoning resulting from a bungled abortion performed by Dr Sparham at Greaves's request. Patterson charged the jury that if they were satisfied that Sparham had, at Greaves's instigation, aborted Burnham and that she had died of blood poisoning caused by that procedure, both would be legally guilty of murder even though they did not intend to cause her death. This followed from the felony-murder rule that relieved the Crown from proving that the accused had the intent to kill: by law, the intention to commit any felony was regarded as 'malice aforethought,' the mental element required for murder.[34] The jury returned a guilty verdict and Patterson imposed the mandatory death sentence, but postponed the execution to 23 June to afford the Court of Common Pleas the opportunity to decide two points of law he had reserved for its consideration.[35]

Patterson's report to the minister made it clear that the prisoners were not convicted of murder because of 'any design of intention to kill' Burnham, but rather because her death resulted from the attempt to procure her abortion, an offence that was classified as a felony: 'This circumstance may not be unimportant in considering the question of commutation; as if the offence of using means to procure abortion had been under the statute a misdemeanour and not a felony, the homicide would have been manslaughter and not murder.'[36]

There were several petitions from Brockville residents pointing out Dr Sparham's heretofore unblemished record and excellent reputation in the community. Also received were the opinions of 'several medical gentlemen of known standing' to support the defence theory that 'while the death resulted from blood poisoning the cause of that blood poisoning was as likely produced by the infection of small pox as from the wound inflicted by the prisoner Sparham.'[37] T. Fournier, the acting minister of justice, concluded that the sentence should be commuted to life imprisonment.[38]

Insanity

Patterson did not hesitate to seek mercy for Charles Mairand, convicted of murder in Belleville in April 1875.[39] Mairand, a solitary and unsettled individual, was charged with the brutal murder of his brother's wife. The victim had been shot with a pistol, beaten with a stove leg, and stabbed several times with a knife. There was little doubt that Mairand was her assailant, but the lack of any apparent motive and the brutality of the crime, together with Mairand's sullen and strange demeanour, raised questions as to his mental capacity. His trial counsel advanced the defence of insanity, but quite ineffectively – the medical evidence he led was that Mairand's mental illness could have been the result of habitual masturbation. The insanity defence failed and the jury convicted Mairand of murder.

Patterson imposed the death sentence, but later, obviously concerned about the justice of the verdict, agreed to stay the execution when the Crown asked him to allow two government-appointed doctors to examine Mairand to determine his mental capacity. The Crown appears to have taken this step, in part at least, because of a concern that 'the question of insanity [was] raised ineffectively by the prisoner's counsel at his trial.'[40]

The two medical experts doubted that Mairand suffered from a recognized mental disorder and they were entirely dismissive of the masturbation defence. They noted that Mairand denied being addicted to the practice and observed that if mental disorder were caused by 'this evil habit ... the number of lunatics in this country would be twenty-fold greater than it is.' Mairand was not technically insane, but his moral and legal responsibility for his acts was questionable. He was 'a man of very inferior intelligence and of very defective mental capacity' and, on the basis that 'a clear perception between right and wrong' are necessary elements for legal sanity and responsibility, the two psychiatrists concluded: 'We should hesitate to declare this convict to be of sound mind.' They saw the case as one for commutation of the death sentence, but with continued incarceration in the interest of protecting the public: 'Certainly, whether deemed to be sane, or insane, we never could recommend his being placed in any position which might afford opportunity for, or present temptation to, repetition of a homicidal act.'[41]

Their recommendation was accepted and Mairand's sentence was commuted to life imprisonment.[42]

Intoxication

Two of Patterson's murder cases involved evidence of intoxication.[43] In both, Patterson made a strong recommendation that the death sentences he had imposed be commuted. In the 1876 case of James Ryan,[44] Justice Patterson reported that the crime was 'unquestionably to be attributed to the effects of drinking.' Patterson's report reveals his understanding of the need to moderate the harshness of the law through the exercise of executive clemency, a process that he regularly used as a judge to achieve justice while remaining faithful to the law, even when the law was harsh. He wrote that Ryan had committed the crime while drunk and that it was 'tolerably certain that in his sober senses he would never have attempted violence of the nature in question.' Patterson explained that while it was 'settled law that drunkenness induced by one's own act does not excuse the commission of a crime' and that 'therefore a conviction for murder committed by reason of intoxication is legally correct,' the same rigid rule need not apply to punishment. Anticipating a legal development that would come years later,[45] Patterson thought that the degree of culpability properly attributable to a drunken act was not the same as that attaching to a sober act. When it comes to punishment, he wrote, 'it may not follow that the same rigid rule should be applied which prevents discrimination between crimes committed when sober and crimes committed when drunk.' Drunkenness leaves 'the technical character of the crime the same,' but as drunkenness 'excluded that deliberation which gives to many crimes their aggravated character,' he agreed with the recommendation for mercy.[46] The sentence was commuted to life imprisonment and Ryan was later released due to ill health.

The Limits of Mercy

Justice Patterson did not see anything in the case of Thomset and Lowder that diminished their moral culpability for the death of Peter Lazier. If they were the men who came to the door of the Jones farmhouse on the night of 21 December 1883, they came armed with two firearms, at least one of which was loaded. The man with the shotgun had either threatened or attempted to inflict violence on Peter Lazier. This indicated that he knew that the escapade might lead to a violent confrontation and that he was prepared to use violence if it did. The man with the pistol fired the fatal shot. Even if they had hoped or intended to carry out their unlawful purpose without killing or injuring anyone, their actions suggested that they came ready to inflict lethal force if necessary.

Thomset and Lowder's plea for mercy was not based on lack of moral culpability or harsh application of the law. It was based on a challenge to the fairness of the trial and the soundness of the jury's verdict. These were not matters likely to cause Justice Patterson to use his influence to save their lives or to attract any sympathy from the Department of Justice. Barring exceptional circumstances – such as in the two cases discussed below – the executive-clemency process simply did not allow for scrutiny of the fairness of the trial or the correctness of the result. The jury was perceived to be the protection against wrongful conviction and the jury's verdict was sacrosanct. And because the process relied so heavily on the views of the trial judge, there was little hope that problems of trial fairness would be exposed or considered by the cabinet. Justice Patterson was hardly likely to point out possible deficiencies in his jury charge or to suggest that his failure to take firmer steps to control the unruly audience in the courtroom might have affected the verdict.

Attacking Wrongful Convictions

Patterson did try two other cases that likely involved wrongful convictions and those cases show the lengths to which a wrongfully convicted person had to go to get a reprieve. In April 1875, Patterson presided over the St Catharine's trial of Mathias Konkle,[47] a fifty-year-old farmer accused of having carnal knowledge of a ten-year-old girl, at the time a capital offence. The defence alleged that the charge had been trumped up by Konkle's stepmother, who had fallen out with him over a dispute concerning his father's estate. Patterson's report[48] noted that there were certain serious inconsistencies in the evidence of the victim and another young girl who testified for the Crown, but he refused to question the correctness of the jury's verdict.

Konkle's defenders, determined to save his life and to see him vindicated, realized that they needed another verdict to contradict or question the first. They initiated conspiracy charges against the stepmother and the mother of the alleged victim for making a false accusation. Konkle, this time able to testify as he did not stand accused of a crime, gave a good impression. The jury acquitted the stepmother and the mother of the victim, but asked the trial judge to inform the governor general that 'having heard the evidence adduced on the part of the Crown ... we are of opinion that although the evidence was insufficient to convict ... on the charge of conspiracy, yet the said evidence strongly impressed our minds with the innocence of the said Mathias Konkle.'[49]

Patterson had initially been reluctant to comment adversely on the jury's verdict, but armed with the second jury's opinion, he was now prepared to say that had it been for him to decide at the first trial, he would have acquitted.[50] The judge who tried the conspiracy case reported that the evidence of the alleged victim of the sexual offence 'was a mass of contradictions,' 'perfectly unintelligible,' and 'totally unreliable,' and that 'there was a strong possibility that this man is innocent of the crime for which he is undergoing punishment.'[51] On the minister of justice's recommendation,[52] Konkle was released.

Less than a year before the Thomset and Lowder trial, Patterson presided over another capital case that quite possibly involved a wrongful conviction. Because the case involved a second judge who took a decidedly different view of the evidence, the prisoner succeeded in attacking his conviction using the process of executive clemency. Henry Russell Greenwood and Henry Hardinge were both convicted of murder at Sandwich, near Windsor, in late October 1883.[53] The cause of death was alleged to be a dose of narcotic administered by the accused for the purpose of robbing the victim, who had been seen with the accused in Detroit on the night of his death and was found dead outdoors on the Canadian side of the border in the middle of winter.

The two accused were first tried before Justice Matthew Crooks Cameron at the Sandwich spring assizes in 1883. The jury failed to reach a verdict. Justice Cameron not only declared a mistrial, but also took the unusual step of expressing his strong opinion that the Crown had no case. Justice Cameron thought that the medical evidence failed to make out a case of narcotic poisoning. The Crown ignored Cameron's advice, and proceeded before Justice Patterson at the fall assizes, when the two men were convicted of murder and sentenced to death. Greenwood escaped, likely back to the United States, and was never found. Hardinge was left to face the death penalty alone.

In his petition to the minister of justice, Hardinge's counsel complained that 'Justice Patterson's charge was so strong against the prisoners that there was little or no alternative left to the jury but to convict which they did with a recommendation [for mercy].'[54] Justice Cameron, asked for his view on account of the mistrial, reported that he 'entertained the very strongest opinion that the deceased Maher died from the effects of exposure and not from poison,' and that while no doubt the accused had 'dishonest designs,' he did not believe that they had caused his death. He cautioned that he had no means of knowing whether the evidence led at the subsequent trial before his colleague Patterson was sufficient to lead to a different result.[55] However, Cameron reported that he and Patterson differed on the law. Cameron did not think there was any evidence that Maher's death had been caused in the commission of another felony and he considered the case to be one of manslaughter rather than murder.[56] In a subsequent report, Patterson defended his legal position, but essentially agreed with Cameron that the key issue was whether or not there was evidence that the accused had administered a narcotic to the deceased. If there was not, neither man could be convicted of murder. Patterson observed that while there were certain weaknesses in the medical evidence, he felt that there was enough of a case to require it to be left with the jury and that he would have been wrong to withdraw it.[57] The Governor General in Council, almost certainly on account of Cameron's doubts about the case, commuted Hardinge's sentence to life in December 1883, six days before the date set for his execution.

Three years later, Hardinge continued to press for his release and took the unusual step of writing to Justice Cameron, now chief justice of the Court of Common Pleas. Justice Cameron's positive response[58] was more than Hardinge could have hoped for. Cameron indicated that he had reviewed the evidence and that 'there was an entire failure in the evidence of the Crown to sustain the charge against you.' Hardinge's letter to Cameron and Cameron's response were sent to the minister of justice.

The Department of Justice officials were not persuaded that Justice Patterson had been wrong to leave the case with the jury and concluded there was enough evidence of Hardinge's participation to prevent him from 'impeaching the technical correctness of the verdict.' But technical legal considerations apart, the minister was prepared to reduce Hardinge's sentence from life to ten years, and with remission he was released in 1891: 'Apart however from any legal consideration there is the question whether his share in the transaction is deserving of life imprisonment. It might also be fairly urged that he ought to get some benefit from the strong view entertained by so eminent a Judge that he was entitled to be discharged.'[59]

'I have no doubt of the successful identification of the men.'

As he had done in his other capital cases, Justice Patterson sat down immediately after the trial of Thomset and Lowder to prepare a thorough, well-written report for the minister of justice.[60] His report was certainly not going to help any effort that might be mounted to save Thomset and Lowder from the gallows. His views were clear and direct: he saw nothing in the case to warrant commutation of the death sentence.

Lazier, the deceased, happened to come, on the evening of 21st December '83, to the home of Gilbert Jones, and remain for the night. Jones, who had fallen and hurt himself in getting hay for Lazier's horse, went to bed early, about 8 ocl. – his room opening off the sitting room where Lazier, Mrs. Jones, and a man named Wallace sat chatting, the door of the bedroom being open to enable Jones to hear and take part in the conversation. A person looking at the bedroom window could have seen Wallace, but could not see Lazier. Shortly before ten o'clock Wallace went away and Lazier went to a bed in a room adjoining that of Jones and also opening from the sitting room. Soon after this and while Mrs. Jones was preparing for bed a knock was heard at the door. She opened it and encountered two men – one evidently disguised having what seemed a linen bag drawn over his head with openings for eye holes – the other apparently disguised also, but seeming to Mrs. Jones like a man with a good deal of dark hair about his face. The latter had a [shot]gun and the former carried a pistol in his hand.

The object of these men was undoubtedly to rob Mr. Jones who had that day received over $500 for hops at the railway station at Bloomfield. Mrs. Jones screamed and rushed to her room which she entered and locked the door. On her way she pushed open Lazier's door and saw him already out of bed, and before she reached her room she glanced back and saw the man with a [shot] gun (who was the convict Lowder) striking Lazier with the [shot]gun.

She had scarcely locked her door when seeing her husband taking down a gun, she unlocked the door again and Jones ran out. While the door was shut a pistol shot must have been fired, because the bullet was found to have glanced off the door and struck the wall of the room when it fell to the floor and was afterwards found. When Jones left his room he saw Lazier apparently struggling with, or keeping back a man. Jones presented his gun, which was not loaded, and the man retreated but fired another shot which entered Lazier's heart. Jones followed the man out of the house and was thus able to shew the route he took, which was of importance when the tracks in the snow were examined, in showing which were the tracks of the man who fired the shot. The neighbours were alarmed and steps were taken in an exceedingly intelligent and judicious manner for following the tracks of both men, who joined each other on the road after leaving Jones' premises, kept together for one or 2 miles, and then separated each making for his own home. It happened that a heavy fall of snow early in the night obliterated all other tracks, and then the snow ceasing, the tracks of these men were easily traced both that night and on the following day, showing where they had loitered about Jones' place and looked in at the windows, apparently waiting till Wallace had gone, and then made the attack supposing that only Mr. and Mrs. Jones, who are both elderly people, were in the house. The identification of the tracks, as those made by the two boots of the two convicts, was very satisfactory, Thomset being the man who fired the shot.

I have alluded to the incident, noticed by Mrs. Jones, of the other man striking Lazier with his gun while Thomset stood by with his pistol, and just before the first shot, which struck the door, was fired, because it was an important piece of evidence to shew that there was a common purpose to use violence if resisted, and thus to fix Lowder with complicity in the murder altho' the fatal shot was fired by his companion.

There was a large amount of evidence apart from that relating to the tracing of the men by means of their tracks in the snow, principally affecting Thomset. By showing his probable knowledge that Jones had the money, and his statements and other times of the ease with which such an enterprise as the robbing of Mr. Jones could be carried out in the very way now attempted, and some other collateral facts and there was evidence to prove an alibi which failed.

I have no doubt of the successful identification of the men.

Your obed. Servt.

C. Patterson

Their Fate Was Sealed

Thomset and Lowder could not appeal to a higher court to assess their convictions. They were left with the process of executive clemency, which depended heavily upon the participation and wisdom of the trial judge. Christopher Patterson, a capable and distinguished judge, regularly used the process of executive clemency to achieve justice in cases where he perceived the letter of the law to be unduly harsh. These cases show how executive clemency worked at its best. But the best was not going to be enough for Thomset and Lowder. Neither Justice Patterson nor the politicians who had the final say were prepared to second-guess the fairness of a jury trial or the correctness of a jury's verdict. The fate of Thomset and Lowder was effectively sealed when the jury of twelve men delivered the guilty verdict.

12

Pleas for Mercy

Thomset and Lowder were consigned to small cells in the Picton jail to await their execution. They were under constant surveillance by gaoler William Patterson, turnkey Ezekiel Harris, and 'death watch' officers Zebulon Sinden and John O'Neil to ensure they remained secure in their cells and that they did not 'cheat' the hangman by taking their own lives. The *British Whig* reported that the condemned men were co-operative and well behaved and 'had nothing but words of kindness to express towards both of the guards, as well as towards the gaoler and turnkey.' They did not appear to be preoccupied with their sentence, but 'conversed freely, ate heartily, and continued to protest their innocence. At times they indulged in a good deal of bitterness against some of the witnesses who gave evidence against them.'[1]

The law provided that condemned prisoners could be visited by medical officers or a 'minister of religion,' but no one else without permission in writing from the trial judge or the sheriff.[2] Thomset and Lowder were regularly visited by two clergymen, Rev. Walter Coulthard, the minister at Picton's Presbyterian St Andrew's Church, and Rev. Edwin Loucks, rector of St Mary Magdalene, Church of England, located a block away from the courthouse and jail. Loucks became rector in 1874 upon the death of the venerable William Macaulay, the wealthy Oxford-educated Loyalist descendant who had been granted 500 acres bordering on the village of Picton and then donated the land for the church, the rectory, the courthouse, and the gaol. He built the church and handsome rectory, now a museum, largely at his own expense, where he lived a 'gracious life' as an 'eminently connected' squire.[3]

Neither Loucks nor Coulthard could hope to match Macaulay's influence, but they were respected clergyman and their support of the two convicted men certainly could not be ignored. They both solemnly believed it to be their duty to convince the two convicted men that their only hope for eternal salvation was to confess their crime. They attended the convicts twice a day to read them scriptures and lead them in prayer and the singing of hymns. The two clergymen used all their influence to try to persuade the men to confess. But neither the threat of hell nor the hope of heaven was enough. Thomset and Lowder both steadfastly and solemnly maintained that they were innocent of the crime.

Loucks was known to be a 'militant churchman' from whom 'evil in every shape and form met with fearless and outspoken denunciation,'[4] a quality amply demonstrated by his determined effort to save the souls and the lives of Joseph Thomset and George Lowder. After spending many hours with the two convicted men, Coulthard and Loucks became convinced that there was good reason to believe them both – although they appear to have been more impressed by Lowder than by Thomset. Coulthard described Lowder as 'a very intelligent man' and Thomset as 'shrewd.'[5] Neither Loucks nor Coulthard opposed capital punishment, but both clergymen felt strongly that these men should not hang.

'The humble petition of the undersigned residents and citizens for the County of Prince Edward'

Loucks and Coulthard decided to mount a petition, addressed to the governor general and the minister of justice, to be signed by as many residents of Prince Edward County as they could convince, to plead for mercy for the condemned men.

The humble petition of the undersigned residents and citizens for [sic] the County of Prince Edward sheweth as follows:

1. That the solemnity attached to request [sic] which your petitioners desire to convey calls forth a greater amount of consideration at your earliest possible moment than could be expected otherwise to warrant the presentation of this petition.
2. That we believe the evidence adduced on behalf of the prosecution rebutted

by the evidence offered by the defence was hardly sufficient to warrant the conviction found by the jury who determined the sad case.

3. That the community at large are we think very desirous that the death sentence pronounced by the learned judge who presided over the trial upon the parties convicted Joseph Thomset and George Lowder should be commuted in some degree even to imprisonment for life.

Your Petitioners therefore pray that Your Excellency through the advice of the Honourable the Minister of Justice may be pleased to order the commutation of the death sentence so pronounced in some degree and your Petitioners will ever pray.[6]

Among the approximately 450 individuals – all male – who signed the petition were several men who had direct involvement in the case. Dr Alan Noxon, the doctor who attended upon Peter Lazier the night he was shot, conducted the coroner's inquest, and testified at the trial, was one of the first to sign. Two more Crown witnesses, Cornelius Mastin and William Leader, added their support to the plea for mercy. Three signatories – William and John Fraleigh and David Conger – bore the title of justice of the peace, and Picton's mayor, Edwards Merrill, a prominent lawyer and future judge, added his support. Gaoler William Patterson and turnkey Ezekiel Harris, the men in daily contact with Thomset and Lowder as they awaited execution, added their names to the long list of those asking for commutation of the sentence. Thomset and Lowder were told of the petition and their spirits were buoyed by the hope of reprieve.

Meanwhile, ten days before the date set for the hangings, Loucks was involved in an incident that displayed his volatile side. Encountering Robert Welsh, one of his parishioners, on the street in Picton, Loucks complained that Welsh had overcharged him for some work he had done. Angry words were exchanged and Loucks knocked Welsh to the ground. The parishioner complained of cuts to his head and body that required medical attention and, alleging a brutal and unprovoked attack, sued Loucks for assault. Loucks insisted that it was he who had been attacked and that he had merely defended himself, but a jury thought otherwise and awarded Welsh $25 damages and costs.[7]

'The verdict of the jury seemed to be an echo of the excited public opinion'

Edwards Merrill, a future county court judge, had sat through the entire trial, and he was profoundly disturbed by what he had seen and heard. Merrill knew Prime Minister Sir John A. Macdonald and wrote directly to him to point out serious weaknesses in the Crown's case and to report that the deplorable conduct of the spectators at the trial likely affected the verdict. Merrill explained that he was not writing 'at the instance of the prisoners or of any of their friends' and asserted that he had 'no further interest in the matter than all citizens might be supposed to have, a desire that no injustice should be done.' His 'wholly unsolicited' letter pleaded for the prime minister's intervention to prevent the death sentence from being carried out:

I attended the trial and paid close attention to the evidence and all was said pro and con by the respective counsel, and if I had been on the jury, would not have felt justified, on the evidence presented, in finding a verdict of guilty.

It was pretty well ascertained or considered as established by a careful consideration of the evidence that the theory of the crown that Thomset fired the pistol is erroneous and it was almost as certainly established that Thomset had left the house before the fatal shot was fired. It is also now generally understood that there were 3 persons engaged in the attempt at robbery, instead of two, and very doubtful to say the least, whether the Lowder that is convicted is the one who was in the house. The verdict of the jury seemed to be an *echo* as it were of the excited public opinion. The whole county was very much agitated over the murder, and the general feeling seemed to be decidedly against the prisoners, and it was on all hands apparently assumed from the first, that they were guilty.

This feeling was especially noticeable at the trial. Every point made, or thought to be made against the prisoners, was greeted with hearty applause by the large audience, until it became necessary for the judge to order the courtroom cleared.

Nor am I confident that under the evidence presented at the trial when carefully analyzed it will be found that there is not only doubt, but *grave* doubt as to the guilt, or the exact measure of guilt of the prisoners, and that they should not have been convicted of *murder*. And I now write in the hope that it may not yet be too late for you, if you will, to give the matter your consideration and if not incompatible with your own views in this behalf, to use your influence in having the sentence commuted.

I have the honor to be Sir
Yours faithfully
E. Merrill[8]

The prime minister was unmoved by Merrill's plea. Macdonald had likely seen or been told of Justice Pattersons's report, and he was not prepared to second-guess the jury's determination that Thomset and Lowder had been properly identified as the intruders. Merrill's letter clearly spelled out the mood of the community, a factor that would not be lost on the shrewd political mind of the prime minister. Macdonald was not prepared to enter the fray of local debate about the case. He refused to venture beyond the strictly legal question of whether both men should be held liable for murder. A criminal lawyer of some considerable experience, he had little doubt that guilty of murder was the proper verdict in law. He wrote a short handwritten note to convey that view to his minister of justice, Alexander Campbell.

My dear Campbell

I have the letter of Merrill. But if these men were of the party going to commit a burglary with deadly weapons to be used in case of resistance, they deserve to be hanged. No matter which of the party fired the deadly shot.

JAMD[9]

'What we humbly ask'

Five days before the scheduled execution, Loucks and Coulthard wrote a joint letter to the minister of justice, Alexander Campbell, explaining why they were convinced the condemned men should not die.[10] In a letter written by Coulthard but signed by both men, they informed the minister that they had sought to impress upon both Thomset and Lowder the solemnity of their situation and endeavoured in every legitimate way to entice a confession, but both men insisted upon their innocence. At this point, the clergymen stopped short of declaring themselves to believe that the prisoners were innocent, but they pointed out that the evidence against them was entirely circumstantial 'and in the judgment of many weak and certainly doubtful, [and] we are impressed that there is a strong doubt in their favour.' The tracking evidence, they wrote, was not consistent and no one had been able to follow the tracks all the way from the scene of the murder to the houses of the two convicted men.

What we humbly ask is the benefit of this doubt to the condemned men. We are deeply impressed that in this case mercy should interpose. We plead not because we are prejudicial, or opposed to capital punishment; we firmly believe that such punishment for a capital crime has the sanction of the word of God. In this case there is certainly a ground to rest the doubt. As ministers of God dealing with the convicted man, we feel it a bounden duty to appeal to you as one of God's servants to administer justice. We most respectfully ask [you] to consider solemnly the whole case, and if it lies within your power as Minister of Justice, to grant or cause to be granted, clemency you would be pleased to do so. To *commute the sentence is all we pray for*. May all-merciful God direct your mind to a just and merciful conclusion. Permit me to state that we have no personal interest in this matter. We feel it a duty that we owe to conscience, and as we believe to God. We, along with the most respectable, and intelligent of this town and county, are deeply impressed that there is a just claim for mercy.

I may further state that the character of the two men, in the past, has by no means been criminal. Even now in their condemned condition they neither act nor speak as criminals. They seem to have a just view of their duty to God and man. They urgently plead their innocence. In the sight of God we are bound to say that there is a strong ground of doubt. We leave the matter to your judgment, earnestly hoping that before Monday evening [the day before that set for execution] we may hear of your clemency.[11]

Justice Patterson had the power as trial judge to grant a reprieve 'as may be necessary for the consideration of the case by the Crown.'[12] The *British Whig* reported that an effort to persuade Justice Patterson to lend his assistance to gain a stay of the death sentence to buy a little more time for consideration of this string of pleas was ineffective.[13]

The local rumour mill was active. Thomset was said to have confessed despite his protestations of innocence.[14] More ominous were rumours that a gang of Thomset and Lowder's friends planned to raid the jail to free them. As well, several people connected with the murder received anonymous letters, 'supposed to have been written by some gang of desperados, to which Thomset and Lowder belonged at the time of the murder.'[15] Such tactics, if indeed employed by friends of the prisoners, were ill conceived, as they could only alarm the community and erode any support the condemned men had been able to garner.

'That the law be allowed to take its course'

Governor General Landsdowne telegraphed Justice Minister Campbell on 6 June to advise that he had approved the necessary order for the executions to proceed.[16] The formal order recited the documents that had been considered and concluded:

The circumstances of this case having been fully considered by His Excellency in Council, together with the Report of the Honorable Minister of Justice adverse to the commutation of the said sentence,

His Excellency has thought fit to order, **AND IT IS HEREBY ORDERED**, that the law be allowed to take its course.[17]

The under-secretary of state informed Loucks that despite his pleas and the petition signed by the residents of Prince Edward County, 'after a careful consideration of the evidence adduced at the trial,' the governor general 'has thought proper to order that the law be allowed to take its course.'[18] A similar message was sent to Sheriff James Gillespie, who would be responsible for seeing that the executions took place as ordered.[19] Gillespie informed the prisoners and the *British Whig* reported that 'wearied with hope deferred, the news seemed to cause them little surprise, as they were evidently prepared for a like announcement.'[20]

'Grave doubts by many of our respectable men'

As the date for the hangings approached, James Simeon McQuaig, a prominent businessman and potentially influential County resident, added his voice to those pleading for mercy. A long-time Macdonald Tory stalwart, McQuaig had been elected to the provincial legislature in 1872 after an unsuccessful federal run for the Tories in 1867. He resigned to run again for parliament, but suffered two more defeats in 1872 and 1874 before finally gaining a seat under the Macdonald banner in 1878. He was again defeated in 1882, and although he was out of office in 1884, he still hoped his voice might be heard at the highest levels in Ottawa.

McQuaig sent a telegram to Minister of Justice Campbell: 'Grave doubts entertained by many of our respectable men of George Lowder's guilt. I concur in this view of the case after the most careful consideration of the whole case.'[21] When McQuaig learned that Sherriff Gillespie had not yet received the letter instructing him to proceed with the executions, he sent another telegram suggesting that the hangings should be reprieved for a few days to reconsider the case of George Lowder.[22]

These last-minute pleas were duly considered, but to no avail. In a telegram to Coulthard, Minister of Justice Campbell advised that his pleas, along with those of Merrill and McQuaig, had been laid before the Privy Council and the case had been 'again considered with the attention its gravity demands.' The cabinet decided not to change its earlier decision: 'The Judge and Jury were satisfied as to the identity of the prisoners, which was the crucial question at the trial. No new facts have been submitted, no new evidence discovered, and we see no grounds which would justify us in seeking to interfere with the execution of the sentence of the court.'[23]

'If possible commute Lowder'

Loucks and Coulthard visited the two condemned men after word had come that the death sentence would not be commuted. Coulthard decided to abandon his effort to save Thomset, but make yet another plea for the life of George Lowder. The reactions of the condemned men led Coulthard to believe that Thomset likely was guilty, but that Lowder almost certainly was not. He sent the following telegram to Minster of Justice Campbell:

Regarding Thomset believe the decision just but having visited Lowder since it was made known that the law must take its course, Lowder declared in the sight of God he is innocent. I am deeply impressed there is truth in his declaration. He has a just view of his responsibility to God and I believe him honest. If possible commute Lowder.[24]

On the day before the execution, Thomset's tearful wife visited him for the last time. She arrived at the jail at noon and asked to see her husband one last time. She was kept waiting until 2 p.m. As she approached the iron door barring the corridor where her husband was held, she let out 'an agonizing, soul-piercing cry: "Oh, God! My poor husband!"' and collapsed. Then, 'nerving herself to the terrible ordeal, she smothered her emotions as best she could that the parting might give her husband as little pain as possible,' and spent three quarters of an hour in the corridor talking to Thomset, who remained in his cell.[25] She was taken away weeping and moaning, leaving Thomset alone and desolate. Thomset's sister had travelled from Rochester with her husband to pay her brother a last visit, but 'her nervous system being unable to withstand such a terrible shock,' her visit was brief.[26]

The entire Lowder family except for Christopher came to bid George farewell. They spent the entire morning in the corridor outside his cell, 'all of them being very much affected, especially the poor old mother who was nearly crazed' with the knowledge that her son 'was about to have his life suddenly cut off in such a cruel manner.' In answer to 'several loving, yet earnest requests to confess his guilt if any,' he repeated his persistent plea of innocence. George's last visitor was Maggie Conger, described as a 'young girl, rather good-looking,' to whom he was said to be engaged.[27]

Early in the afternoon any hope of a last-minute reprieve was dashed. Minister Campbell acknowledged Coulthard's telegram, but advised that both men would be executed. 'The responsibility which is very great for all concerned in the administration of justice has been discharged with painful solicitude. I have no power further to interfere.'[28]

At about 3:30 p.m. on 9 June, Sheriff Gillespie received a telegram from Ottawa instructing him that the death sentence was to be carried into effect the next day. The sheriff gave the telegram to Gaoler Patterson, who took it to the prisoners. They read it carefully but, already resigned to their fate, displayed little reaction.[29]

13

The Day of Execution Approaches

Thomset and Lowder were painfully aware that preparations were under way to ensure that they hanged on the appointed day. Sheriff James Gillespie and carpenter H.V. Carson travelled to Kingston to take the plan of the Kingston scaffold. A week before the date set for the execution, Carson started to erect the gallows outside a range of cells on the upper corridor of the jail. Thomset and Lowder, in the cells on the ground floor, could hear the carpenter at work. The plan was to let the men drop from the upper to the lower corridor. A double trap door was cut in the floor and a heavy oak beam mounted on an oak frame was placed over the trap door. As the day of their execution approached, the condemned men could hear the digging of their graves in the yard of the jail.

Apparently resigned to the fact that neither man could be saved from the gallows, the Thomset and Lowder families turned their attention to the distressing fact that they would not be given the bodies of their loved ones for burial. The only letter to be found in the file of documents considered by the cabinet from lawyer Nehemiah Gilbert is a plea for a direction to the sheriff 'to permit the relatives receiving the bodies for interment' rather than burying them in unmarked graves in the prison yard.[1] That request was rejected. With meticulous attention to detail, parliament had specifically provided that 'the body of every offender executed shall be buried within the walls of the prison within which judgment of death is executed' unless the lieutenant governor, 'being satisfied that there is not, within the walls of any prison, sufficient space for the convenient burial of offenders executed therein, permits some other place to be used for the purpose.'[2]

The condemned men spent the rest of the day attended by Loucks, reading religious scriptures and in prayer, and ate a hearty dinner. During the day, Loucks led a special service at St Mary Magdalene. When interviewed by reporters at the jail in the evening, Loucks expressed his personal conviction of Lowder's innocence, and a rather more cautious doubt as to Thomset's guilt: 'I believe that Lowder is as innocent as I, myself, and I was not there, and if I am to believe the statement of a man who is going into eternity, I must certainly believe that Thomset is innocent.'[3]

Loucks described the prisoners as being 'calm and thoroughly resigned to their fate,' and reported that they had had 'not a shadow' of a hope of commutation. He told a reporter:

They assume a quiet dignity, remarkable for people so near the end. There is not the slightest bravado about them, but on the contrary, they seem to be calmly waiting for the final stroke, confident their end shall be peace. I cannot but admire the self-respect which they appear to have … The prisoners have made no confession. On the contrary they assert their innocence. I talked to them about going to eternity without telling the truth. They called God to witness their statement that they had taken no part whatsoever in the murder of Peter Lazier. Their friends have begged of them to make a confession but their only reply is that they are innocent.[4]

Loucks took a swing at the press and those in the community who welcomed the death sentence, saying to another reporter: 'The men have been most cruelly maligned by the papers. They have been trodden upon by a relentless public.'[5]

John O'Neil, one of the jailers on the 'death watch', told the *Intelligencer* reporter that Thomset had insinuated to him on several occasions that he had been at the Jones' the night of the murder, but that he had not fired the fatal shot and that Lowder was not there.[6] The Picton *Gazette* claimed that Thomset also told his sister the same story – that he was at the Jones farm, but that he was not the one who fired the fatal shot.[7] Shortly before the day of the execution, George Lowder was reported to have cried out across the corridor to Thomset that if he knew anything about the murder, for God's sake tell it, to which Thomset made no reply.[8]

Death Watch

The condemned men went to bed at 9:30 p.m. and rose at 4:45 a.m. to face their death at the appointed hour of 8 a.m.[9] A reporter with access to the jailers wrote that the condemned men slept well despite the fate that awaited them. 'The death watches sat opposite each cell while a faint light glimmered from a lamp and near at hand stood two bouquets – the last tribute and tokens of affection – from Thomset's wife and Lowder's mother.' Thomset woke up at about 3:30 a.m., asked O'Neil what time it was, and 'on receiving the desired information he turned over again and went to sleep.'

Shortly after they arose, they were attended by Loucks and later Coulthard. A plentiful breakfast was provided – toast, pie, eggs, and tea, of which Thomset partook heartily but Lowder ate very little. When Coulthard left, 'the parting was most affecting – both the prisoners as well as the clergyman showing unmistakable signs of great agitation.' When they came out of their cells, carrying the flowers they had been given by their relatives, Thomset said to Lowder: 'It is difficult to die but there is no help for us.' As they said their farewells, Thomset added ominously: 'If I am guilty I hope I'll die hard and hang for an hour.'

Several reporters were allowed to interview the prisoners between seven and eight o'clock. Thomset was composed and anxious to talk: 'I knew nothing regarding the death of Peter Lazier until after I was arrested at my home. I was at Lowder's house till ten o'clock the night before the murder and I call God Almighty to witness my dying words that I am innocent of murder. That night I was at Lowder's. This is the truth, so help me God, as these are my dying words.' When asked 'How do you feel,' Thomset replied: 'Oh, I am happy and have made my peace with God whom I am ready to meet. I hold no spite against the public and I forgive all my enemies. I love everybody, even as Jesus loves me. (*A heavy sigh.*) The officers have treated me like a brother.' He began to speak about the evidence against him, but was checked by the jailer. He added, however: 'I wish to deny that I ever killed a man. I never was arrested, never was fined, and never was in the gaol before.' George Lowder stated: 'I know nothing about the affair. I was not present when the man was shot, and I am not a murderer at heart. I have written a few lines for the public, and Mr. Loucks will publish them and the papers can copy them. There is no use saying anything for the public will not believe me. I was at home at the time of the murder.'

'Favoured individuals'

Until 1870, public hangings were common, and in notorious cases, such as the 1869 execution of Patrick James Whelan in Ottawa for the assassination of politician D'Arcy McGee, large crowds attended the grisly scene.[10] Even after the abolition of public hangings, executions attracted an audience. Tickets were routinely issued to a select number of reporters, police officers, justices of the peace, and other local worthies to witness the execution. Where hangings were conducted within the walls of the local jail but out of doors, the curious often climbed trees or found places in surrounding buildings to watch.

A number of people assembled in the yard outside the Picton jail, but only about thirty were issued passes to permit them to gain entry to the jail where they would witness the execution. Those admitted – described by the press as 'favoured individuals'[11] – included newspaper reporters from the Picton *Gazette*, Belleville *Intelligencer*, Kingston *British Whig*, Napanee *Beaver*, and Trenton *Courier Advocate*, several justices of the peace, Dr Noxon and, of course, Hugh McKinnon, there to witness the final chapter of the story he had helped write.[12]

Walk to the Gallows

Sheriff Gillespie arrived at the jail at 7 a.m. The morning was appropriately dull and gloomy. Loucks had the difficult task of ministering to the condemned men as they faced execution. He ordered the bell at St Mary Magdalene to start to toll at 7:45. When Thomset and Lowder were led out of their cells five minutes later, he was at the jail to walk with them as the sheriff and the other jailers led them to the gallows. Both men were wearing their own suits rather than their prison garb. The prisoners were visibly shaken, but managed to walk up the stairway unassisted.

The hangman, unidentified but said to be from London, hooded and wearing prison clothes, had preceded them to the gallows. Loucks, in surplice, read from the burial service: 'I am the resurrection and the life; he that believeth in me, though he were dead, yet shall he live: and whosoever liveth and believeth in me shall never die.'

The scene was one which few would care to witness and horrific for those who did. As Loucks read the prayer, Sheriff Gillespie asked the prisoners to make themselves ready. The prisoners rose from the kneeling position and their hands and feet were pinioned. The hangman placed black hoods over their heads and adjusted the nooses. Loucks continued to read: 'Into thy merciful hands I commend my spirit; for thou hast redeemed me, O Lord, thou God of Truth.'

Sheriff Gillespie then said: 'If either of you have anything to say you can speak now.' Thomset said nothing, but Lowder, showing intense grief, exclaimed in a supplicating tone interrupted by his desperate sobs:

Oh God, grant that I might not be lost in eternity. I am innocent of this crime and I pray that I may remain steadfast. I am ready to go to meet my God. I am trusting in Jesus. Oh Jesus, be with me to the last. Oh be with me and take me to that happy home above where I will see no more sorrow. God be with me for ever more I trust, Amen.

Standing side by side on the trap door, and not knowing the moment the bolt would be drawn, they grasped each other by the hand and Lowder said, 'Good bye, Joe.' Thomset remained silent.

Loucks recited the Lord's prayer, and when he reached: 'Thine is the kingdom, the power and the glory ...' Sheriff Gillespie gave the hangman the signal to spring the trap door. The witnesses soon realized to their horror that the hangman had bungled his task. They watched the condemned men dangle alive at the end of the ropes as they slowly strangled to death. Lowder struggled briefly, but then stopped moving. Thomset kicked and moved about so violently that he broke the rope that bound his legs. He continued to kick for almost two minutes. The black hoods were dislodged and their faces could be seen turning blue. Lowder was pronounced dead at nine minutes after 8:00. Thomset took an additional five minutes to die. The hangman quickly slipped away, knowing that if he remained, he would be condemned for the appalling suffering he had inflicted.

If a hanging was properly conducted, the cervical vertebrae were dislocated and death was relatively painless. However, much depended upon the skill and expertise of the hangman and there were many bungled hangings – some say as many as a third to one half – caused by misplacement of the rope or miscalculation of the appropriate drop, resulting in strangling or decapitation or, in cases where the unfortunate prisoner survived, a second hanging.[13]

At 8:20, the bodies were cut down and placed in plain pine coffins.

The coroner held the required inquest. The bodies (and the flowers given by Thomset's wife and Lowder's mother) were taken out to the yard of the jail, where they were buried in unmarked graves.

'A few lines before I die'

There were many who wept when they saw the black flag flying from the staff at the courthouse to signal that the sentence had been carried out. There were certainly those who thought that justice had been done, but Lowder's protestations of innocence resonated with many, and the efforts of Loucks, Coulthard, Merrill, McQuaig, and the many citizens who signed the petition to save his life revealed a deep split in the community.

Both men wrote letters shortly before they died that were intended for general publication after the hanging. George Lowder's letter was addressed: 'To the inhabitants of Prince Edward County.'

I thought I would write to you a few lines before I die. I do not suppose anything I might say would cause you to change your mind regarding guilt or innocence and even if I could it would be too late to rectify any mistake and bring me back to earth again. God is my witness that I am innocent of having anything to do with the murder of Peter Lazier and when I am hung for that crime the innocent is punished for the guilty. I die bearing neither spite nor malice against anyone and my wishes are that all my enemies may be forgiven as truly as I hope to be forgiven for all my sins. Believe me, I do not die a murderer nor with a murderer's heart. If I knew who were guilty of the crime for which I am to suffer death I would make it known. I have not owned a revolver for two years past, and I have not fired one for upwards of one year. I did not have a gun in my hands for six weeks previous to my arrest, and I was not in Mr. Gilbert Jones house nor on his premises in my life to my knowledge. These are my last and dying words.

George Lowder[14]

Thomset's semi-literate letter, addressed to his mother, but apparently intended for public consumption, was also published after he met his death.

Dear, kind, and loving mother – These are my last dying words I never knew that fatal shot was fired, nor of that man was killed nor nothing of that murder nor my boots never made the tracks but the jury says I must die to pay some man's penalty. I am ready to die, but I die for something I never did. You want me to confess that I never will to a crime I am not guilty of. I never was in Gilbert Jones house in 15 years, nor I never was at the door in four years. I never saw Jones get any money at the station, but I must say that it is like all the stories that is told about me. They will not let me alone and let me die in peace with the world they won't let my old father rest in the grave. You know father never had to pay one dollar for any wrong I ever did but I forgive all those who swore false against me. I forgive all my enemies. I want them to forgive me. With all the reports no man can say I ever done them any wrong, nor took anything from them. But my shoulders have borne many wrongs that I never did. Mrs. Jones swore at the examination the men was larger than we and at the trial we look just like the men. She said the man that fired the shot had on a grey suit of tweed I had on my black clothes that day. They say I fired the shot but Thank God I was not there to fire any shot so I can not confess to that crime nor I never will. If they will let me die in peace I have made my peace with God. I would rather go to meet my reward than go to prison for life so don't weep for me Dear Mother sister wife and daughter for I am going to a better world … Believe me I am innocent – I declare to my God these my last words … I die an innocent man … My heart aches for my sweet little girl but God will take care of her and you all til he think it best to call you home to a better world and me … Don't think I am the cause of this disgrace on you for I am not. Good bye and farewell for ever til we meet in a better world. Your loving son brother husband and father.

Joseph Thomset[15]

Sheriff James Gillespie submitted his claim for the expenses for the hanging of $96.34, the most significant items being $35.35 paid to a carpenter for 'furnishing material and building the scaffold' and the hangman's fee of $40.00 plus 6.50 for 'refreshments,' duly paid despite his bungling.[16] Loucks, no doubt deeply saddened by the fact that he had not been able to save their lives, had one satisfaction: the death certificates of both men declared them to be members of the Church of England.[17]

Death by Hanging

The only protest to emerge from the hanging of Thomset and Lowder in relation to capital punishment was a plea for greater skill on the part of the hangman. Two days after the execution, the Trenton *Courier Advocate* reported: 'The murder was something new in Prince Edward County and the execution stirred the people as they had not been stirred for years,' adding: 'The hangman did not understand his business, and the case will strengthen the agitation for the appointment of one skilled in the dreadful work of death by hanging.'[18] Kingston's *British Whig* expressed similar outrage and pleaded: 'A competent hangman should be appointed by the Government.'[19] Newspaper reporters were given remarkable access to the condemned men shortly before the hanging and then allowed to witness the execution itself. The poignant reports of Thomset and Lowder's last hours and the horrific eyewitness accounts of the grizzly scene at the hanging likely contributed post-trial to the swing in the public's attitude about the case. If the *Gazette*'s reports fuelled public hostility towards Thomset and Lowder before and during the trial, the published accounts of the hanging confronted the community with the horror that hostility had produced.

The issue of capital punishment was debated in Canada in the nineteenth century and there was at least one attempt to have the death penalty abolished,[20] but for the most part, capital punishment opponents appear to have focused their efforts on narrowing the list of offences attracting execution. In pre-Confederation Canada, capital punishment was the penalty for most serious criminal offences. By 1867, the list of capital offences was reduced to murder, rape, treason, and piracy. While prisoners convicted of rape were sometimes sentenced to death, none was executed after 1867. Only one man – Métis leader Louis Riel in 1885 – was hanged for treason.[21] So for all practical purposes, from 1865 until its abolition in 1976, capital punishment was reserved for those convicted of murder.

There was an effective abolitionist movement in the nineteenth century in the United States and several states abolished capital punishment.[22] Caesar Beccaria's pioneering work *An Essay on Crimes and Punishments*, first published in 1764, was translated into English and had considerable influence in the United States.[23] Beccaria, the father of the study of criminology, argued that capital punishment was morally indefensible, 'pernicious to society, from the barbarity of the example it affords'[24] and less effective as a deterrent than a lengthy term of incarceration. Beccaria's basic premise was that to be just, a punishment 'should have only that degree of severity which is sufficient to deter others'[25] and that capital punishment failed that test: 'The death of a criminal is a terrible but momentary spectacle, and therefore a less efficacious method of deterring others than the continued example of a man being deprived of his liberty, condemned, as a beast of burden, to repair, by his labour, the injury he has done to society.'[26]

Some religious groups – notably Quakers – opposed capital punishment in principle, and in England, the Quaker-inspired Society for the Abolition of the Death Penalty urged abolition. Public debate on the issue of capital punishment in England resulted in the appointment of a royal commission on capital punishment in 1866. A number of prominent lawyers and judges, including influential criminal law reformer and codifier James Fitzjames Stephen, gave evidence supporting retention, primarily on the ground of deterrence. The commissioners, who included committed abolitionists, were divided. A significant minority were of the view that 'Capital Punishment might, safely, and with advantage to the community, be at once abolished,'[27] but the majority supported creating a new category of serious murder cases for which the death penalty would be retained.

The debate over capital punishment in the United States and England was followed with sceptical interest in Canada.[28] The anti–death penalty movement was not strong in Canada and the Canadian legal establishment, like the English, favoured retention, largely on the grounds of deterrence. Abolition of capital punishment in Iowa in 1872 was described in the *Canada Law Journal* as a 'dangerous experiment.'[29] There was really no concerted effort to eliminate the death penalty in Canada until well into the twentieth century,[30] and the abolition movement did not begin in earnest until after the Second World War.

Even then, progress was slow.[31] A royal commission was appointed in England in 1949 following public concern over the questionable conviction of Timothy Evans. It recommended retention of the death penalty, as did the *Report of the Joint Committee of the Senate and House of Commons on Capital Punishment* in Canada in 1956. The next year saw the election of Prime Minister John Diefenbaker, a former defence lawyer who, having endured the hanging of two clients, was opposed to capital punishment. During Diefenbaker's term in office, from 1957 to 1963, the rate of commutation increased. Death by hanging remained the mandatory sentence for all cases of murder until a Criminal Code amendment in 1961 that restricted the death penalty to cases of 'capital murder,' defined as planned and deliberate murder, murder committed during the commission of certain specified offences, and murder of a police officer or prison guard in the execution of their duties.

The last hangings in Canada took place in 1962 in Toronto when two men were hanged back to back for two separate murders.[32] In 1967, parliament enacted a five-year moratorium on the death penalty, except for the murder of police officers and prison guards, a measure that was continued in 1973. By this time, there was a growing international movement towards abolition, but popular support in Canada for the death penalty continued. On a free vote in 1976, against the weight of public opinion but with a strong push from Prime Minister Pierre Elliott Trudeau, parliament abolished capital punishment for all criminal offences. Another free vote to restore capital punishment was defeated in 1987.

There is a vast body of literature tracking public debate over the efficacy and morality of the death penalty that falls outside the scope of this case study. For present purposes, the arguments may be summarized as follows. Those supporting capital punishment relied primarily on deterrence and the need for public protection against professional criminals, the appropriateness of just retribution and the need to mark society's abhorrence of murder, and the specific need to protect those on the front line of crime control, police officers and prison guards. Those opposed to capital punishment disputed its deterrent effect, considered retribution to be nothing more than revenge, unworthy of a civilized state, and argued that the infliction of the death sentence was morally repugnant, undermined the sanctity of life, and demeaned the administration of justice.

As late as the 1950s, these conflicting arguments produced a stalemate insufficient to overcome the strong popular support for capital punishment. As the joint Senate–House of Commons committee reported in 1956: 'The abolition of a penalty traditionally accepted as a just and effective deterrent could only be recommended if the evidence clearly established that the ordinary citizen's view of its efficacy was demonstrably wrong.'[33]

What does bear upon the Thomset-Lowder case is the concern over the risk of wrongful conviction. Even the most stalwart supporter of the death penalty must be horrified by the execution of an innocent person. The frequent pleas for the lives of allegedly innocent prisoners, including Thomset and Lowder, did not displace faith in the rigours of the adversarial trial, confidence in the common sense of the average jury, and, all else failing, the capacity of the residual prerogative of mercy to remedy an injustice. As late as 1956, the joint Senate–House of Commons committee confidently reported: 'The fact that there was no known Canadian instance of the execution of an innocent person indicated the effectiveness of present procedures by way of trial and executive review and this suggests that the risk of error does not present a reasonable argument for abolition in Canada.'[34]

The myth of the infallibility of the justice system was shattered in the second half of the twentieth century by a depressingly long string of demonstrated wrongful convictions in Canada and elsewhere.[35] In the face of this evidence, it has become difficult to accept that the trial, appeal, and review processes are now, or ever were, capable of sustaining a level of confidence sufficient to support the use of capital punishment. The Supreme Court of Canada has stated that 'the unique feature of capital punishment is that it puts beyond recall the possibility of correction.'[36] In refusing to sanction the extradition of two men charged with murder to the United States absent assurances that the death penalty would not be imposed, the Court observed: 'The recent and continuing disclosures of wrongful convictions for murder in Canada, the United States and the United Kingdom provide tragic testimony to the fallibility of the legal system, despite its elaborate safeguards for the protection of the innocent.'[37]

14

Community Conscience

Was justice done in the Lazier murder case? Justice Patterson, an experienced and able judge, was convinced that the jury reached the right result, and the prevailing view of the legal establishment was that both men were properly convicted. The media also supported the verdict. The *Daily Ontario* reported that 'the general belief is that both men died with a lie on their lips.'[1] The *British Whig* expressed confidence in the outcome and suggested that those who were doubting the correctness of the verdict seemed to be ignoring some important facts: the circumstantial evidence 'pointed strongly towards' the executed men as the guilty parties; 'they were accorded a fair trial, which lasted over a period of four days and a half'; 'they were defended by two of the best criminal lawyers in Ontario'; the jury 'was composed of 12 honest and intelligent men to whom counsel for the prisoners took no exception'; and Justice Patterson had 'expressed his full concurrence in the verdict rendered.'[2] Not surprisingly, Hugh McKinnon 'talked boldly about the affair' shortly after the hanging and 'severely arraigned the clergymen who had questioned the guilt of the men' and 'even imputed to them cranky notions.'[3]

But the confidence of the media and the legal establishment was not shared by everyone. At the time of the murder, it seemed that the entire community was out for blood. As soon as they were arrested, Joseph Thomset and George Lowder were presumed to be guilty. That opinion had not abated by the time of the trial. However, as the trial proceeded, and especially after the death sentence was passed, public opinion shifted, or at least divided, and a significant segment of the community was horrified by what had happened.

The community did not divide along the lines of social class and standing that one might expect. Thomset and Lowder were rural working people with limited means and little education. The crime they were accused of posed a serious threat to the peace and tranquillity of Prince Edward County's prosperous land owners. Yet their principal defenders and supporters came from the well-to-do and educated elite – Picton's mayor, Edwards Merrill, former Conservative Member of Parliament James McQuaig, and Reverend Coulthard and Rector Loucks. Coulthard and Loucks claimed to speak for 'the most respectable, and intelligent of this town and county.' The petition they mounted was signed by many prominent members of the community. McQuaig purported to reflect the views of 'many of our respectable men' and Merrill complained of the 'excited' and 'agitated' mood that prevailed in the community and in the courtroom. These words indicated that the educated elite considered those responsible for the deplorable atmosphere in the courtroom and the hostile mood of the community to be ignorant rowdies and ruffians.

A Judge's Angry Outburst

Prince Edward County Court Judge Robert Jellett was outraged by the sympathy generated for Thomset and Lowder. He was alarmed by the extent of the support for the executed men and he regarded criticism of the verdict and sentence as an attack on the courts, the administration of justice, and the integrity of the entire legal system. A few days after the hangings, Judge Jellett addressed the grand jury summonsed for the General Sessions of the Peace, over which he would preside. Jellett confessed that 'in speaking on this matter I can scarcely restrain myself.' Those whose 'minds are not judicious' had nothing but 'the evidence of the scoundrels themselves' upon which to base their criticism of the verdict. Their 'flimsy pretence of sympathy for the men condemned to death endangers society.' Jellett urged 'faith in justice, in juries, in the law of the land,' not 'the mad utterances of these fanatics based upon the words of the criminals themselves.' He described as 'almost criminal' the efforts of those who, 'in their excitement, their idiocy, I might almost call it,' tried to stay the process.[4]

Jellett's views were extreme and extravagant but, regrettably, not uncommon in the face of allegations of wrongful conviction. Too often, the response of the legal establishment has been to man the barricades and to regard criticism of a contested verdict as an attack on the entire apparatus of law and social protection rather than to ask calmly and dispassionately whether a mistake was made and how to avoid similar mistakes in the future.[5]

The *Globe* had reported Jellett's outburst and within two days published an editorial describing his comments to the grand jury as 'extravagant and unnecessarily severe.' The editorial writer shared Jellett's assessment that 'the strong pleas of innocence put forward by the men in their dying hours must be taken for what they are worth,' but argued that there was room for honest difference of opinion on the outcome and pointed out that the 'sentence was carried out in a brutally bungling manner.'[6]

Lingering Doubts

Doubts about the verdict have never abated, and the case continues to cast its shadow to this day. It has become part of the local lore and popular culture, the frequent subject of newspaper and magazine articles, lectures, walking tours, and popular local histories.[7] The case is even sometimes the subject of levity. In 2008 Grant Howe's County Cider Company launched a brew labelled the 'Thompsett-Louder' beer and Reid Pickering of the band Tin Roof Rusted performed his song 'Thompsett and Lowder Swung' in a Picton bar.[8]

In the years following the hanging, there emerged a widespread, persistent, but unproven belief among many County residents that George Lowder's father John was the real culprit[9] and that George was either not involved or that he played a limited role as the driver of a rig that carried Thomset and John Lowder to the Jones farmhouse. Within six months of the hanging, the *New York Times* published an article asserting that John Lowder had made a death-bed confession stating that he was the guilty party and that George's only involvement was driving him to the Jones house on the night of the murder.[10]

If true, that story could have saved George from the gallows, although if the Crown could prove that he knew of his father's plan for the armed robbery and the use of force if necessary to carry out that plan, it is certainly conceivable that he would still have been liable as a party to the murder. If John and George Lowder were both somehow involved in the murder that would explain why no one in the Lowder family spoke out to save George by pointing the finger of guilt at John; that would have condemned John without exonerating George. On the other hand, if George had driven his father and Thomset to the Jones farm and abandoned them there when he learned what they were up to, he would lack the required knowledge or intent to make him a party to the crime they committed.[11]

Stories have continued to circulate over the years of John's guilt and George's tangential involvement in the crime, and of another West Lake resident who might have been involved. However, John Lowder certainly did not make a death-bed confession in 1884. He did not die until 7 June 1910 at the age of 87 when a piece of timber fell and struck him on the head in a shack where he was living at the Sandbanks.[12]

There was also speculation that George's brother Christopher may have been involved. He was the only member of the family not to visit George before the execution and he appears to have left the County shortly afterwards, never to be heard from again. David Lowder lived in the County another sixty years until his death in 1944, apparently without shedding any light on the crime for which he was acquitted.

A Case of Wrongful Conviction?

It is impossible to say, a century and a quarter after the fact, whether or not Joseph Thomset and George Lowder committed the crime of murdering Peter Lazier on 21 December 1883. All that can be said is that the case against them was far from clear.

The case certainly presents many troubling features that correspond with documented cases of wrongful conviction.[13] The first was the enormous public pressure to apprehend, and then convict, the suspects. The jury was almost certainly influenced by the community's prejudgment of the case. Prince Edward County was a small, close-knit, and relatively isolated community with a strong sense of its own identity and values. It is difficult to disagree with D'Alton McCarthy's fear of the 'magnetic' effect of the extremely hostile mood of the community and the deplorable behaviour of the courtroom attendees. The twelve men on the jury would have been keenly aware of exactly how the community felt. Lawyers, judges, and popular culture revered juries as palladiums of liberty, capable of standing strong against the arbitrary power of the state. But when the threat to liberty and fair play came from the community itself, could the jury be relied on to resist the very community it represented? Edwards Merrill, an experienced lawyer and a man who had deep roots in the community and understood the pull of popular opinion, was profoundly troubled by the hostile mood in the courtroom and described the verdict as an 'echo ... of the excited public opinion.'

There is also evidence of what has been labelled as 'noble cause corruption,' where the police believe that it is justifiable to fabricate or distort evidence or in some other manner bend the rules to secure the conviction of someone they believe to be guilty.[14] In this regard, the imposing figure of Hugh McKinnon casts a large shadow over the case. He was a man anxious to build his reputation as a relentless and clever crime-buster, and he was prepared to use dubious tactics in the process. He almost certainly coached key witnesses such as Margaret Jones to shade their evidence in favour of the prosecution and his open use of deception with regard to Mrs Thomset suggests he may well have been prepared to go even further.

Related to this are the 'tunnel vision' and 'rush to judgment' problems that arise when the authorities narrowly focus their attention on a viable suspect and fail to pursue all reasonable lines of inquiry, keeping an open mind to anything that points the finger of blame elsewhere.[15] The investigation focused immediately and exclusively on Joseph Thomset and the Lowder family. No consideration was given to the possibility that someone else might have committed the crime. McKinnon saw his job as being to gather the evidence necessary to convict the accused men, not to conduct a thorough and dispassionate investigation into the crime.

While the speed and efficiency of the criminal process in the late nineteenth century was in some respects admirable when compared to the sometimes glacial pace of modern criminal trials and appeals, one is left with a lingering feeling that there was something of a rush to judgment that simply did not allow for careful reflection and deliberation. Just as public opinion was building in their favour less than six months after the crime had been committed and one month after the death sentence had been imposed, the day of execution arrived with no reprieve. Recent experience shows that it often takes years to build a case demonstrating a wrongful conviction and to establish special procedures, ranging from appeal to ad hoc commissions of inquiry or, as in England, a permanent statutory Criminal Cases Review Commission,[16] to assess such cases.

Unreliable expert evidence is a distressingly common source of injustice and wrongful conviction.[17] The investigative method employed by McKinnon with respect to identifying the tracks in the snow was amateurish and failed to comply with the standards of the day. While their work perhaps did not rise to the level of expert evidence, both McKinnon and George Pope were presented by the Crown as being experienced in tracking, and their evidence was clothed with an air of weight and authority it almost certainly did not deserve.

Inadequate disclosure by the prosecution is another common cause of wrongful convictions.[18] In 1884 the Crown was not required to disclose its entire case to the defence, and Clute certainly gained an advantage by springing the surprise evidence of Thomset's alleged statement to Phoebe Cunningham that he was planning to rob Gilbert Jones as well as the evidence that Thomset had been seen with a pistol.

Related to this was the relative lack of preparation by defence counsel. Inadequate defence work has been recognized as a potential cause of wrongful convictions.[19] While D'Alton McCarthy and George Dickson were certainly experienced and competent to take on the defence of this case and while they performed admirably, they were retained at the last moment and lacked the time required to prepare adequately. Their lack of preparation and time to absorb all the details of the case and their arrival after key witnesses had already testified almost certainly affected the efficacy of the defence.

And of course there were features of nineteenth-century criminal law that worked to the disadvantage of the condemned men. Thomset and Lowder were denied the right to testify and to proclaim their innocence from the witness stand, and they had no right to have their convictions reviewed by a higher court. The last two legal deficiencies were strongly contested even at the time and could well have been factors in the result in this case.

The case against Thomset was certainly stronger than that against George Lowder. The footprints in the snow could not be precisely traced to Thomset's door, but they did lead in the direction of his home at West Lake and they were made by boots similar to his. Thomset was at the station when Gilbert Jones was paid for his hops and likely knew that he had received a large sum of money. There was evidence of two statements he made indicating that he considered Jones to be a wealthy man and that he planned to rob him. There was also some evidence that he possessed a pistol.

On the other hand, Margaret and Gilbert Jones' description of the appearance and height of the man with the pistol did not match that of Thomset and might well have excluded him. And it is difficult to understand why neither the Crown nor the defence explored the implications of the fact that the man with the pistol appeared to be left-handed and that he had a distinctive gait or limp when he ran off. If Thomset had had these characteristics, they would likely be known or at least discoverable by the diligent Hugh McKinnon. If he was not left-handed and had no limp, the defence could have introduced those facts to exclude him as the killer. After the hangings, it was reported that while the man who fired the fatal shot was left-handed, the jailers decided that both Thomset and Lowder were right-handed 'as in whitewashing the gaol, the condemned men could not use their left hands with any skill at all.'[20]

The timing and circumstances of Thomset's visit to Alfred and Delia Hicks on the night of the murder lean in his favour. He was calm, showed no sign of having just travelled in a rush on foot over several miles in the snow after shooting someone, and the clothes Mrs Hicks described did not correspond to the clothes Mrs Jones saw the intruder wearing. The trackers only found one set of tracks between Lowder's home and the Hicks establishment, and Babbitt's evidence that the tracks led away from Thomset's house seems very odd. Another piece of evidence that favoured Thomset was his reaction when first confronted by Constable Edmund Bedell. He immediately denied any involvement and provided an explanation for his whereabouts the night of the crime that was entirely consistent with his brief conversation with David Lowder a few minutes later and with the alibi defence advanced at trial.

For what they are worth, the newspaper reports of Thomset's statements to his guards as he awaited his death indicate that although he may not have been the shooter, he did play a role in the commission of the crime. If, as those statements suggest, Thomset was present that night at the home of Gilbert and Margaret Jones, it seems much more likely that he was the second man with the dark beard who fled the scene before the fatal shot was fired. If that were the case, Thomset could still be guilty of murder, although not on the Crown's theory that he fired the fatal shot. By using or attempting violence against Lazier, the man with the shotgun had actively participated in the attempted robbery, and that participation could make him a party to the murder actually committed by the other intruder.[21]

George Lowder's conviction is more troubling. The only evidence against him was the tracks in the snow that matched his patch-bottom boots. Even if one assumes that the tracks in the snow provide an adequate basis upon which to conclude that one of the culprits came from the Lowder household, which Lowder was the guilty party? George's father and two of his brothers wore the same size and style of boots. George's behaviour and statements on the day following the murder suggest that the patch-bottom boots were his. But if he was one of the culprits, he was astonishingly naive to go looking for the very boots he wore the night before, knowing that the constables and concerned citizens had been out all night and into the next day trying to follow the tracks left by the killer's boots and that the boots had been seized by the authorities as evidence. Could his pursuit of the boots not be seen as evidence of innocence?

With no evidence other than the boots and tracks to link him to the crime, George Lowder's conviction seems highly dubious. And if the man with the shotgun did have a dark beard, not a false beard, that excluded George Lowder as one of the intruders. An unspoken factor that may have sealed George's fate could well be that the members of the jury thought that the tracks indicated that the crime had been committed by one of the Lowders. The jury may not have been prepared to acquit George in the absence of any explanation as to who else in the Lowder household had committed the crime. But this ignores the fact that under the law of the day, George Lowder could not testify in his own defence. Even if he did have an explanation or was prepared to point the finger at another family member, the law required him to remain mute.

A Community's Sense of Guilt

In the twenty years following the Lazier murder, there were five homicides in Prince Edward County, three involving manslaughter charges and two in which the accused were charged with murder.[22] Roger Clute returned to prosecute both murder cases. The Crown's case was strong in both. But never again did Clute persuade a Prince Edward County jury to convict an accused charged with a capital offence. The reason was, at least in part, the community's sense of guilt over the Thomset-Lowder case and the fear of sending another innocent man to his death on the pleading of the same lawyer.

In August 1888, a father and son, Peter and Wellington Loveless, were charged in the shooting death of Leslie Church near Carrying Place. The Lovelesses were described as 'poor farmers ... decently attired in common tweed clothes, which have apparently seen considerable service.'[23] Peter, the sixty-five-year-old father, was charged with counselling murder and Wellington, the eighteen-year-old son, with murder. Despite their humble situation, the prisoners retained D'Alton McCarthy's partner, B.B. Osler, who ranked as one of the country's leading criminal trial lawyers.[24]

The only available accounts of the two-day trial at the 1888 Picton fall assizes are sparse,[25] but it is difficult to see what legal defence Wellington Loveless could have that would justify or excuse the killing of Leslie Church in the circumstances. However, B.B. Osler's address to the jury was described as 'the grandest effort ever made in the Picton courthouse' and 'much affected' the audience. While the skilful Clute 'made an able address to the jury,' he could not persuade the jury to convict. The trial judge's 'complete and very painstaking' jury charge was thought to favour the prisoners,[26] and Wellington and his father were acquitted on all charges.

The explanation for the Loveless acquittals perhaps becomes more apparent when one turns to Roger Clute's next murder trial in the County. Fifteen years after the Church trial and almost twenty years after the Lazier trial, Roger Clute, by then a KC and the senior partner in a Toronto firm, returned to Picton to prosecute a third murder case.[27] Again, the Crown was confident of obtaining a conviction: Clute described it as 'a very strong case.'[28] Edward Clark, a member of a travelling circus company, was charged with the murder of a fellow circus worker. Both the accused and the victim were black. The case had obvious racial overtones. Neither the Picton community nor the jury could identify with either the victim or the accused, who both came to town as temporary visitors from another world. But more troubling for the prospect of conviction was that 'in Picton, Clute's name was clouded by his association with [an] infamous case of injustice.'[29] Clute presented strong evidence that Clark was the killer, but the Picton jury refused to convict. Both Clute and the trial judge, Justice James Teetzel, were surprised and unsettled by the jury's verdict and by the 'vociferous cheering' that greeted it in the courtroom.[30]

J. Roland Brown, the local crown attorney, realized that the Crown had made a serious error by retaining Clute to prosecute the case. Brown regarded the verdict as 'a miscarriage of justice' and attributed it to lingering misgivings about the Thomset-Lowder verdict. He explained to Deputy Attorney General Cartwright: 'There has always been a suspicion in the minds of a number of people in this county that one of the last two men who were executed here might have been innocent. I refer to one Lowder.' Brown thought that the jury was simply not prepared to be persuaded by Roger Clute to send another man to the gallows, particularly as the case 'was simply one alien negro killing another alien negro.' He reported that the Thomset-Lowder case had created 'a strong and increasing feeling against capital punishment' in Prince Edward County, adding that if the penalty had been imprisonment rather than death, the jury likely would have convicted.[31]

Brown may well have been right. Justice Patterson was the last judge to pronounce the death sentence in the Prince Edward County Courthouse.

Community Justice

The British 'Tory'-inspired model of community justice in the hands of lay magistrates, coroners, and volunteer constables was fast fading in late-nineteenth-century Ontario at the time of the Lazier murder. Local constables, like Babbitt and Bedell, were gradually giving way to trained professionals, like Hugh McKinnon. The institution of the coroner, once a key element in the local administration of justice, was declining in importance and succumbing to the general shift towards a more centralized and professional model. But the County community did speak in the Lazier murder case – in a loud voice that condemned Joseph Thomset and George Lowder to the gallows. Upon reflection, that community had second thoughts, leading to doubt and shame over what it had done. A perceived miscarriage of justice left an indelible stain on the community's conscience.

Until recently, the cells where Thomset and Lowder were held in the old Picton jail housed the Prince Edward County Archives. Exhibits from the 1884 trial could be viewed in a display case to be found only a few metres from the spot where Thomset and Lowder met their death. The archives have been moved to another location, but the double-gallows still stand hovering over the trap door that was sprung in front of the invited witnesses who watched in horror as Joseph Thomset and George Lowder met their painful deaths by strangulation. The gallows were never used again – Thomset and Lowder were the last men to face the executioner in Prince Edward County. The gallows remain as a chilling reminder of the fragility of the adversarial criminal trial process, and of the brutality and the terrible finality of the capital sentence that was carried out on 10 June 1884 to a community's profound regret.

'Hanged Unjustly'

A crudely handcrafted gravestone was recently uncovered in the pau-
pers' corner of Picton's Glenwood cemetery. It was likely placed there
some time after the hanging by George Lowder's friends and family. It
is almost certain that George Lowder was not buried under the stone. A
little over a week after the hangings, J.S. McQuaig wrote to the minister
of justice at the request of the Lowder family, stating that 'Lowder's
body was interred in the gaol yard,' and asking if his body could be
exhumed and given to the family for burial. McQuaig observed that
'the mother particularly feels the anguish natural to the parents.'[32] No
response to this letter has been found, but given the letter of the law, it
seems unlikely that Campbell could have agreed to the request.

The 'natural anguish' and bitterness of George Lowder's family and
friends is evident from the inscription on the stone:[33]

G. LOUDER
HANGED
1884
UNJUSTLY

Notes

1: Introduction

1 The contemporary records and newspaper reports contain various spellings of these names – 'Thomsett,' 'Thomsitt,' and 'Lauder' are common. I have used the spellings that are used in the court documents and the Capital Case File, LAC, RG 13, vol. 1420, file 184A.

2 Samuel Williamson, 'Seven Ways to Compute the Relative Value of a U.S. Dollar Amount, 1790 to Present,' Measuring Worth, 2010, http://www .measuringworth.com/uscompare/.

3 *Annual Report of the Bureau of Industries, Province of Ontario*, 1883, 37. The annual provincial tradesman's wage was $452.

4 See Jim Phillips, 'Why Legal History Matters' (2010) 41 *Victoria University of Wellington Law Review* 393.

5 A.W. Brian Simpson, *Leading Cases in the Common Law* (Oxford: Oxford University Press, 1995) 12.

6 See, e.g., A.W. Brian Simpson, *Cannibalism and the Common Law: The Story of the Tragic Last Voyage of the Mignonette and the Strange Legal Proceedings to Which It Gave Rise* (Chicago: University of Chicago Press, 1984); Patrick Brode, *The Odyssey of John Anderson* (Toronto: Osgoode Society and University of Toronto Press, 1989); Robert Sharpe, *The Last Day, the Last Hour: The Currie Libel Trial* (Toronto: Osgoode Society and University of Toronto Press, 1988); Robert Sharpe and Patricia McMahon, *The Persons Case: The Origins and Legacy of the Fight for Legal Personhood* (Toronto: Osgoode Society and University of Toronto Press, 2007); Judy Fudge and Eric Tucker,

eds, *Work on Trial: Canadian Labour Law Struggles* (Toronto: Osgoode Society and Irwin Law, 2010).

7 See, e.g., Jim Phillips and Rosemary Gartner, *Murdering Holiness: The Trials of Franz Creffield and George Mitchell* (Vancouver: UBC Press, 2003); Constance Backhouse, *Carnal Crimes and Sexual Assault Law in Canada, 1900–1975* (Toronto: Osgoode Society and University of Toronto Press, 2008); Reinhold Kramer and Tom Mitchell, *Walk towards the Gallows: The Tragedy of Hilda Blake, Hanged 1899* (Toronto: Oxford University Press, 2002); Martin L. Friedland, *The Case of Valentine Shortis: A True Story of Crime and Politics in Canada* (Toronto: Osgoode Society and University of Toronto Press, 1986); Martin L. Friedland, *The Trials of Israel Lipski* (London: Macmillan, 1984).

8 See Phillips and Gartner, *Murdering Holiness* 2–4; Natalie Davis, *The Return of Martin Guerre* (Cambridge: Harvard University Press, 1983).

9 See chapter 14.

2: The Crime

1 Tom Cruickshank, Peter John Stokes, and John de Visser, *The Settler's Dream: A Pictorial History of the Older Buildings of Prince Edward County* (Picton: Corporation of the County of Prince Edward, 1984) 147–8.

2 Arthur Garratt Dorland, *Former Days & Quaker Ways* (Belleville: Mika Studio, 1972), 5.

3 And in litigation involving Quaker affairs. See below, chapter 6.

4 Dorland, *Former Days & Quaker Ways* 74.

5 A full transcript of the trial is found in the Capital Case File ['CCF'], Lowder, George, and Thomset, Joseph, LAC, RG 13, vol. 1420, files 183A and 184A (1884).

6 Unless otherwise indicated, all quotations are taken from the trial transcript, CCF.

7 The role of constables is more fully explored in chapter 3.

8 Hallowell Township Census 1861, Prince Edward County Archives (PECA).

9 Ibid.

10 George had a twin brother, Albert, of whom there is no record after the age of one – presumably he died as a child. I am grateful to Doreen Dolleman for providing me with her genealogy of the Lowder family.

3: Hugh McKinnon, Detective

1 Deputy attorney general to Low, 21 February 1884, PECA, Walmsley Papers, box 5, item 9d.

2 Robert L. Fraser, 'McKinnon, Hugh,' *Dictionary of Canadian Biography Online*; Frank W. Anderson, *Oldtime Eastern Sheriffs and Outlaws* (Humbolt, SK: Gopher Books, 1999); Harry Mulhall, 'Hugh McKinnon: the Strongest Strong Arm of the Law,' in Nick and Helma Mika, eds, *Belleville: The Good Old Days* (Belleville: Mika Publishing, 1975).

3 Fraser, 'McKinnon.'

4 Ray Fazakas, *The Donnelly Album* (Toronto: Macmillan, 1977) 83ff.

5 *Illustrated Historical Atlas of the Counties of Hastings and Prince Edward* (Toronto: H. Beldon & Co., 1878; reproduced Belleville: Mika Silk Screening Ltd, 1972) iii.

6 Mulhall, 'Hugh McKinnon' 70.

7 *Justices of the Peace Act*, C.S.C. 1859, c. 100, ss. 1 and 3, requiring justices to be in 'possession of absolute property ... of or above the value of one thousand two hundred dollars.'

8 Discussed below, chapter 5.

9 Paul Romney, *Mr Attorney: The Attorney General for Ontario in Court, Cabinet, and Legislature 1791–1899* (Toronto: Osgoode Society and University of Toronto Press, 1986) 231–9.

10 Municipal Institutions Act, CSUC 1859, c. 54, s. 373 fixed the stipend at not less than $400 per annum.

11 Police Magistrate George Spencer to Deputy Attorney General J.G. Scott, 19 January 1882. The source for the correspondence referred to here and in notes 13 to 27 is: Ontario Sessional Papers (no. 91), 1884. For judges' salaries, see chapter 7, note 6 and for tradesmen's wages, see chapter 1, note 3.

12 Greg Marquis, *Policing Canada's Century: A History of the Canadian Association of Chiefs of Police* (Toronto: Osgoode Society and University of Toronto Press, 1993), ch. 1; Romney, *Mr Attorney* 231–9.

13 Deputy Attorney General J.G. Scott, 14 January 1882.

14 Perth County Crown Attorney John Iddington to deputy attorney general, 18 January 1882.

15 Police Magistrate George Spencer to deputy attorney general, 19 January 1882.

16 Haldimand Sheriff Robert H. Davis to deputy attorney general, 21 January 1882.

17 John Mercer to deputy attorney general, 20 January 1882.

18 H.H. Loucks to deputy attorney general, 18 January 1882.

19 Sheriff James Gillespie to deputy attorney general, 19 January 1882.

20 Wm. H. Wilkinson to deputy attorney general, 30 January 1882.

21 G.M. Boswell to deputy attorney general, 23 January 1882.

22 Brant County Court Judge S.J. Jones to deputy attorney general, 26 January 1882.

23 W.T.P. Williams to deputy attorney general, 23 January 1882.
24 Hugh McKinnon to deputy attorney general, 27 January 1882.
25 Judge Robert P. Jellett to deputy attorney general, 18 January 1882.
26 Sheriff James Gillespie to deputy attorney general, 19 January 1882.
27 Chief Constable H.N. Babbitt to deputy attorney general, 20 January 1882.
28 See chapter 4.
29 Systemic change at the provincial level was still years away. It was not
    until 1896 that county councils were required to appoint and pay a chief
    constable, and not until 1909 that the Ontario Provincial Police came into
    being: Romney, *Mr Attorney* 239.
30 W.F. Boys, *A Practical Treatise on the Office and Duties of Coroners in Ontario*,
    2nd ed. (Toronto: Hart & Rawlinson, 1878) 123.
31 *R. v. Gavin* (1885) 15 Cox 656 at 657; David Bentley, *English Criminal Justice
    in the Nineteenth Century* (London: Hambeldon Press, 1998) 230–5.
32 Bentley, *English Criminal Justice* 230–5.

4: A Place Apart

1 *Intelligencer*, 24 December 1883.
2 *Pioneer Life on the Bay of Quinte* (1904; repr. Belleville: Mika Silk Screening
   Ltd, 1972) 978–83.
3 Nick and Helma Mika, *The Settlement of Prince Edward County* (Belleville:
   Mika Publishing Co., 1984).
4 *Intelligencer*, 24 December 1883.
5 Trenton *Courier Advocate*, 27 December 1883.
6 *Intelligencer*, 24 December 1883.
7 Arthur Meighen used the phrase 'a place apart' as a metaphor for the independence of the judiciary: see Martin L. Friedland, *A Place Apart: Judicial
   Independence and Accountability in Canada* (Ottawa: Canadian Judicial Council, 1995) xiii.
8 Richard and Janet Lunn, *The County* (Picton: Picton Gazette, 1972) 303.
9 *Illustrated Historical Atlas of the Counties of Hastings and Prince Edward* (Toronto: H. Beldon & Co., 1878; reproduced Belleville: Mika Silk Screening
   Ltd, 1972) xii.
10 Lunn, *The County* 335–7.
11 Ibid. 178.
12 *Illustrated Historical Atlas* xii.
13 Ibid. xv.
14 Donald Creighton, *John A. Macdonald: The Young Politician* (Toronto: Mac-
    millan, 1952) 31.

15 A copy of the entry in the court records is in PECA, Walmsley Papers, box 5-4.
16 David Taylor, *History of the County of Prince Edward Courthouse and Gaol* (Picton: Prince Edward Historical Society, 1992); David Warwick, 'John A. Macdonald's First Recorded Trial in 1834 Upper Canada: Old World Privilege versus New World Ideals' (2010 draft article for future publication).
17 Alan Capon, 'Sir John No Stranger to the County,' *County Weekly News*, 20 October 2000.
18 Supplement to the Picton *Gazette*, c. 1861.
19 Lunn, *The County* 390.
20 J.K. Johnson, *The Canadian Directory of Parliament 1867–1967* (Ottawa: Public Archives of Canada, 1968).
21 Picton Jail Register, AO, RG 20, vol. 1-C F-33 (Oct. 1876 – Oct. 1907).
22 'Criminal Statistics' (1877) 13 *Canada Law Journal* n.s., 265.
23 Alan R. Capon and Margaret E. Haylock, *More Stories of Prince Edward County* (Belleville: Mika, 1982) 9–13.
24 *Intelligencer*, 18 May 1880.
25 *Intelligencer*, 21 May 1880.
26 Letters from Deputy Attorney General J.G. Scott, Judge Robert P. Jellett, Sheriff James Gillespie, and Chief Constable H.N. Babbitt, Ontario Sessional Papers (no. 91), 1884.

5: Coroner's Inquest

1 Coroner's Act, R.S.O. 1877, c. 79.
2 Myles Leslie, 'Reforming the Coroner: Death Investigation Manuals in Ontario 1863–1894' (2008) *Ontario History* vol. C, no. 2, 221.
3 W.F. Boys, *A Practical Treatise on the Office and Duties of Coroners in Ontario*, 2nd ed. (Toronto: Hart & Rawlinson, 1878) 3. The evolution in the late nineteenth century of the role of the coroner from a local investigative function and 'escape valve for village gossip' to a centrally controlled 'prefilter for the provincial justice system' is considered by Leslie, 'Reforming the Coroner.'
4 Ibid. 4.
5 John A. Kains, *'How Say You?' A Review of the Grand Jury Question* (St Thomas: The Journal, 1893) 58.
6 Coroner's Act.
7 Boys, *A Practical Treatise* 112. The quotations that follow are on pp. 120–7.

8 John Iddington to Deputy Attorney General J.G. Scott, 18 January 1882, Ontario Sessional Papers (no. 91), 1884.
9 *Intelligencer*, 24 December 1883.
10 Trial transcript.
11 *Intelligencer*, 24 December 1883.
12 Boys, *A Practical Treatise* 142.
13 Ibid. 105.
14 *Intelligencer*, 24 December 1883.
15 Ibid.
16 Trenton *Courier Advocate*, 23 December 1883.

6: Committal Proceedings

1 David Bentley, *English Criminal Justice in the Nineteenth Century* (London: Hambeldon Press, 1998) ch. 3.
2 *Illustrated Historical Atlas of the Counties of Hastings and Prince Edward* (Toronto: H. Beldon & Co., 1878; reproduced Belleville: Mika Silk Screening Ltd, 1972) xxii.
3 'Phillip Low,' Law Society of Upper Canada Past Member Database, Law Society of Upper Canada Archives.
4 Crown Attorneys Act, S.C. 1857, 20 Vict., c. 59. See Paul Romney, *Mr Attorney: The Attorney General for Ontario in Court, Cabinet, and Legislature, 1791–1899* (Toronto: Osgoode Society and University of Toronto Press, 1986) 214–31.
5 Romney, *Mr Attorney* 214–15.
6 *Intelligencer*, 28 December 1883.
7 Justices – Indictable Offences Act, (1869) S.C. 32–33 Vict., c. 30, s. 54.
8 Judith Farbey and R.J. Sharpe, *The Law of Habeas Corpus*, 3rd ed. (Oxford: Oxford University Press, 2011) 150.
9 Justices – Indictable Offences Act, s. 35.
10 Arthur Garratt Dorland, *Former Days & Quaker Ways* (Belleville: Mika Studio, 1972) 5–6.
11 *Dorland v. Jones* (1884), 7 O.R. 17.
12 *Dorland v. Jones* (1886), 12 O.A.R. 543.
13 *Jones v. Dorland* (1887), 14 S.C.R. 39.
14 *Intelligencer*, 29 December 1883.
15 Ibid.
16 Ibid.
17 *Intelligencer*, 10 January 1884 contains only a very brief report suggesting that no evidence of significance was presented at this point.

7: Picton Spring Assizes, 1884

1 Biographical details from 'Obituary: Mr. Justice Patterson' (1893) 29 *Canada Law Journal* 500; *The Supreme Court of Canada and Its Justices* (Ottawa: Supreme Court of Canada, 2000) 84; and John Charles Dent, *The Canadian Portrait Gallery*, vol. 4 (Toronto: John B. Magurn, 1881).
2 'Obituary.'
3 'Law Reform Commission' (1871) 7 *Canada Law Journal* 232.
4 For the details of the establishment of the Court of Error and Appeal, see Margaret Banks, 'The Evolution of the Ontario Courts 1788 to 1981,' in David H. Flaherty, ed., *Essays in the History of Canadian Law*, vol. 2 (Toronto: The Osgoode Society, 1983) 515.
5 See chapter 1, note 3.
6 'Judicial Salaries' (1887) 23 *Canada Law Journal* 62.
7 'Judicial Salaries' (1883) 19 *Canada Law Journal* 183.
8 Justice Patterson Bench Books, AO, RG 22-479-3-6, box 4.
9 *Intelligencer*, 8 May 1884.
10 Marion MacRae and Anthony Adamson, *Cornerstones of Order: Courthouses and Town Halls of Ontario, 1784–1914* (Toronto: Osgoode Society, 1983); David Taylor, *History of the County of Prince Edward Courthouse and Gaol* (Picton: Prince Edward Historical Society, 1992).
11 I am indebted to Justice Richard Byers for this information.
12 Picton *Gazette*, undated clipping, PECA.
13 *British Whig*, 10 June 1884.
14 See chapter 6.
15 W.S. Herrington, 'Sir Glenholme Falconbridge, C.J.K.B.' (1925) 3 *Canadian Bar Review* 229.
16 For discussion of this case, see Martin L. Friedland, *A Century of Criminal Justice: Perspectives on the Development of Canadian Law* (Toronto: Carswell, 1984) 242–5.
17 'Mr. Justice Clute' (1905) 25 *Canada Law Times* 164; Henry James Morgan, *The Canadian Men and Women of the Time* (Toronto: William Briggs, 1912) 243.
18 Mark Kadish, 'Behind the Locked Door of an American Grand Jury: Its History, Its Secrecy, and Its Process' (1996) 24 *Florida State University Law Review* 1; John A. Kains, *'How Say You?' A Review of the Grand Jury Question* (St Thomas: The Journal, 1893).
19 Patrick Brode, 'Grand Jury Addresses of the Early Canadian Judges in an Age of Reform' (1989) 23 *Law Society of Upper Canada Gazette* 130.
20 Mary Stokes, 'Grand Juries and "Proper Authorities": Low Law, Soft Law

and Local Government in Canada West/Ontario, 1850–1880,' at http://ssrn.com/abstract=1674089.

21 Peter Oliver, *Terror to Evil-Doers: Prisons and Punishment in Nineteenth-Century Ontario* (Toronto: Osgoode Society and University of Toronto Press, 1998) 320.

22 R. Blake Brown, *A Trying Question: The Jury in Nineteenth-Century Canada* (Toronto: Osgoode Society and University of Toronto Press, 2009) 206–10. See also Kains, *'How Say You?,'* focusing on the efforts of Senator James Robert Gowan, formerly a county court judge; Paul Romney, *Mr Attorney: The Attorney General for Ontario in Court, Cabinet, and Legislature, 1791–1899* (Toronto: Osgoode Society and University of Toronto Press, 1986) 298–311.

23 Quoted in Kains, *'How Say You?'* 11.

24 Brown, *A Trying Question* 209.

25 *Intelligencer*, 7 May 1884.

26 *Globe*, 7 May 1884.

27 *Daily Ontario*, 6 May 1884.

28 *Globe*, 7 May 1884.

29 *Daily Ontario*, 6 May 1884.

30 *Globe*, 7 May 1884.

31 The Consolidated Jurors Act (1883), S.O. 46 Vict., c. 7, s. 103.

32 Ibid. s. 3. The required property value was $600 for residents of cities.

33 Robert Sharpe and Patricia McMahon, *The Persons Case: The Origins and Legacy of the Fight for Legal Personhood* (Toronto: Osgoode Society and University of Toronto Press, 2007), chap. 3.

34 An Act Respecting Procedure in Criminal Cases (1869), S.C., 32–33 Vict., c. 29, s. 37.

35 Ibid. s. 38.

36 PECA, Walmsley Papers, box 5, item 9.d.

37 *Daily Ontario*, 7 May 1884.

38 *R. v. Dowling* and *R. v. Lacey* (1848), 3 Cox 509 and 517; David Bentley, *English Criminal Justice in the Nineteenth Century* (London: Hambeldon Press, 1998) 95.

39 See, e.g., the description of jury selection in Jim Phillips and Rosemary Gartner, *Murdering Holiness: The Trials of Franz Creffield and George Mitchell* (Vancouver: UBC Press, 2003) 141–54, and Martin L. Friedland, *The Death of Old Man Rice: A True Story of Criminal Justice in America* (Toronto: University of Toronto Press, 1994) 130–3.

40 See *R. v. Sherratt*, [1991] 1 S.C.R. 509 at para. 66, allowing for challenges for cause where 'the particular publicity and notoriety of the accused

could potentially have the effect of destroying the prospective juror's indifference.'

41 *R. v. Williams*, [1998] 1 S.C.R. 1128.

42 The members of the jury were: W.R. Babcock, yeoman from Ameliasburg, Wm. H. Kinnear, yeoman from Ameliasburg, Stephen N. Seeds, clerk from Picton, Jas. N. Wright, Mark R. Burlingham, grocer from Picton, Jonathan Clark, yeoman from Hallowell, J.H.W. Bedford, dentist from Picton, Albert Huff, yeoman from Ameliasburg, Thos. E. Wright, yeoman from North Marysburg, David J. Barker, yeoman from Picton, Charles Pettingill, yeoman from Hillier, and J.W. Fegan, merchant from South Marysburg.

43 Act Respecting Procedure in Criminal Cases, s. 57.

44 Justice Patterson's Bench Books, AO, RG 22-479-3-6, box 4.

45 PECA, Walmsley Papers, box 5.

46 The opening address was not transcribed. The following is based on a report in the Picton *Gazette*, undated clipping, PECA.

47 See George W. Burbidge, *A Digest of the Criminal Law of Canada* (Toronto: Carswell, 1890) 44. The current law of parties to offences is more restrictive: Criminal Code, s. 21(2): 'Where two or more persons form an intention in common to carry out an unlawful purpose and to assist each other therein and any one of them, in carrying out the common purpose, commits an offence, each of them who knew or ought to have known that the commission of the offence would be a probable consequence of carrying out the common purpose is a party to that offence.' In *R. v. Logan*, [1990] 2 S.C.R. 731; *R. v. Rodney*, [1990] 2 S.C.R. 687, the Supreme Court of Canada held that on a charge of attempted murder or murder, the words 'or ought to have known' are inoperative, as they are inconsistent with the minimum degree of *mens rea* (intention) required for the offences by s. 7 of the Charter of Rights and Freedoms.

48 See Christopher Moore, *McCarthy Tétrault: Building Canada's Premier Law Firm 1855–2005* (Vancouver: Douglas & McIntyre, 2005) 13–40; Larry L. Kulisek, 'McCarthy, D'Alton,' in *Dictionary of Canadian Biography Online*; J.R. Miller, '"As a Politician He Is a Great Enigma": The Social and Political Ideas of D'Alton McCarthy' (1977) 58 *Canadian Historical Review* 399.

49 'D'Alton McCarthy Jr.,' Law Society of Upper Canada Past Member Database, Law Society of Upper Canada Archives.

50 Quoted in Moore, *McCarthy Tétrault* 32.

51 See *Citizens Insurance Company v. Parsons* (1881–2), 7 App. Cas. 96; *St. Catherine's Milling and Lumber Co. v. The Queen* (1888), 14 App. Cas. 46; *Barrett v. City of Winnipeg* (1892), A.C. 445; *Hodge v. The Queen* (1883), 9 App. Cas. 117.

52 Miller, '"As a Politician He Is a Great Enigma"' 421.
53 Moore, *McCarthy Tétrault* 31.
54 Miller, '"As a Politician He Is a Great Enigma"' 402, quoting *Canadian Law Times*, June 1898, 134.
55 Edward J. Noble, 'D'Alton Who?' *Canadian Lawyer*, April 1982, 12.
56 Miller, '"As a Politician He Is a Great Enigma"' 409.
57 *Intelligencer*, 8 May 1884.
58 *Intelligencer*, 7 May 1884.
59 Ibid.
60 *Intelligencer*, 8 May 1884.
61 *Gazette*, undated clipping.
62 Ibid.
63 Justice Patterson Bench Books, AO, RG 22-479-3-6, box 4.
64 *Intelligencer*, 8 May 1884; *Globe*, 9 May 1884.

8: Surprise Evidence

1 *Gazette*, undated clipping, PECA.
2 David Bentley, *English Criminal Justice in the Nineteenth Century* (London: Hambeldon Press, 1998), 40 and 300
3 *R. v. Stinchcombe*, [1991] 3 S.C.R. 326.
4 Ibid., 332.
5 *Gazette*, 9 May 1884.
6 Ibid.
7 Justice Patterson Bench Books, AO, RG 22-479-3-6, box 4.

9: The Defence

1 'Testimony of Persons Accused of Crime' (1867) 3 *Upper Canada Law Journal* n.s. 88.
2 Geoffry Gilbert, *Evidence*, 6th ed. (London: W. Clarke, 1756) 106.
3 'The Law of Evidence' (1868) 4 *Canada Law Journal* n.s. 82.
4 'Testimony of Persons Accused of Crime,' 91.
5 'Every Prisoner His Own Witness' (1886) 22 *Canada Law Journal* n.s. 177.
6 Prisoners' Counsel Act 1836, R.S.U.C. Wm. IV c. 44.
7 David Bentley, *English Criminal Justice in the Nineteenth Century* (London: Hambeldon Press, 1998) 156–9.
8 Ibid. 176–82.
9 Travers Humphries, *Criminal Days: Recollections and Reflections* (London: Hodder, 1946) 45.

10 The debate was closely followed in Canada: see 'Testimony of Parties in Criminal Prosecutions' (1866) 2 *Upper Canada Law Journal* n.s. 60; 'Testimony of Defendants in Criminal Prosecutions,' ibid. 286; 'Testimony of Persons Accused of Crime' (above); 'Testimony of Parties in Criminal Prosecutions' (1867) 3 *Upper Canada Law Journal* n.s. 120; 'Statements of Prisoners through Counsel' (1884) 20 *Canada Law Journal* n.s. 20; 'Statements by Prisoners and Their Counsel' ibid. 53; 'Statements by Prisoners' Counsel' ibid. 141.

11 Criminal Procedure Act, R.S.C. 1886, c. 174, s. 216.

12 Canada Evidence Act, 1893, S.C. 1893, c. 31.

13 Criminal Evidence Act, 1898 (U.K.).

14 *Gazette*, 10 May 1884.

15 *Intelligencer*, 9 May 1884.

16 See chapter 14.

17 *R. v. Whitehouse*, [1941] 1 D.L.R. 683 (B.C.C.A.).

18 *Gazette*, 10 May 1884.

19 Ibid.

10: Verdict

1 *Gazette*, 10 May 1884.

2 *Intelligencer*, 12 May 1884.

3 *Gazette*, 10 May 1884.

4 Ibid.

5 The court reporter did not transcribe the closing arguments, and what follows is based upon reports of the proceedings in *Intelligencer*, 10 May 1884; *Gazette*, 10 May 1884; and *Daily Ontario*, 10 May 1884.

6 Justice Patterson Bench Books, AO, RG 22-479-3-6, box 4.

7 *Intelligencer*, 12 May 1884.

8 Ibid.

9 *Gazette*, 10 May 1884.

10 *Globe*, 12 May 1884.

11 As with counsel's closing addresses, the judge's jury charge was not transcribed. What follows is drawn from the same newspaper reports used as the source for the closing arguments of counsel.

12 This would not be required today. The Crown is not required to specify the nature of an accused's participation in the offence and the jury can convict even if they find that the crime was accomplished in a manner other than that advanced as the theory of the Crown at trial: *R. v. Thatcher*, [1987] 1 S.C.R. 652; *R. v. Pickton* 2010 SCC 32.

13 (1838), 2 Lewin 227, 168 E.R. 1136.

14 The Canadian courts followed *Hodge's case* until the decision in *R. v. Cooper*, [1978] 1 S.C.R. 860 held that such a direction was no longer mandatory. See also *R. v. Griffin*, [2009] 2 S.C.R. 42 and Benjamin Berger, 'The Rule in Hodge's Case: Rumours of Its Death Are Greatly Exaggerated' (2005) 84 *Canadian Bar Review* 47.

15 David Bentley, *English Criminal Justice in the Nineteenth Century* (London: Hambeldon Press, 1998) 74, 274–5.

16 James Fitzjames Stephen, *A History of the Criminal Law of England*, vol. 1 (London: Macmillan, 1883) 455–6.

17 *Globe*, 13 May 1884.

18 Ken Leyton-Brown, *The Practice of Execution in Canada* (Vancouver: UBC Press, 2010) 22 suggests that it was 'common knowledge' that juries did not like to see two or more people hang where there was only one victim.

19 'Flotsam and Jetsam' (1878) 14 *Canada Law Journal* 277; Leyton-Brown, *The Practice of Execution in Canada* 25.

20 PECA, Walmsley Papers, AR 983.006.005(9).

21 *Intelligencer*, 12 May 1884.

22 *Gazette*, 10 May 1884.

11: Last Hope

1 James Fitzjames Stephen, *A History of the Criminal Law of England*, vol. 1 (London: Macmillan, 1883) 308–18.

2 Ibid. 312. In 1868, the writ of error was apparently still available in Canada but said to be 'rather out of the common': 'Criminal Procedure' (1868) 4 *Canada Law Journal* n.s. 274.

3 David Bentley, *English Criminal Justice in the Nineteenth Century* (London: Hambeldon Press, 1998) 283; Vincent M. Del Buono, 'The Right to Appeal in Indictable Cases: A Legislative History' (1978) 16 *Alberta Law Review* 446; C.H. O'Halloran, 'Development of the Right of Appeal in England in Criminal Cases' (1949) 27 *Canadian Bar Review* 153; *R. v. E.(A.W.)*, [1993] 3 S.C.R. 155.

4 The Criminal Procedure Act 1869, S.C. 32–33 Vict., c. 29, s. 80. That provision repealed a right of appeal that had been given by An Act to extend the right of Appeal in Criminal Cases in Upper Canada 1857, S.C. 20 Vict., c. 41.

5 Bentley, *English Criminal Justice* 284.

6 O'Halloran, 'Development of the Right of Appeal' 153.

7 See Bentley, *English Criminal Justice* 282–96; Benjamin Berger, 'Criminal

Appeals as Jury Control: An Anglo-Canadian Historical Perspective on the Rise of Criminal Appeals' (2006) 10 *Canadian Criminal Law Review* 1.

8 See below, note 12.

9 Bentley, *English Criminal Justice* 286.

10 R. Blake Brown, *A Trying Question: The Jury in Nineteenth-Century Canada* (Toronto: Osgoode Society and University of Toronto Press, 2009).

11 See, e.g., testimony of the Rt. Hon. S.H. Walpole, *Royal Commission on Capital Punishment together with the minutes of evidence and appendix* (Parliamentary Papers, Session 1866, vol. 21), 485, advising against appeals and referring to the view that there were no cases, 'or if there were any there were very few cases indeed in which a man had been wrongly convicted upon questions of fact. The real difficulty in courts of law which justified appeals was in cases with regard to property, and not in cases with regard to crime.' See also the conclusion reached by the *Report of the Joint Committee of the Senate and House of Commons on Capital Punishment*, 27 June 1956, 15, discussed below in chapter 13.

12 Adolf Beck Inquiry Report Parliamentary Papers, 1905 (Cmnd 2315), and the case of George Edalji, which is the subject of Julian Barnes, *Arthur and George* (London: Cape, 2005).

13 See Desmond Brown, *The Genesis of the Canadian Criminal Code of 1892* (Toronto: Osgoode Society and University of Toronto Press, 1989).

14 The rights of appeal conferred by the 1892 Code are discussed by Berger, 'Criminal Appeals as Jury Control' 35–40.

15 S.C. 1923, c. 23.

16 In cases where no transcript was available, the trial judge's report constituted the record of the case for further consideration: *R. v. E.(A.W.)*, [1993] 3 S.C.R. 155.

17 The process of review is discussed in Jonathan Swainger, *The Canadian Department of Justice and the Completion of Confederation, 1876–78* (Vancouver: UBC Press, 2000) chap. 4; Carolyn Strange, ed., *Qualities of Mercy: Justice, Punishment, and Discretion* (Vancouver: UBC Press, 1996); Carolyn Strange, 'The Lottery of Death: Capital Punishment, 1867–1976' (1996) 23 *Manitoba Law Journal* 594; Carolyn Strange, 'Mercy for Murders: An Historical Perspective on the Royal Prerogative of Mercy' (2001) 64 *Saskatchewan Law Review* 559; and Martin L. Friedland, *The Case of Valentine Shortis: A True Story of Crime and Politics in Canada* (Toronto: Osgoode Society and University of Toronto Press, 1986) 119–63.

18 Registrar, Court of Appeal to Secretary of State, 22 May 1884, CCF.

19 Women convicted of capital crimes benefited from gender discrimination. Of 58 women condemned to death only 12, or just over 20%, were hanged: statistics derived from Lorraine Gadoury and Antonio Lechasseur, *Persons*

Sentenced to Death in Canada: 1867–1976. An Inventory of the Case Files in the Fonds of the Department of Justice (Ottawa: National Archives of Canada, 1994) 26. For consideration of gender issues, see F. Murray Greenwood and Beverly Boissery, *Uncertain Justice: Canadian Women and Capital Punishment, 1754–1953* (Toronto: Osgoode Society and Dundurn Press, 2000); Aritha Van Herk, 'Driving towards Death,' in Elspeth Cameron and Janice Dickin, eds, *Great Dames* (Toronto: University of Toronto Press, 1997); Tom Mitchell, '"Blood with the Taint of Cain": Labouring Children, Manitoba Politics, and the Execution of Hilda Blake' (1993–4) 28 *Journal of Canadian Studies* 49; Scott M. Garfield, 'Justice Not Done: The Hanging of Elizabeth Workman' (2005) 20 *Canadian Journal of Law and Society* 171; Reinhold Kramer and Tom Mitchell, *Walk toward the Gallows: The Tragedy of Hilda Blake, Hanged 1899* (Toronto: Oxford, 2002).

20 See Tina Loo, 'Savage Mercy: Native Culture and the Modification of Capital Punishment in Nineteenth Century British Columbia,' in Strange, ed., *Qualities of Mercy*. A good example is an 1884 British Columbia case (Haatq (Aht), LAC, RG 13, vol. 1421, file 190A), where the white victim had violated a tribal custom and knew of the reaction that could provoke. The trial judge wrote that he 'could not allow these considerations to go to a jury, but it would be very unwise for the pardoning power not to consider the matter' (Henry Creasy to Secretary of State, 15 December 1884), and the sentence was commuted to one of ten years' imprisonment.

21 In two other 1884 British Columbia murder cases involving aboriginals, racism worked against the accused: see William Robertson, LAC, RG 13, vol. 1419, file 177A. The trial judge had no sympathy with the jury's recommendation for mercy in a case involving a man he described as a 'half-breed' and of 'weak intellect,' and pointed out that there had been several unsolved murders in which 'probably Indians have been involved.' See also Edward Lemon (Lamont), LAC, RG 13, vol. 1420, file 182A, where British Columbia's Chief Justice Begbie reported that had the accused been a white man he would have expected a manslaughter verdict. 'I think that the evidence scarcely justifies the verdict. It was a very bad case of manslaughter ... I believe that sometimes juries will not convict white men of wilful murder in cases where they would convict Indians.' However, the local Indian agent wrote: 'There is a strong feeling amongst the Indians of the coast that Indians are always hung for the crime of murder but others get acquitted by the juries.' The European settlers wanted a hanging 'as a warning to the very lawless class of half breeds of whom there are so many on this coast,' and who felt that if the condemned man were pardoned, 'some natives it is feared will go back to their old customs and take a life for a life having very little regard as to whether the person they kill

is the guilty one or not' (W.H. Lomas to G.W. Powell, 17 April 1884). The cabinet refused to interfere and the death sentence was carried out.

22 The lack of clear and consistent standards is revealed by a report of Deputy Minister of Justice George Burbidge to Justice Minister Alexander Campbell stating that his predecessor had told him that 'in practice it had always been considered that a sentence from I think ten or twelve years to twenty years according to the nature of the case was considered equivalent to a life term and that some time between those limits life terms are usu-ally commuted.' He added that he had tried to look into how other coun-tries handled these matters, but with little or no success. 'Sometime when I have more time I will pursue that matter further as it is most desirable that we should have well established rules.' William H. Greaves, LAC, RG 13, vol. 1413, file 93A (1874–87), Memorandum, Geo. W. Burbidge to Camp-bell, 21 February 1885.

23 Strange, 'The Lottery of Death.'

24 These statistics are derived from Gadoury and Lechasseur, *Persons Sen-tenced to Death in Canada*. For case descriptions of capital cases resulting in hangings from 1867 to 1923, see Jeffery Pfeifer and Ken Leyton-Brown, *Death by Rope: An Anthology of Canadian Executions* (Regina: Centax Books, 2007).

25 *Capital Punishment: Material Relating to Its Purpose and Value* (Ottawa: Queen's Printer, 1965) 98.

26 The following biographical details are taken from Donald Swainson, 'Alexander Campbell,' in *Dictionary of Canadian Biography Online*.

27 1 June 1881, vol. 17, no. 11.

28 Ibid.

29 The following table shows commutations per minister of justice in murder convictions from Confederation to 1884. The figures for ministers of justice preceding Campbell are taken from Swainger, *The Canadian Department of Justice* 66, and the figures for Campbell are based on the information con-tained in Gadoury and Lechasseur, *Persons Sentenced to Death in Canada*.

Minister	Total cases	Number commuted	Percentage
Macdonald	36	16	44.4
Dorion	7	2	28.6
Fournier	14	12	85.7
Blake	20	12	60
Laflamme	8	6	75
Total of above	85	48	56.5
Campbell	38	15*	39.5

*No record of commutation or execution in 1 case.

30 Gadoury and Lechasseur, *Persons Sentenced to Death in Canada*.

31 LAC: William H. Greaves, RG 13, vol. 1413, file 93A (1874–87); Henry Russell Greenwood, RG 13, vol. 1419, file 175A (1883–91); Henry Hardinge, RG 13, vol. 1419, file 176A (1883–91); Austin Humphrey, RG 13, vol. 1415, file 117A (1877); John Josey, RG 13, vol. 1413, file 88A (1875); Mathias Konkle, RG 13, vol. 1413, file 87A (1875–6); George Lowder, RG 13, vol. 1420, file 184A (1884); Charles Mairand, RG 13, vol. 1413, file 91A (1875); James Ryan, RG 13, vol. 1415, file 113A (1876–8); Eric Benzel Sparham, RG 13, vol. 1413, file 92A (1874–80); Joseph Thomset, RG 13, vol. 1420, file 183A (1884).

32 LAC: Eusébie Boutet (Tremblay), RG 13, vol. 1420, file 185A (1884–98); Francis Bowie, RG 13, vol. 1420, file 186A (1884–8); Haatq (Aht), RG 13, vol. 1421, file 190A (1884–5); Edward Lemon (Lamont), RG 13, vol. 1420, file 182A (1884); Luke Phipps, RG 13, vol. 1420, file 181A (1884); William Robert Robertson, RG 13, vol. 1419, file 177A (1883–4); Charles Joseph Rogers, RG 13, vol. 1420, file 188A (1885); Cook Teets, RG 13, vol. 1420, file 187A (1884); Jess Williams, RG 13, vol. 1420, file 180A (1884); Sulwhalem, (alias Jim), RG 13, vol. 1420, file 189A (1885).

33 See Eric Benzel Sparham and William H. Greaves, note 31.

34 See George W. Burbidge, *A Digest of the Criminal Law of Canada* (Toronto: Carswell, 1890) 216–17. In *R. v. Vaillancourt*, [1987] 2 S.C.R. 636 and *R. v. Martineau*, [1990] 2 S.C.R. 636, the Supreme Court of Canada struck down the 'constructive murder' provisions of the Criminal Code, derived from the felony-murder rule, as a violation of the minimum level of fault required for murder, as guaranteed by the Charter of Rights and Freedoms, s. 7.

35 One involved the admissibility of two statements from the victim that tied the accused men to her death as falling under the 'dying declaration' exception to the rule against hearsay. The second point of law was whether the Crown had properly been allowed to call reply evidence of the precautions taken by the physician attending Burnham's brother to avoid spreading smallpox. The court concluded that Burnham's statements and the Crown's reply evidence had been properly admitted: *R. v. Sparham and Greaves* (1875), 25 U.C.C.P. 143.

36 Patterson to Secretary of State, 3 June 1875, see Sparham and Greaves, note 31.

37 Report of T. Fournier, 9 June 1875, ibid.

38 Efforts to secure Dr Sparham's release continued. In 1876, a book was published outlining his defence to the charge and pleading his innocence: *A Defence of Dr. Eric Benzel Sparham* (Brockville: Leavitt and Southworth

Printers, 1876). From his cell in Kingston Penitentiary, Sparham continued to write letters to Prime Minister Sir John A. Macdonald and Justice Minister Sir Charles Tupper protesting his innocence. In 1880, Justice Patterson was asked to review the matter once again. Patterson characteristically approached the case from a strictly legal perspective: Patterson to the Minister of Justice, 17 February 1880, see Sparham and Greaves, note 31. He refused to question the propriety of the conviction, but allowed that the circumstances might affect the sentence and added that at the time of the trial he was satisfied with the verdict. Again, the Department of Justice recommended no further clemency. Sparham, said by the prison doctor to be in a constant state of depression, was finally released in November 1882 after serving a little over seven years of his life sentence.

39 See note 31.
40 Report of T. Fournier, 10 June 1875, see Charles and Mairand, note 31.
41 Report of Dr Joseph Monkman and Dr John Dickson, 28 May 1875, ibid.
42 Report of T. Fournier, 10 June 1875, ibid.
43 John Josey and James Ryan, see note 31.
44 Ibid.
45 See *D.P.P. v. Beard*, [1920] A.C. 479 for discussion of the evolution of the consideration of drunkenness as a factor reducing murder to manslaughter and *R. v. Robinson*, [1996] 1 S.C.R. 683 for the post-Charter law on the consideration of the evidence of drunkenness in murder cases.
46 Patterson to Secretary of State, 6 November 1876, see Ryan, note 31.
47 Ibid.
48 Patterson to Secretary of State, 20 April 1875, see Mathias Konkle, note 31.
49 Undated note to Justice Burton signed by the twelve jurors. Ibid.
50 Patterson to Secretary of State, 13 January 1876, ibid.
51 Burton to Secretary of State, 22 January 1876, ibid.
52 Report, 26 January 1876, approved by Lord Dufferin 29 January 1876, ibid.
53 Ibid.
54 S. White to Alexander Campbell, 29 October 1883. Henry Hardinge, see note 31.
55 Cameron to Geo. Burbidge, Deputy Minister of Justice, 7 November 1883. Ibid.
56 Cameron to Campbell, 19 November 1883, ibid.
57 Patterson to Campbell, 4 December 1883, ibid.
58 Cameron to Hardinge, 12 August 1886, ibid.
59 Report, 24 January 1890, ibid.
60 Patterson to Secretary of State, 12 May 1884, CCF.

12: Pleas for Mercy

1 *British Whig*, [n.d.] June 1884.
2 Act Respecting Procedure in Criminal Cases (1869), S.C. 32–33 Vict., c. 29, s. 108.
3 Richard and Janet Lunn, *The County* (Picton: Picton Gazette,1972) 187–8.
4 Alan R. Capon, *A Goodly Heritage* (Picton: Church of St Mary Magdalene, c. 1980) 85.
5 *Intelligencer*, 10 June 1884.
6 Undated petition, CCF.
7 *Daily Ontario*, 31 May 1884; Capon, *A Goodly Heritage* 52.
8 Merrill to Macdonald, n.d., CCF.
9 Macdonald to Campbell, n.d., CCF.
10 Coulthard and Loucks to A. Campbell, 5 June 1884, CCF.
11 Ibid.
12 Act Respecting Procedure in Criminal Cases, s. 107.
13 *British Whig*, [n.d.] June 1884.
14 *Daily Ontario*, 22 May 1884.
15 *Daily Ontario*, 5 June 1884.
16 Landsdowne to Campbell, 6 June 1884, CCF.
17 Order, 6 June 1884, CCF.
18 G. Powell to Loucks, 9 June 1884, CCF.
19 G. Powell to Sheriff, 9 June 1884, CCF.
20 *British Whig*, [n.d.] June 1884.
21 McQuaig to Campbell, 9 June 1884, CCF.
22 J.S. McQuaig to Campbell, 9 June 1884, CCF.
23 Campbell to Coulthard, 9 June 1884, CCF.
24 Coulthard to Campbell, 9 June 1884 CCF.
25 *Daily Ontario*, 10 June 1884.
26 Ibid.
27 Ibid.
28 Campbell to Coulthard, 10 June 1884, CCF.
29 *Daily Ontario*, 10 June 1884.

13: The Day of Execution Approaches

1 Gilbert to Minister of Justice, n.d., CCF.
2 Act Respecting Procedure in Criminal Cases (1869), S.C. 32–33 Vict., c. 29, s. 117. Ken Leyton-Brown, *The Practice of Execution in Canada* (Vancouver: UBC Press, 2010) 136–8 discusses how this was applied. The provision was

changed with the 1892 Criminal Code, s. 945, which gave the lieutenant governor a general discretion to allow for burial outside the prison walls.

3 *Intelligencer*, 10 June 1884.

4 *Daily Ontario*, 10 June 1884.

5 *Globe*, 10 June 1884.

6 *Intelligencer*, 10 June 1884.

7 As reported in the *British Whig*, 31 May 1884.

8 *Daily Ontario*, 10 June 1884.

9 What follows is based on reports from the *British Whig*, 11 June 1884, and the *Daily Ontario*, 10 June 1884.

10 Leyton-Brown, *The Practice of Execution in Canada* 104–17; Frank W. Anderson, *A Concise History of Capital Punishment in Canada* (Calgary: Frontier Publishing, 1973) 27; John Melady, *Double Trap: The Last Public Hanging in Canada* (Dundurn: Toronto, 2005) describes a public execution in Goderich, Ontario, watched by some 300 people.

11 *Daily Ontario*, 10 June 1884.

12 PECA, Walmsley Papers, box 5, items 9f and 9h.

13 Jeffery Pfeifer and Ken Leyton-Brown, *Death by Rope: An Anthology of Canadian Executions* (Regina: Centax Books, 2007) 7; Leyton-Brown, *The Practice of Execution in Canada* 98. The *Report of the Joint Committee of the Senate and House of Commons on Capital Punishment*, Ottawa, 27 June 1956, rejected abolition of the death penalty, but recommended that hanging be replaced with electrocution: 'one of the principal objections to hanging was that so much depended upon the competence of the hangman, leaving a greater margin for error than in the case of execution by electrocution or the gas chamber' (21).

14 *Globe*, 12 June 1884; *Daily Ontario*, 11 June 1884.

15 *Daily Ontario*, 11 June 1884; *Globe*, 12 June 1884. There is a photocopy of a handwritten copy of the letter, likely in Thomset's hand, in the Taylor Papers, PECA, A1985.004.24d 16d.

16 PECA, Walmsley Papers, box 5, item 9 h.

17 PECA, Joseph Thomset and George Lowder, Death certificates.

18 12 June 1884.

19 *British Whig*, 11 June 1884.

20 Paul Romney, *Mr Attorney: The Attorney General for Ontario in Court, Cabinet, and Legislature 1791–1899* (Toronto: Osgoode Society and University of Toronto Press,1986) 204, referring to an unsuccessful bill in Upper Canada in 1823.

21 See Carolyn Strange, 'The Lottery of Death: Capital Punishment 1867–1976' (1996) 23 *Manitoba Law Journal* 594 at n. 20. One other man, Louis

Letendre, a Fenian, was convicted in 1871 of treason and sentenced to death, but the sentence was commuted: LAC, RG 13, vol. 1409, file 45A. Eight aboriginal participants in the Northwest Rebellion were hanged, but for murder, not treason: see Ted McCoy, 'Legal Ideology in the Aftermath of Rebellion: The Convicted First Nations Participants, 1885' (2009) 42 *Histoire Sociale/Social History* 175.

22 Herbert H. Haines, *Against Capital Punishment: The Anti-Death Penalty Movement in America, 1972–1994* (Oxford: Oxford United Press, 1996) 7–16.

23 Philadelphia: Philip Nicklin, 1819.

24 Beccaria, *An Essay on Crimes and Punishments* 104.

25 Ibid. 100.

26 Ibid. 99.

27 *Royal Commission on Capital Punishment* (Parliamentary papers, Session 1866, vol. 21) li.

28 See, e.g., 'The Report of the Capital Punishment Commission' (1866) 2 *Upper Canada Law Journal* 36; 'On the Report of the Capital Punishment Commissioners,' ibid. 147.

29 (1872) 53 *Canada Law Journal* 209.

30 David B. Chandler, *Capital Punishment in Canada: A Sociological Study of Repressive Law* (Toronto: McClelland and Stewart, 1976). The first significant abolition effort in Canada started with the efforts of Montreal Liberal MP Robert Bickerdike in 1914, and continued with Alberta Labour party MP William Irvine in the 1920s and Liberal MP Ross Thatcher in the 1950s. See also Frank W. Anderson, *A Concise History of Capital Punishment in Canada* (Calgary: Frontier Publishing, 1973) 78.

31 See Carolyn Strange, 'The Undercurrents of Penal Culture: Punishment of the Body in Mid-Twentieth Century Canada' (2001) 19 *Law and History Review* 343.

32 Robert J. Hoshowsky, *The Last to Die: Ronald Turpin, Arthur Lucas, and the End of Capital Punishment in Canada* (Toronto: Dundurn Press, 2007).

33 *Report of the Joint Committee* 15.

34 Ibid.

35 See Bruce MacFarlane, 'Convicting the Innocent: A Triple Failure of the Justice System' (2005–6) 31 *Manitoba Law Journal* 403; *Royal Commission on the Donald Marshall, Jr., Prosecution: Findings and Recommendations* (Halifax: The Commission, 1989); *Reference re Milgaard (Can.)*, [1992] 1 S.C.R. 866; *Report of the Commission on Proceedings Involving Guy Paul Morin* by the Honourable F. Kaufman (Toronto: Ontario Ministry of the Attorney General, 1998); *Inquiry Regarding Thomas Sophonow* by the Honourable Peter de-Carteret Cory (Winnipeg: Manitoba Justice, 2001); *The Lamer Commission of*

Inquiry into the Proceedings Pertaining to: Ronald Dalton, Gregory Parsons and Randy Drunken: Report and Annexes (St John's: Government of Newfoundland and Labrador, 2006); *Report of the Commission of Inquiry into Certain Aspects of the Trial and Conviction of James Driskell* (Winnipeg: Department of Justice, 2007); *Truscott (Re)* (2007), 225 C.C.C. (3d) 321 (Ont. C.A.); *R. v. Mullins-Johnson* (2007), 87 O.R. (3d) 425 (C.A.); *Inquiry into Pediatric Forensic Pathology in Ontario: Report* by the Honourable Stephen Goudge (Toronto: Ontario Ministry of the Attorney General, 2008); *R. v. Phillion* (2009), 241 C.C.C. (3d) 193 (Ont. C.A.); Sam Chaiton and Terry Swinton, *Lazarus and the Hurricane: The Untold Story of the Freeing of Rubin 'Hurricane' Carter* (Toronto: Viking, 1991).
36 *United States v. Burns*, [2001] 1 S.C.R. 283 at para. 1.
37 Ibid. at para. 117. Yet public opinion polls indicate a surprising level of support for capital punishment: 'Canadians take a fresh look at capital punishment,' *Globe and Mail*, 22 January 2010, A4.

14: Community Conscience

1 10 June 1884.
2 *British Whig*, [n.d.] June 1884.
3 Ibid. 11 June 1884.
4 *Globe*, 11 June 1888.
5 The classic example is the Dreyfus Affair in late-nineteenth-, early-twentieth-century France, on which there is a vast literature: see, e.g., Jean-Denis Bredin, *L'Affaire* (Paris: Julliard, 1983) translated as Jean-Denis Bredin, *The Affair: The Case of Alfred Dreyfus* (New York: George Braziller, 1986).
6 13 June 1888.
7 See David Taylor, 'New Light on the Peter Lazier Murder,' *County Magazine* 66 (Winter 1992) 18; Peter Lockyer, 'Walking Back in Time: Gallows and Graveyard Walking Tours,' *County and Quinte Living*, Summer 2009, 38; Alan Capon, 'Facts and Fiction about Picton's "Bungled Hanging of '84,"' in *Stories of Prince Edward* (Belleville: Mika Publishing, 1973); Steve Campbell, Janet Davies, and Ian Robertson, *Prince Edward County: An Illustrated History* (Bloomfield: County Magazine, 2009) 66–7; Alan Capon, 'Was the Wrong Man Hanged?' Kingston *Whig Standard*, 1 May 1973; Peter Lockyer, 'Justice or Vengeance? Picton's 1884 Double Hanging,' *Watershed: Life in Northumberland, Prince Edward County and Quinte* 10, no. 37 (Summer 2010); Alan Capon, 'Prince Edward County Courthouse Featured in History Exhibit,' Kingston *Whig Standard*, 16 September 1982.
8 *The County Weekly News*, 1 August 2008.

9 Arthur Garratt Dorland, *Former Days & Quaker Ways* (Belleville: Mika Studio, 1972) 73.

10 *New York Times*, 22 December 1884.

11 See chapter 9, note 17.

12 Dorland, *Former Days & Quaker Ways* 74.

13 See chapter 13, note 35.

14 Bruce MacFarlane, 'Convicting the Innocent: A Triple Failure of the Justice System' (2005–6) 31 *Manitoba Law Journal* 441.

15 See *Report of the Commission on Proceedings Involving Guy Paul Morin* by the Honourable F. Kaufman (Toronto: Ontario Ministry of the Attorney General, 1998); *Inquiry Regarding Thomas Sophonow* by the Honourable Peter deCarteret Cory (Winnipeg: Manitoba Justice, 2001).

16 Criminal Appeal Act, 1995, c. 35.

17 See *Inquiry into Pediatric Forensic Pathology in Ontario: Report* by the Honourable Stephen Goudge (Toronto: Ontario Ministry of the Attorney General, 2008); *R. v. Mullins-Johnson* (2007), 87 O.R. (3d) 425 (Ont. C.A.).

18 See *R. v. Phillion* (2009), 241 C.C.C. (3d) 193 (Ont. C.A.); *Inquiry Regarding Thomas Sophonow*.

19 MacFarlane, 'Convicting the Innocent' 470–2.

20 *British Whig*, 11 June 1884.

21 See chapter 7, note 47.

22 The Picton Jail register (AO, RG 20, vol. 1-C F-33) shows the following: William and Peter Loveless were acquitted of the murder of Leslie Church in November 1889 (discussed below); William Goodwin was charged with manslaughter in October 1890 (no disposition given); George Aulthouse was charged and convicted of manslaughter and sentenced to one year in October 1899; and Edward Clark was acquitted of murder in October 1903 (discussed below). In addition, Philip M. Kellar was charged with manslaughter in February 1898. That case ended when the grand jury returned 'no bill': see AO, RG 4-32, nos. 1132, 1903.

23 *Intelligencer*, 31 October 1888.

24 Christopher Moore, *McCarthy Tétrault: Building Canada's Premier Law Firm 1855–2005* (Vancouver: Douglas & McIntyre, 2005) 28.

25 *Intelligencer* and *Globe*, 31 October and 1 November 1888.

26 *Intelligencer*, 1 November 1888.

27 Carolyn Strange and Tina Loo, 'Spectacular Justice: The Circus on Trial, and the Trial as Circus, Picton, 1903' (1996) 77 *Canadian Historical Review* 159.

28 Clute to Cartwright, 23 October 1903, Department of the Attorney General, Central Registry Files, AO, RG 4-32, nos. 1132, 1903.

29 Strange and Loo, 'Spectacular Justice' 167.
30 Clute to Cartwright, 23 October 1903.
31 Brown to Cartwright, 22 October 1903, Department of the Attorney General, Central Registry Files, AO, RG 4-32, nos. 1132, 1903.
32 J.S. McQuaig to Minister of Justice, 19 June 1884, CCF.
33 The inscription spells George's last name 'Louder,' while the court documents spell it 'Lowder': see chapter 1, note 1.

Index

PUBLICATIONS OF THE OSGOODE SOCIETY FOR CANADIAN LEGAL HISTORY

2011 Robert J. Sharpe, *The Lazier Murder: Prince Edward County, 1884*
Philip Girard, *Lawyers and Legal Culture in British North America: Beamish Murdoch of Halifax*
John McLaren, *Dewigged, Bothered, and Bewildered: British Colonial Judges on Trial, 1800–1900*
Lesley Erickson, *Westward Bound: Sex, Violence, the Law, and the Making of a Settler Society*

2010 Judy Fudge and Eric Tucker, eds., *Work on Trial: Canadian Labour Law Struggles*
Christopher Moore, *The British Columbia Court of Appeal: The First Hundred Years*
Frederick Vaughan, *Viscount Haldane: 'The Wicked Step-father of the Canadian Constitution'*
Barrington Walker, *Race on Trial: Black Defendants in Ontario's Criminal Courts, 1858–1958*

2009 William Kaplan, *Canadian Maverick: The Life and Times of Ivan C. Rand*
R. Blake Brown, *A Trying Question: The Jury in Nineteenth-Century Canada*
Barry Wright and Susan Binnie, eds., *Canadian State Trials, Volume III: Political Trials and Security Measures, 1840–1914*
Robert J. Sharpe, *The Last Day, the Last Hour: The Currie Libel Trial* (paperback edition with a new preface)

2008 Constance Backhouse, *Carnal Crimes: Sexual Assault Law in Canada, 1900–1975*
Jim Phillips, R. Roy McMurtry, and John T. Saywell, eds., *Essays in the History of Canadian Law, Volume X: A Tribute to Peter N. Oliver*
Greg Taylor, *The Law of the Land: The Advent of the Torrens System in Canada*
Hamar Foster, Benjamin Berger, and A.R. Buck, eds., *The Grand Experiment: Law and Legal Culture in British Settler Societies*

2007 Robert Sharpe and Patricia McMahon, *The Persons Case: The Origins and Legacy of the Fight for Legal Personhood*
Lori Chambers, *Misconceptions: Unmarried Motherhood and the Ontario Children of Unmarried Parents Act, 1921–1969*
Jonathan Swainger, ed., *A History of the Supreme Court of Alberta*
Martin Friedland, *My Life in Crime and Other Academic Adventures*

2006 Donald Fyson, *Magistrates, Police, and People: Everyday Criminal Justice in Quebec and Lower Canada, 1764–1837*

Dale Brawn, *The Court of Queen's Bench of Manitoba, 1870–1950: A Biographical History*

R.C.B. Risk, *A History of Canadian Legal Thought: Collected Essays*, edited and introduced by G. Blaine Baker and Jim Phillips

2005 Philip Girard, *Bora Laskin: Bringing Law to Life*

Christopher English, ed., *Essays in the History of Canadian Law: Volume IX – Two Islands: Newfoundland and Prince Edward Island*

Fred Kaufman, *Searching for Justice: An Autobiography*

2004 Philip Girard, Jim Phillips, and Barry Cahill, eds., *The Supreme Court of Nova Scotia, 1754–2004: From Imperial Bastion to Provincial Oracle*

Frederick Vaughan, *Aggressive in Pursuit: The Life of Justice Emmett Hall*

John D. Honsberger, *Osgoode Hall: An Illustrated History*

Constance Backhouse and Nancy Backhouse, *The Heiress versus the Establishment: Mrs Campbell's Campaign for Legal Justice*

2003 Robert Sharpe and Kent Roach, *Brian Dickson: A Judge's Journey*

Jerry Bannister, *The Rule of the Admirals: Law, Custom, and Naval Government in Newfoundland, 1699–1832*

George Finlayson, *John J. Robinette, Peerless Mentor: An Appreciation*

Peter Oliver, *The Conventional Man: The Diaries of Ontario Chief Justice Robert A. Harrison, 1856–1878*

2002 John T. Saywell, *The Lawmakers: Judicial Power and the Shaping of Canadian Federalism*

Patrick Brode, *Courted and Abandoned: Seduction in Canadian Law*

David Murray, *Colonial Justice: Justice, Morality, and Crime in the Niagara District, 1791–1849*

F. Murray Greenwood and Barry Wright, eds., *Canadian State Trials, Volume II: Rebellion and Invasion in the Canadas, 1837–1839*

2001 Ellen Anderson, *Judging Bertha Wilson: Law as Large as Life*

Judy Fudge and Eric Tucker, *Labour before the Law: The Regulation of Workers' Collective Action in Canada, 1900–1948*

Laurel Sefton MacDowell, *Renegade Lawyer: The Life of J.L. Cohen*

2000 Barry Cahill, *'The Thousandth Man': A Biography of James McGregor Stewart*

A.B. McKillop, *The Spinster and the Prophet: Florence Deeks, H.G. Wells, and the Mystery of the Purloined Past*

Beverley Boissery and F. Murray Greenwood, *Uncertain Justice: Canadian Women and Capital Punishment*

Bruce Ziff, *Unforeseen Legacies: Reuben Wells Leonard and the Leonard Foundation Trust*

1999 Constance Backhouse, *Colour-Coded: A Legal History of Racism in Canada, 1900–1950*
G. Blaine Baker and Jim Phillips, eds., *Essays in the History of Canadian Law: Volume VIII – In Honour of R.C.B. Risk*
Richard W. Pound, *Chief Justice W.R. Jackett: By the Law of the Land*
David Vanek, *Fulfilment: Memoirs of a Criminal Court Judge*

1998 Sidney Harring, *White Man's Law: Native People in Nineteenth-Century Canadian Jurisprudence*
Peter Oliver, *'Terror to Evil-Doers': Prisons and Punishments in Nineteenth-Century Ontario*

1997 James W.St.G. Walker, *'Race,' Rights and the Law in the Supreme Court of Canada: Historical Case Studies*
Lori Chambers, *Married Women and Property Law in Victorian Ontario*
Patrick Brode, *Casual Slaughters and Accidental Judgments: Canadian War Crimes and Prosecutions, 1944–1948*
Ian Bushnell, *The Federal Court of Canada: A History, 1875–1992*

1996 Carol Wilton, ed., *Essays in the History of Canadian Law: Volume VII – Inside the Law: Canadian Law Firms in Historical Perspective*
William Kaplan, *Bad Judgment: The Case of Mr Justice Leo A. Landreville*
Murray Greenwood and Barry Wright, eds., *Canadian State Trials: Volume I – Law, Politics, and Security Measures, 1608–1837*

1995 David Williams, *Just Lawyers: Seven Portraits*
Hamar Foster and John McLaren, eds., *Essays in the History of Canadian Law: Volume VI – British Columbia and the Yukon*
W.H. Morrow, ed., *Northern Justice: The Memoirs of Mr Justice William G. Morrow*
Beverley Boissery, *A Deep Sense of Wrong: The Treason, Trials, and Transportation to New South Wales of Lower Canadian Rebels after the 1838 Rebellion*

1994 Patrick Boyer, *A Passion for Justice: The Legacy of James Chalmers McRuer*
Charles Pullen, *The Life and Times of Arthur Maloney: The Last of the Tribunes*
Jim Phillips, Tina Loo, and Susan Lewthwaite, eds., *Essays in the History of Canadian Law: Volume V – Crime and Criminal Justice*
Brian Young, *The Politics of Codification: The Lower Canadian Civil Code of 1866*

1993 Greg Marquis, *Policing Canada's Century: A History of the Canadian Association of Chiefs of Police*
Murray Greenwood, *Legacies of Fear: Law and Politics in Quebec in the Era of the French Revolution*

1992 Brendan O'Brien, *Speedy Justice: The Tragic Last Voyage of His Majesty's Vessel Speedy*
Robert Fraser, ed., *Provincial Justice: Upper Canadian Legal Portraits from the Dictionary of Canadian Biography*

1991 Constance Backhouse, *Petticoats and Prejudice: Women and Law in Nineteenth-Century Canada*

1990 Philip Girard and Jim Phillips, eds., *Essays in the History of Canadian Law: Volume III – Nova Scotia*
Carol Wilton, ed., *Essays in the History of Canadian Law: Volume IV – Beyond the Law: Lawyers and Business in Canada, 1830–1930*

1989 Desmond Brown, *The Genesis of the Canadian Criminal Code of 1892*
Patrick Brode, *The Odyssey of John Anderson*

1988 Robert Sharpe, *The Last Day, the Last Hour: The Currie Libel Trial*
John D. Arnup, *Middleton: The Beloved Judge*

1987 C. Ian Kyer and Jerome Bickenbach, *The Fiercest Debate: Cecil A. Wright, the Benchers, and Legal Education in Ontario, 1923–1957*

1986 Paul Romney, *Mr Attorney: The Attorney General for Ontario in Court, Cabinet, and Legislature, 1791–1899*
Martin Friedland, *The Case of Valentine Shortis: A True Story of Crime and Politics in Canada*

1985 James Snell and Frederick Vaughan, *The Supreme Court of Canada: History of the Institution*

1984 Patrick Brode, *Sir John Beverley Robinson: Bone and Sinew of the Compact*
David Williams, *Duff: A Life in the Law*

1983 David H. Flaherty, ed., *Essays in the History of Canadian Law: Volume II*

1982 Marion MacRae and Anthony Adamson, *Cornerstones of Order: Courthouses and Town Halls of Ontario, 1784–1914*

1981 David H. Flaherty, ed., *Essays in the History of Canadian Law: Volume I*